Caregiving Our Loved Ones
Stories and Strategies
That Will Change Your Life

Nanette J. Davis, Ph.D.

Caregiving Our Loved Ones:
Stories and Strategies That Will Change Your Life

©2012 Nanette J. Davis, Ph.D.
A House of Harmony Press Publication
Bellingham, WA
www.houseofharmonypress.com

Publisher's Cataloging-in-Publication Data

Davis, Nanette J.

    Caregiving our loved ones : stories and strategies that will change your life / Nanette J. Davis. — Bellingham, WA : House of Harmony Press, c2012.

    p. ; cm.

    ISBN: 978-0-9838299-3-5 (print) ; 978-0-9838299-2-8 (ebk.)

    Revised and expanded from the author's 2008 book, "Blessed is she".

    Includes bibliographical references.

    Summary: Aimed at helping adult long-term and elder caregivers and their families, it features the narratives of 60 women who looked after spouses, siblings, parents, grandparents and friends; including the author's own experiences caring for her dying husband.

    1. Women caregivers—United States. 2. Older caregivers—United States. 3. Caregivers—Psychological aspects. 4. Older people—Care—United States. 5. Aging parents—Care—United States. 6. Spouses—Death. 7. Terminal care—United States. 8. Bereavement—Psychological aspects. I. Title. II. Title: Blessed is she.

HV1461 .D395 2012   2012940699
362.63—dc23   2012

Design and typesetting for print and ebook by Kate Weisel,
www.weiselcreative.com

To Burl… the wind beneath my wings.

Cover Design: The Nautilus

The nautilus is an ancient symbol of the spiral of our lives—the ups and downs, the twists and turns over the life cycle. As long as we have had stick and charcoal, humans have been trying to reproduce the many, and ever growing, chambers of this illusive denizen of the deep. As the nautilus grows it continually builds new chambers to its shell and closes off the previous chambers. Thus, we take who we are with us through life, but with no returning. Yesterday is gone. We can only grow in one direction. This sea creature also demonstrates that growth is inevitable as long as we are alive.

Contents

Preface

The national news about elder caregiving has not changed substantially since I published my first study on 61 women caregivers in 2008. Women still remain the primary family caregivers when their elderly parents, spouses or other relatives need help. This means women, often without support, continue to bear the brunt of the financial, physical and emotional burden of this undertaking. A commitment to caregiving is not solely a woman's issue, though. Entire families experience disruption for months or years, as adult children grieve over an elderly parent who merely lingers on, too debilitated in mind or body to respond. Older people, hanging on to the remnants of their dignity and family honor, persist in looking after their frail loved one, sometimes alone in their struggle. And the costs of care keep rising, with no end in sight.

I believed then I had covered the bases and predicted a home run with *Blessed is She... Elder Care: Women's Stories of Choice, Challenge and Commitment.* The world would now be a better place with a greater understanding of what to expect when an aging loved one requires care. Now I know the situation has become, if anything, more complex, and caregiving even less visible as a critical public issue, despite the dozens of books and interminable Internet chatter on the subject. So, what started as a revision of *Blessed is She* has become a re-envisioning of the original book.

Talking to dozens of female and male caregivers since the book's publication convinced me that I needed to explore this issue in even greater depth. Subsequently, a number of new and highlighted themes have emerged about the nature of caregiving itself. Above all, I bring out the contradictory character of giving care: the incredible joys and sorrows; the nearly unspeakable highs and lows. Most of all, I discovered the gifts of caregiving that made every sacrifice worthwhile.

Another principal concern for all caregivers is wrestling with emotions—their own feelings, their elderly loved one's moods and their family members' emotional states. Anger, sadness, fear, grief and guilt imbue the caregiving experience with lifelong consequences. To address this, I include a chapter on grief and a final chapter further exploring these crucial emotions.

Hands-on caregivers—who provide the day-in, day-out physical, financial, emotional and social functions that keep their elderly loved one surviving—rarely reflect on the *gifts* of caregiving. What consoles them? What makes it all worthwhile? What sustains them in times of crisis and death? How do they renew themselves both during the caregiving period and after the loved one's death? Gifts are the spiritual rewards caregivers receive when they persist in an intentional, mindful state. I pay credence to these benefits because without transcending the difficult and dreadful aspects of caregiving, we caregivers are laid waste—sick in body and soul.

This book, *Caregiving Our Loved Ones: Stories and Strategies that Will Change Your Life,* incorporates a more expanded version of my own four-year caregiving involvement than my first book on elder care. As a memoir, the writing takes a turn away from the analytical to the intimate and the sentimental, perhaps less event-centered than self-encounter. Without a doubt, living through long-term caregiving changed my life. My perspective hovered somewhere between the here-and-now and eternity during those caregiving years. Whereas, before caregiving, my sense of direction was up—invariably future oriented. Now, almost a decade after active caregiving, I can see more clearly that *up* can also mean *down* or *out*—as in my *own* decline and eventual death.

Believe it or not, this book is not morose. These stories about caregiving offer subtle humor, profound insights, practical tips and invaluable self-help strategies. Caregivers everywhere will be able to relate to the simple, everyday situations, and hopefully gain greater understanding and awareness.

But let's be realistic. Long-term care is a topic that will not go away in our lifetime. The entire developed world confronts a revolution in aging that includes as a core element, protracted dying. Scientific discoveries, medical technology and pharmaceutical breakthroughs have radically altered the way we live—and the kind of end-of-life experience we will have. Regrettably, many of these advances have not eased the edges of the last stage of life. It behooves us to seriously consider how we might prepare ourselves for a softer landing.

My husband, Burl Harmon, provides sing-along sessions in nursing homes, assisted living facilities and other venues where the elderly, sick and dying congregate. I frequently accompany him in song with his guitar and vocal offerings, and afterwards chat with residents, patients, staff and family caregivers who have joined loved ones. What stands out for me is the kindness and compassion of both family members and staff who accept the facts of human decline, but are not limited by them. We could all certainly benefit from a visit to our neighborhood assisted living or extended care facility or talk to a home care agency to do some advance planning for our older family members or ourselves. The life we save is not merely our own, but the whole network of family, friends and supporters who will surely be part of the end-of-our life drama.

One word on terms: I frequently refer to "elder," "elderly," "aged" and "aging" throughout the book. Some would say these are no longer appropriate terms for describing older people who are sick and dying. But these references also point to time-honored traditions, as when church leaders are called "elders" (even when they are only middle-aged) or where "aged" refers to one's older and deeply respected relatives in traditional cultures. The word, "aging" is, of course, merely generic—we are all of us aging as we move from birth to death. Thus "aging" has a neutral character.

Another perspective: Dr. Oz of television fame characterizes age in two ways: "real" age, which is how you feel and act, and calendar age. You may be looking forward to your 55th birthday party, but behave like 45, a difference of 10 years. It also works in the reverse. A sickly person with Parkinson's disease may be only 73, but his "real" age may be closer to 85. Real age is determined by a person's health, strength, cardiovascular functioning and other components. Although I don't have a clue about my sister Marilyn Clement's *real* age, I do know she plays a mean game of tennis at the ripe age of 77. So, age is a relative matter, after all.

Acknowledgements are always in order. First, to my daughters Patricia Davis and Susan Browne, a published author herself, who serve as editors *par excellence*. A better team could not be found. Burl's pithy observations about aging and life in general have kept me plugging away despite the sometimes blood, sweat and tears of the writing. Special plaudits go to my writers' group—Evelyn Wright, Lynne Masland, Troy-Faith Ward and Iris Jones—master writers all. Professor Bill Smith provided just the right touch with a male point of view toward caregiving. Additionally, his meticulous editing could not be equaled. I am always grateful to those other readers who have read all or part of the book, and offered their personal insights and suggestions.

Finally, I salute the caregivers, who opened their hearts to me, both those who provided the original interviews, and those with whom I spoke informally over the last decade. We all need to salute the millions of caregivers who continue to grapple with the often grim details of caregiving, even while they summon the depths of compassion to do the very best within their capacity for their beloved elder.

To all caregivers, consider this: To the world you may be just one caregiver, but to that suffering elder, you may be the world.

May 2012
Bellingham, Washington

Introduction

The Talmud teaches: One must bless God for the bad in life as well as for the good. In the act of blessing God, we begin the deeply personal journey from senseless pain to meaningful challenge.

– Rabbi Saul Goldman

Do Opposites Attract?

In extreme situations all of our emotions are exaggerated. Having a new baby, being in love and securing that dreamed-about first job after college gets us in touch with those superb highs. Conversely, what happens when we fall into the lowest of lows: the baby constantly keeps us awake at night and has a bad case of colic, the love interest has been disloyal or disappeared, or we get fired from that great job? If change occurs too rapidly, and one incident is piled on another, we find it hard to catch our breath. What was exciting is now distressing. What once thrilled us now seems out of control—even perilous.

Caregiving is a similarly intense undertaking. Those new to caregiving enter this arena with hope, love and the belief that they can make a difference. Their loved one will get better, they can ease up on the vigilance and chronic worry, life can continue as before. Few are prepared for the roller coaster ride that often ensues.

Many caregivers express surprise when they discover how truly overwhelming giving care can be. They are unprepared for having their lives completely turned around. The father becomes the willful child, the husband changes into an ogre, the mother a pitiful version of her former charming self. A caregiver's cherished self-image as calm, competent and organized begins to deteriorate, as she copes with round-the-clock home supervision. The constant sense of responsibility is ever-present: "Everything rides on me. What if he dies and it's my fault?"

A different set of emotions surfaces, as well, and sometimes concurrently: "She depends on me, and I'm proud I can rise to the occasion." "This is the high point of my life and I'm still healthy enough and have the stamina to take care of my sick husband." "What joy there is in giving care to a person who has given so much to me over the years." These contradictions reveal themselves at all points along the caregiving journey.

Contradictions in Caregiving: Opportunity versus Ordeal

Possibilities and opportunities await the caregiver. Simply facing the necessity to *change* routines can be life-altering. The caregiver learns to make adjustments in the everyday schedule. Along with the organizational skills required for renovating the care receiver's home for his greater comfort, the caregiver discovers she may need to make changes, as well—those long-awaited New Year's resolutions to overhaul less than productive habits.

Accomplishing the fine art of juggling the caregiver role, along with maintaining a meaningful life, can lead to a reawakening of old skills and practices: that long abandoned daily walk, the quiet time with knitting, more frequent visits with friendly neighbors. The necessity to bring the family together for home visits and decisions about their loved one's care could initiate a sense of renewal and promise—a return to friendly sibling exchanges or the sense of family unity that adult children haven't felt in years. And what most caregivers initially underestimate is the incredible opportunity of living more deeply with their loved one in his or her final, vulnerable moments.

The distressful side of caregiving must also be recognized. You may find yourself challenged by these caregivers' stories. You may feel repelled by some highly questionable caregiver decisions. Why give care to a parent who abused you? Why do caregivers contradict themselves? In one breath, they say, "It's too much, I don't have what it takes to do this." Or "it's too hard, and my job and marriage are faltering." Instead of quitting, though, they keep on giving care?

Consider the incredible difficulty of confronting the torment of watching a loved one become ill, frail and dying. Likewise, the sheer misery of witnessing the unraveling of a precious mind and spirit can be unbearable. Add to this the trial caregivers must endure to cope with learning new skills and ways of *being*. Then, reflect for a moment on the untold suffering of losses and pain—both physical and emotional—in their loved one and themselves. The stress of caregiving itself must be recognized, which can go on for months or years. The financial, social and psychological hardships become a cumulative burden. All of these adversities become the everyday reality for caregivers.

These colliding emotions are an integral part of elder caregiving, and must be acknowledged as a single coin with two distinct sides. This contradiction accounts for the multiple instances when caregivers said:

"I'm so confused. I don't know what to think/feel/be."

"I feel so uncertain about everything."

"I'm on a roller coaster ride, and I can't get off, but I'm not staying on very well either."

Of course, a way *can* be found to live with these profound inconsistencies. Here's the secret: Live in the moment! But for most caregivers, this is something that must be painfully learned as they move through the caregiving experience.

Once we master the fine art of living, of being in the Now, you and I—and all caregivers—can simply be grateful witnesses to the last drama of our loved one's journey, as all of us learn to live with the reality of a longer life. A new old age beckons, and these final experiences of a loved one's life made fragile and quixotic by great old age is a totally new occurrence in a youth-driven culture. We need to pay attention to these profound changes.

Caregiving is More than a Private Concern

Caregiving for the elderly has recently entered the public domain and can even be found in contemporary fiction (*A Map of True Places* by Brunonia Barry, for example). It's no wonder. Across the country 61.6 million Americans struggle with caring for their older relatives and friends.

People of all ages are providing care. Among the 60 caregivers in this book the ages ranged from 15 years old at the time they gave care (for a father) to 90 years old (for a husband). The average age of these working caregivers caring for parents was 57, while retired caregivers had an average age of 74. Thirty percent of these caregivers worked full-time, while the others were retired or semi-retired, some because of the caregiving work load.

Caregiving exacts a heavy toll. The average number of hours per week involved in giving care was more than 57 for these caregivers. For nearly half of them, their work was unremitting—a 24/7 undertaking. Because the majority of care receivers suffered from severe medical conditions—advanced cancer, Alzheimer's disease, stroke, Parkinson's disease, heart disease, depression and other ailments of frail old age—medical demands are continuous.

Caregiving for the elderly also demands years of commitment. For these caregivers, the average is about five and one-half years. For one caregiver in my book whose husband has Parkinson's, caregiving has lasted nearly the duration of the marriage (30 years).

More than half of the caregivers had previously provided care to at least one other family member. I found that families have informally targeted certain women in the family—wife, granddaughter, daughter, daughter-in-law—to serve as the "designated caregiver" when an elderly family member is stricken.

Gender and Caregiving

Is this commitment to care for a disabled elder a socialized response restricted solely to women? Certainly, men find themselves equally challenged to give care to their aging mother or sick wife. In our culture, though, it is primarily women who are expected to take on the caregiving duties, and are more likely to sacrifice careers, hopes and dreams to care for the younger—or in this case—older generation.

A special report by the Family Caregiver Alliance (FCA) from 2006 on the status of women caregivers emphasizes that although men also provide assistance, female caregivers may spend as much as 50 percent more time providing care than do male caregivers.

Caregiving involves well-defined gender styles, which are clearly portrayed in my book. Women are far more likely to intensify their care, investing more time and being more psychologically involved. I have observed that men who give care to their wives take a different path, tending to delay retirement to bolster declining family finances.

Moreover, women's tendency toward intense care contributes to significant economic losses—a point we cannot overemphasize. My research on financial security among older women shows that caregiving places a significant strain on women's retirement incomes. So too do decreased work hours, failure to receive job promotions or training, and/or being forced to quit jobs or take early retirement. Smaller pensions, as well as reduced Social Security amounts and other retirement payments, are the consequences of both reduced hours on the job and fewer years in the workforce. Gender matters: Women are much less likely to receive a pension than men, and when they do, their pension is about half of what men receive.

The toll caregiving takes is not only a financial one. Higher levels of depression, anxiety and other mental health challenges are common among these women. A four-year study by Langa and Associates in "The Journal of General Internal Medicine" (2001) found that middle-aged and older women who provided care for an ill or disabled spouse were **six times** more likely to suffer symptoms of depression and anxiety than were women who were not caregivers.

Compounding this dismal picture, the study shows that physical ailments are a common problem. More than one-third of caregivers provide ongoing care to others while suffering from poor health themselves. Elderly women caring for a loved one with dementia may be particularly susceptible to the negative health effects of caregiving, due largely to significantly less help from family members for their own impairments.

Aside from gender, consider the fact that minority and low-income caregivers face special challenges. Among the lower income caregivers I interviewed, having access to paid sources of care was especially difficult. They usually could not count on either family or friends, either. Langa and Associates observed that lower-income caregivers are **half as likely** as higher-income caregivers to have paid home health care or assistance with their caregiving duties.

Nanette's Story

I have chosen to introduce the book with my own narrative. I discovered that while every caregiver's story is hers alone, each echoes that of other caregivers. I also weave my story throughout the rest of the chapters to demonstrate my personal connection to caregiving. Here, I emphasize how the road I have traveled is like that of so many others. I am not alone.

A heart attack in 1998 on Jim's 78th birthday alerted me to the precarious state of my husband's health. As he was wheeled into surgery by the "swat team" of intervention specialists, he continued a refrain I would hear for weeks—"I don't even feel as though I've had a heart attack—I can't believe I've had a heart attack." And once released from the hospital, he continued "business-as-usual" without taking the precautions necessary to avoid another attack, because, after all, he felt he wasn't at risk.

The doctor's initial prognosis was excellent—stent installed, patient stabilized, family relieved, job done. Jim resumed his normal life, seemingly without missing a beat. On the other hand, I was apprehensive and vigilant, as he had waited to seek medical care for days after his initial symptoms, thinking the pain and lethargy would pass. I feared the worst. Less than four months later, the day after Thanksgiving, with all the family assembled at the house for the holiday, we received a call from the hospital. Jim had had another, more serious heart attack, after collapsing on the first hole of his favorite local golf course. Hope appeared futile; the crisis had begun.

Over the next few years, as his condition deteriorated, physicians continued to add more drugs to his cornucopia of medicines, and attempted different treatments—all to no avail. Medical crisis followed medical crisis. Trips to the hospital, as well as to various doctors and care centers accelerated. I was in shock, as were our children.

What can we expect? Will our beloved husband and father emerge from these trials alive or dead? We did not know then that the answer would be: both alive *and* dead. Jim was alive, in that his heart beat, he retained the power of speech, he ate (little), slept (even less) and eliminated (only with difficulty). He was dead, as well—dead to the significance of his relationship to himself, family, friends and the world. Dead to cherished roles, dead to a lifelong commitment to scholarship and writing, dead to independence and creativity, dead to physical wholeness, dead to the possibilities of a future or even a present that had meaning and purpose. He survived, but without strength, without joy, without courage, and most tragically, without hope.

This personal tragedy started me on a journey that has brought much grief, yet much heart-opening wisdom. My experience has been nothing less than transforming, taking me deep into the recesses of myself and my capacities for coping. It also opened my eyes to the profound contradictions surrounding elders and their caregivers within our culture.

Part of my healing process involved reaching out to other caregivers for interviews. I sought to determine if their experiences were similar or different from my own. I discovered a remarkable coincidence in all our stories. I also found all of us experienced clear-cut shifts over time invariably related to our level of experience with caregiving.

During the year I spent interviewing caregivers, I delved deeply on a face-to-face level into the losses and joys of other caregivers. I was initially unprepared for the emotional connection I developed with these women, and frequently felt overcome by their hardships. Once I pounced on the idea that we were sisters-in-caregiving, I could lean back and accept the flow of experiences they were so willing to share. I provide a brief profile of these caregivers in an Epilogue.

All names have been fictionalized, except for Anne Mikkelsen, my research assistant, Margaret Shipp, my friend and temporary nurse for Jim, and my name. The next chapter features my story, and subsequent chapters highlight various caregivers' accounts, and my personal remembrances and reflections.

Chapter 1

Transitions

Keep your face to the sunshine and you cannot see the shadow.
— Helen Keller, *The Promise of a New Day*

At the Beginning

My journey into caregiving began on a sunny August morning. While still in bed, I noticed that Jim seemed to be having trouble breathing. He also reported feeling "out of sorts," which was unusual for him. I got up, dressed, and began buzzing around the kitchen, having dismissed his comments as a passing irritation. When I returned to the bedroom, I found Jim slumped in the easy chair, his face sweating and contorted with pain. I knew this was serious, but I also realized that confronting a man who typically resisted doctors was well beyond my persuasive abilities. His background in Christian Science led to a certain avoidance of medical matters.

I asked him to describe his symptoms. Grudgingly, he listed what turned out to be the classic signs of heart attack. I dashed to the phone to call our physician, but he was on his way out of town. In his haste, the doctor failed to provide the name of his replacement, perhaps because I was nearly hysterical and he was in a rush to hang up.

With the news that his family physician was not available, Jim shut down emotionally. He refused to let me drive him to the hospital emergency room, and thought it was far too much "trouble" to call an ambulance. So, there we sat from Friday through Sunday with Jim's symptoms worsening, and my panic accelerating. Watching him clutching his chest, I desperately sought a workable plan that would goad Jim into cooperating. Dragging my suitcase out of the closet, I raised my voice, and announced: "If you won't go to the hospital, then I'm leaving. I'm not going to stay here and watch you die." The ploy worked. My perpetually stubborn husband finally relented. But the crisis was not over, and was to repeat itself a few months later in a more intense and damaging heart attack. I had backed into the caregiving role without warning or preparation.

Everything Changes

When you have an older parent, spouse, grandparent, other relative or friend, it's almost inevitable that they will become ill and/or frail at some point. Yet, for most of us, we are utterly surprised when we get "the call." And it's when we least expect it that the dreaded event happens. A brother texts you: "Mom's had a fall and is in the hospital." Or your mother writes a hasty e-mail, "Your dad's cancer has returned and he'll need 24/7 care over the next six months." Or, in my case, an attending nurse calls, "Your husband's had a massive heart attack on the golf course, and we're doing what we can to minimize the impact."

How will you respond to this crisis? Undoubtedly, you will have a number of questions. Where do I go from here? Is this my wake-up call? What will be expected of me? How can I give care or immediate help without totally disrupting my routines, my everyday life? Can I return to an oblivious state of denial, only to be rudely awakened when financial, emotional and social demands are thrust upon me?

Caregiving is **not** what most of us plan to undertake. In fact, I've often listened to women repeat my own remarks: "I didn't have a clue." "I simply have been in a state of shock about this whole thing." "Why did **this** happen?" We live in a society that rejects both aging and death. It's no wonder so many caregivers—myself included—were wholly ignorant of the final stages of life: illness, frailty, dependency, losses, and dying.

I found that a commitment to compassionate care appeared to have clear shifts over time, depending on a variety of conditions. Among them: my husband's changing health and mental capacity, my ability to adapt to new circumstances, medical and drug issues, level of social supports, and more importantly, my willingness to learn *new* coping skills. Transitions are never easy. My first instinct was to resist, deny or ignore change, rather than open up, surrender and accept it.

Looking back on my personal caregiving experience, I can identify a distinct set of stages: Crisis, Hope, Despair, Victim, Resignation and Acceptance. A final stage, Renewal, occurred in the weeks following Jim's funeral.

After the initial flood of emotions during the Crisis period, I found solid ground in Hope, a transition that carried me through the first months of diagnosis and medical treatment. But the ground soon gave way to a more entrenched period of Despair. I simply could not, nor would not, accept the physical and mental onslaughts that were happening to my strong, courageous husband. Over the agonizing months of waiting for a more positive outcome, I gradually woke up to the reality that Jim's illness was permanent. His heart had been severely damaged, and worse, his brain was impaired by repeated ischemic strokes. Then, the inevitable occurred: Jim became an invalid.

This new awareness carried me into a different, very disgruntled state—that of Victim—which lingered for a couple of years. I took on the burdens of caregiving, filled with resentment and anger. I had a number of targets: Jim, for one, whom I silently accused of contributing to his own illness because of poor diet and neglecting his medical care. I felt deeply let down by doctors, who were evasive about his prognosis and seemed to have nothing to offer in terms of a cure. I also aimed my rancor at certain family members I was convinced weren't contributing enough. Even friends, I thought, could never understand my miseries. What pulled me out of this was time. As the months wore on, I became weary of my guilt and enforced isolation. Additionally, I was experiencing painful burn-out.

Once I became Resigned to the role of full-time caregiver, though, many of the more highly stressful feelings fell away. Yet, I was not ready to let go of my negative emotions. Only after I pushed myself to find help did I fully move into a resolution of my situation and acceptance. Hospice played a large part in this process. Jim's protracted time on Hospice (18 months) and my awakening to his slow dying helped me through those last months. A final stage, Renewal, began with family and friends gathered at the funeral and continued for more than a year, as I adjusted to my loss and to opening up my life to embrace new roles and relationships.

Transitions through caregiving among the 60 women I feature in this book took varying forms. I was surprised to discover that some caregivers leaped over stages. For example, one older caregiver moved from hope to acceptance at the outset of her husband's illness, while many others remained fixed at a particular stage, viewing themselves as perpetual victims, or simply resigning themselves to their fate. In a few cases, caregivers experienced two stages at once. They may have continued to hope their loved one would recover—only to be disappointed when he or she continued to decline. At the same time, the caregivers remained resigned to the burden of long-term caregiving.

What I—and most caregivers—have come to recognize is that with experience and patience, the confused and negative stages pass. The caregiver sooner or later comes to an awareness of a deeper understanding of the caring process and acceptance of herself, as well as her loved one. For the fortunate few, developing a co-partnering role in which caregiver and care receiver work harmoniously together provide enormous satisfaction.

Crisis

Every caregiver I spoke with can give you a myriad of details about the moment when the medical disaster was revealed: heart attack confirmed, cancer diagnosis clarified, Alzheimer's disease identified, stroke acknowledged. In my case, I knew the heart attack needed my immediate attention—every minute counted. However, I had no power to make things happen. After Jim's first heart attack, I had to confront an array of bewildering and unfamiliar medical procedures and treatments. I relied on Jim to continue his masterful management of the situation as he had throughout our marriage.

Before Jim's illness, we had an intellectual partnership. Not only did he review my manuscripts multiple times, but he was also far more adept at completing my book indexes and handling final editing, with his careful attention to detail. Because we had a commuting marriage for almost 20 years, he had developed the art of household management. He oversaw the finances, cars and home repairs, as well as shopping and endless errands—all without skipping a beat on his own academic work. Somehow, he maintained a rigorous schedule of research and writing for hours each day, along with taking an active community leadership role and fitting in a daily golf game. He was a leading expert in his field. He was called on for interviews from regional and national media to speak on the American presidency during many elections—that is, until he became quite ill. The family remembers the Bill Clinton–Monica Lewinsky meltdown in 1999, with more than the usual shock. Their father no longer had the capacity to respond to the media's requests for interviews, which worsened his depression and our impending sense of disaster.

Hope

After Jim's second heart attack, the cardiologist presented us with a "newer and better" angioplasty, which was less likely to lead to yet another heart attack. At this point, Jim had only about five percent functioning in one of his cardiac arteries. Moreover, he was now comatose in the intensive care unit, lacking any semblance of life. Our grown children and I wanted the best medical care possible, but our limited knowledge kept us from asking some key questions. We failed to inquire about heart surgery, instead of the angioplasty. We missed the mark in not asking about the prognosis for our loved one. We completely failed to notice how the severely weakened heart could no longer sustain Jim as a scholar, teacher, husband, father, friend and golfer. Throughout this first critical period, our family merely reacted to the situation without a guide or even a notion about what the future would hold.

Despite what I recognized as a painful setback, I felt utterly optimistic about my husband's heart condition, as did our children. We lived in a community with a specialized heart center, and medical knowledge of heart disease continues to be nothing less than encyclopedic. Our cardiologist radiated an overwhelmingly positive picture of Jim's condition, as he showed us images of his successfully completed upgraded angioplasty. I truly believed it was only a matter of days, at most, weeks, until Jim would return to normal. In fact, after his first heart attack, Jim refused to take his situation seriously, resuming his often unhealthy diet and failing to complete the exercises suggested by his doctor. Only after his second heart attack on the golf course did his mood shift, and a sobering reality swept over all of us: This is serious business, and we're not sure where we're headed. My natural propensity for keeping everyone's spirits up blinded us to the devastating physical, psychological and social toll this second heart attack would take.

If the cardiologist had offered to perform open heart surgery at this early stage, I believe Jim would have embraced the idea, despite the risks. After heart failure had set in, it was clearly too late to make that decision. Instead, Jim was outfitted with a defibrillator, a device implanted in the chest that records the heart rate and identifies such heart irregularities as atrial fibrillation, which could cause clot formation. We were told the patient experiences an electric shock when the device restores the heart to its normal rate. We all had great faith that this treatment would work.

During this early period, I acknowledged fatigue, but not depression; recognized sorrow, but never anguish; and remained open to joy while rejecting signs of despondency. That period of hope began to fade after three months, once unmistakable signs of heart disease emerged. Jim's steady decline brought with it a profound depression and withdrawal from family and friends. In practical terms, this led to a sharp increase in the caregiving work load along with a certain loss of interest by some family members. I now had to confront the sheer exhaustion of caregiving without a cure in sight. Once this situation became the new normal, I began a shift into the next—and clearly the worst—stage.

Despair

Despair has many sides that all suggest dead-ends in our caregiving journey. I felt so helpless about Jim's profound losses—physical, intellectual, emotional and spiritual. I grieved moment by moment as he coped with his ongoing pain. I had to confront my own sense of futility over and over—what good was any of this medical intervention doing? My own losses and pains were always close to the surface, and sometimes left me staggering with fear that this dreadful situation would never end.

Despite the family's best efforts to buoy up his spirits and deal with his weakened state, I could not overcome or overlook Jim's continuous loss of energy, talents, mental capacity and his growing physical infirmity. Within a few months I succumbed to an overwhelming sense of desolation—the bleakness of failure. The "nothing can be done" conviction extended to Jim's physical and emotional pain. Even when Jim remained stoical about all of the medical interventions we pursued, I could feel his hopelessness. His misery became my misery, his desperation, my desperation, his losses, my losses. Now, the despair circle was complete.

I now faced futility. After Jim's rapid physical and mental withdrawal—despite repeated medical help—I lacked the energy to try new approaches. When Jim pushed his food and medicine away, I simply stared at him, not believing he could be so uncooperative. When he buried his head in his arms on the kitchen table for hours at a time, I sat passively without speaking. When the children declared how their Dad would rub his forehead after his stroke, hour after hour, I slipped into the bathroom and silently wept. To this day, I regret my passivity, my utter capitulation to grief and apathy. Jim could no longer help himself, and I had failed him in his moment of need.

At this juncture, my sense of personal losses began to accumulate. Sacrifices were inevitable. I gave up writing, my vocation and avocation. I recognized that our mutual dreams of being together in old age to nurture and love one another were an impossible dream, as Jim was only on the receiving end of nurturing (or so I thought at the time). I watched our bank account dwindle, while at the same time I lost my primary advisor in life and money matters. I felt completely bereft of the kind of support I had experienced when Jim was well. I was inconsolable.

In between a series of hospital emergency room visits and post-hospital rehabilitation attempts, I took care of Jim at home. I made every effort to get regular household assistance to help with Jim's bathing, administer medications, cope with his incontinence and clean up the sick room, as well as provide me with respite care, however limited. But I was faced with a revolving door situation. Mark, a well-trained care provider, worked a few months, and then began drinking on the job. Brett, a very competent medical student, assisted me for a while over the summer, but other demands soon filled his life, and he left after a few weeks. My friend, Margaret, a trained nurse, offered to help me, but after one evening with Jim, concluded he was "too much to handle." Local agency help turned out to be a disaster, as one care provider recommended Gatorade for his dehydration, which only succeeded in putting Jim in shock.

With Jim at home, I suffered from sleep deprivation. Or I forgot to eat or continually postponed meals until I could "finish" my duties. Grief and anguish haunted me, even while I carried out ordinary tasks. The notion that no one else could understand my hopeless situation kept me isolated and fearful. Rather than sharing my losses, I tried to bury them under the mask of silence. During this stage, I felt as if I were drowning, trapped, facing closed doors and had no options. I seemed unable to overcome this downward spiral. What pushed me into the next stage was my decision, after much agony, to take a two-week respite trip to Italy, and place Jim in an assisted living facility during my absence.

Being a Victim

While the Despair stage may be likened to a free fall with no landing, the next stage, that of victim, opened up the possibility of simply living with my husband's disease and discomfort. Still, the sense of intense loss haunted me. After my return from that glorious trip to Tuscany, I was determined to practice self-denial. Since I lacked self-awareness, it just made me feel embittered. A "poor me" self emerged that was preoccupied with the logic of martyrdom: "My life is wasted, but at least I can give something back to my loved one. I have no life so what difference does it make? When will this ever end? Nobody cares about me—the phone has been silent for days. We're just being hung out to dry—or die." Stress, anger and futility now governed my life. Routines that once seemed lifesaving now appeared obsolete or inadequate for the enormity of the tasks. Yet, my efforts to develop new, more viable coping mechanisms seemed overwhelming. Fatigue and remorse followed me—with no end in sight.

I realize now that my primary frustration centered on Jim's heart disease. I lacked solid information about the trajectory of the ailment. What was really going on? I understood that Jim's heart attacks had weakened his heart, but the physician did not inform me how these events would also affect his lungs and brain, as well as greatly increase the risk of more strokes. His frequent hospitalizations with heart failure, where each time death seemed imminent, generated a growing sense of terror as we watched the life squeezed out of him. In November 1999, when I felt he was so close to dying, we invited our former priest to administer last rites. I seem to recall the priest saying: "I've never seen anyone this close to death, but then survive."

After the fourth hospitalization in six weeks, I felt even more closed in. How could I leave the house? He could die in my absence. Invite friends over? Impossible. I might have to call 911. Should I let the children know how genuinely ill he was? No, I thought, because they might overreact—either avoiding a visit to their dad or becoming obsessed with spending what could be their final hours with him.

Guilt stalked my days. It seemed that I was responsible for everything that happened. The heart attack was my fault because I refused to see the signs, and lacked a strategy to force him into earlier treatment. Later, I viewed the heart failure as something I caused, because I had been a smoker for years, and that's why Jim's breathing was so impaired. I blamed myself for every setback. His inability to sleep was my error. I couldn't settle him down at night. His failure to eat or take his medicine means I forgot to give him a pep talk beforehand. Or, the food choices I made were all wrong. I knew he had zero tolerance for health food. As for his depression, it must be something I said or did that created such a black mood. At no time did Jim verbally attack or blame me for his miseries. I only wish he could have mustered the physical and emotional energy for an outburst. Instead, an unrelenting depression left him mute and disoriented.

Finally, I had to face up to my own physical pain and inability to maintain the schedule of care. I experienced energy depletion, chronic exhaustion, a badly damaged shoulder (from repeatedly lifting Jim out of bed), thyroid disease, and at one point, I was too ill with pneumonia to visit Jim in the nursing home. At the same time, I felt intense shame for my weakness and inability to carry on.

In the face of Jim's passivity—so unlike the active, even heroic role he played as husband and father—the family seemed to settle on one unified approach: kindness. All of us treated Jim with great solicitude—we didn't know how else to behave. When I became edgy (which was frequent), I reined myself in. I remembered Jim's loving, sweet care of the children when they were younger. He was never too tired, even after sleepless nights with crying infants, to cook them hot cereal or make toast laden with jam. Our domestic life had always been so crowded with six children, but the days were unvaryingly happy, busy with work or teaching, and for Jim, creating one of his 12 scholarly treatises in political science. Perhaps the most tragic part of our family drama is that I couldn't share any of these beautiful memories with him. Jim showed little interest in opening his heart—the disease had truly claimed him: body, mind and soul.

Resignation

What happens to a caregiver after months or years of caring for a sick elder who will never get better? I found giving care over the long-term most closely associated with an attitude of resignation. After more than two years, I had abandoned hope for a better tomorrow. I felt that nothing I did could make a significant difference in Jim's life or my own. After repeated hospitalizations, Jim had finally stabilized into a perpetually frail condition with chronic dementia. His physician assured me that "Jim could easily last another 10 years." It was an assurance I did not want to hear. In this era of high-tech medicine where a person can suffer for years with debilitating illness, family members mourn their loved one over and over and over again.

Our family's great hope in the defibrillator had proven a double-edged sword. On one side, I learned that a heart patient, like Jim, can be assured he will *not* die from heart disease. On the other, he *cannot* die from his disease. So long as he has the implanted device, he will be shocked over and over into existence. For Jim, the intensity of the electric shock was similar to "being kicked by a horse." This additional pain, compounded with continual anxiety because "the shock" can occur at any moment, proved relentlessly debilitating.

Death, then, must be ordered, so to speak, demanding a counter surgery to have the defibrillator removed. We made the decision to remove the implant once Jim entered Hospice.

Taking a submissive stance—"what will be, will be"—did not bring inner peace, though. Subservient to the demands of the illness, quietly accepting my situation without attempting to change the direction of my life or routine, I spiraled downward into the tedium of the everyday burdens that would keep me and my loved one alive. I was now forced to view not only Jim, but also myself, as vulnerable. I frequently wondered if Jim's situation could also bring me to the brink. My greatest fear was a pervasive apprehension that the children could lose *two* parents.

At one level, I discovered that resignation was far more comfortable than actively despairing or feeling victimized about the losses I had experienced. I suppose my dominant feelings were that of numbness, frozen into the role of providing physical care, or when Jim was hospitalized or in rehabilitation, visiting for hours a day. Being passive implied not merely giving up on my life, but in another sense, giving up hope that either Jim or myself could ever reanimate our marriage or experience the love and joy we had known. I must admit that on some days, I failed to enlist either a sense of charity or compassion. I wanted to do a good job, but fatigue seemed to overwhelm me. Thus, I slouched through my days without delight, joyless in the face of tragedy.

Acceptance

I made three decisions that turned out to keep me sane. First, I continued to teach full-time for financial security and sense of accomplishment. Despite sleep shortages and frustrations with scheduling because I wanted to have more time with Jim, the teaching proved to be a soul remedy.

Second, I began sessions with an innovative counselor, who each week straightened out my confused and distressed psyche. After almost three years of being overwhelmed, I discovered this highly unusual therapist in a workshop I had attended. Seth had been trained by an Indian guru, unconventional by Western standards. At this point I truly began my healing process with breath exercises and wise advice. Seth's recipe: Enlightenment through deep and sustained breathing, and letting go of expectations. Acceptance meant living in the moment: the eternal Now.

And, third, I energetically took on the advocate role in institutions, as Jim entered a new phase of his illness. His polio, contracted in infancy, had resurfaced, and he was now required to use a wheelchair. The family now encountered a new routine. For me, it was monitoring his care on a daily basis in a nursing home. For the children, it was learning to deal with someone who was like a stranger, and whose behavior was persistently structured by his disease and even worse, arbitrary institutional mandates.

My daughter, Susan, recalled trying to elicit some of his early childhood memories. "I remember trying to get him to reminisce at the assisted living place at dinner," Susan said. "When I coaxed him to reveal his own dad's favorite tune, it was like a precious gift when he responded. But those moments were so rare, like once every six months."

I had always considered *acceptance* to be a passive psychological state. I was wrong. *Acceptance* was wholly opposed to my earlier feelings of submission and lack of resistance. Instead, it involved an active intellectual, emotional and spiritual connection with me and others. This stage embodied prior stages, but also transcended them. Hope became the perfect gift for day-to-day coping, as I realized I was creating a legacy for my children. A glimpse of Despair reminded me to stay in the moment, and breathe deeply to enhance the feeling of aliveness. When the Victim threatened to re-emerge, I sought to cultivate possibilities. And, when that overly resigned mood began to set in, I stopped and asked: "What can be done? How can I best carry it out?" In a word, acceptance involved strategies—workable solutions to life as it is, and the resolution of accumulated grievances.

If the doctor said, "There's no other medication for this symptom," (oxycodone led to hallucinations and panic attacks, for example), I insisted on stopping it. Or, when the disease threatened to overtake my husband, I recognized that there were a variety of ways to live with illness, other than medical. Emotional and spiritual growth was an unexpected gift. I even tried admitting the worst: "I'm only too well aware of the reality, but I have no intention of succumbing to self-pity." During this final transition, six major strategies came into play that allowed me to acquire the ease and calm I needed for myself and my family.

First, I recognized that my husband's journey was one that I willingly and lovingly *shared*, and given in the spirit of generosity, but *I was not Jim, and I could not fall into the fallacy of losing myself in his suffering.* I could only give within my limits and capacities. At the same time, I realized how expansive these capacities and abilities had become over the course of my caregiving journey.

Second, I realized that role reversal was normal and timely, given the nature of Jim's illness. The idea of my making unilateral decisions about Jim's health and well-being would have once evoked an outrage. In his pre-illness state, Jim would never have allowed me to "call the shots," as it were, and treat him as a dependent. I have yet to meet a more autonomous, self-determining and stubborn man than Jim Davis, whose age superiority (11 years my senior) was played out in all of our interactions over a 50-year marriage. Ultimately, I sadly acquiesced to the reality that Jim would never again resume his previous roles as parent or partner.

Third, I had to understand the basics of self-care, which required developing a routine for managing *my* health, wealth and well-being. Eating well, sleeping soundly and exercising regularly had to be built into the daily schedule. I realized that learning to live at ease entailed time out every week with friends or just to be alone. I recognized that leaving family and friends behind had to be assiduously avoided, as these people were my support system. I also acknowledged that I needed time off. A few months before Jim died, I took a much-needed week's vacation in Mexico. As I understood over time, good self-care raised not only my mood and level of energy, but had a profoundly positive impact on Jim. Ultimately, I came to realize that I, along with other family members, set the tone and quality of the relationship, especially as Jim continued to lose cognitive abilities.

Fourth, being adaptive to Jim's physical, mental and emotional changes was essential for my caregiving success. I learned that each chronic disease has its own trajectory, and for heart disease complicated by stroke, severe debilitation and dementia were normal. For Jim, everyday fears could easily turn into terrors. Showers became a nightmare for him, because they were preceded by the "sling," a mechanical conveyance that rapidly swings the patient high in the air after extracting him from the bed, and unceremoniously dumping him into a wheelchair. Once I put a stop to this procedure, Jim gratefully received all future baths in the safety of his bed.

Fifth, looking within was the only way I was going to maintain balance and equanimity. Fortunately, I knew a variety of spiritual strategies but had let them lapse at earlier stages of my caregiving—among them, attending weekly church services, daily prayer, meditation and yoga. I also needed to continually retool my thinking to overcome the illusion that life would ever be "normal" again. When the Hospice social worker emphasized that in the spirit of normality I should just act as a "happy wife" to my now withdrawn and confused husband, I actually laughed out loud. I did not find such counsel consoling or healing at all. Her advice seemed to negate the years of adapting and internal transformations I had been through. Today, I have come to appreciate her words, and recognize I still had much learning and growing ahead of me, much of which happened after his death.

Finally, I learned to enjoy those few moments when Jim was mentally cogent. My children remind me even today how essential I was to their father—"you were the light in our father's eyes." In Jim's last months, I came to deeply acknowledge his heartfelt response when I entered his room at the nursing facility. His eyes lit up to embrace me. His gratitude was palpable.

Renewal

Funerals are typically considered—yes, funereal—grippingly sad, intensely gloomy, very solemn, if not dismal, affairs. One can only *endure* such a depressing event. I was wrong again. Bringing the family together, the presence of my sweet brother and sister-in-law, the many supportive friends, along with Jim's former colleagues, the incredibly moving statement made by our son, Timothy, the wonderful meal put on by our church—all were deeply cherished experiences. Despite my exhaustion, I could feel my spirits lifting. I knew I could survive this, too, with its dreadful aftermath of sending out death certificates and completing all of Jim's affairs.

Over time, I renewed friendships, and made new ones. In a few years, I encountered a heart connection that turned into a joyous marriage. My life has come full circle. I no longer yearned for the old adage: "The best is yet to come." I realized with profound gratitude that "the best is here and now."

Lessons Learned

A quote in *Daily Wisdom*, a collection of Buddhist-inspired writings, helped me to clarify how the caregiving journey can be eased. One friend inquires of another:

> "How, dear sir, did you cross the flood?"
> "By not halting, friend, and by not straining, I crossed the flood."
> "But how is it, dear sir, that by not halting and by not straining you crossed the flood?"
> "When I came to a standstill, friend, then I sank, but when I struggled, then I got swept away. It is in this way, friend, that by not halting and by not straining I crossed the flood."

How did the caregivers I interviewed face the flood that confronted them? We'll be looking more deeply at this issue in upcoming chapters.

Chapter 2

Caregiver Burden and Opportunity

It is not unusual for family members to feel alone in their struggle with a chronic illness. People may drift away... it may seem impossible to get out of the house, and life narrows down to a tight circle of lonely misery.

– The Thirty-Six Hour Day,
Nancy L. Mace and Peter V. Rabins

There is no remedy for love but to love more.

– Thoreau

Caregiving as Opportunity

Certainly, long-term care can be described as burdensome, a yoke that, if not borne lightly, breaks us physically and mentally. But there's another side to the story. Let's start with the positive part of caregiving. Hard as it is, caregiving offers a genuine opportunity—a once-in-a-lifetime chance to make a deep connection with a loved one.

Joanne is a middle-aged woman confronted with the long-term care of a mother who was never there for her. Like most caregivers we interviewed, she had an all-consuming sense of responsibility. Her story begins with abandonment at age five by a mother who dropped her off at an older sister's, and showed her little or no support throughout her life.

I never really lived with my mother. That was part of my mental problem with her.

Many years later, she encountered her mother again—a feeble 80-year-old woman, suffering from mini-strokes, heart problems and osteoporosis. Helping her mother required that Joanne seek a more secure housing situation for her. She found an assisted living facility two states away, a solution that appeared to work for two to three years. At one point, Joanne realized her mother was not receiving adequate care.

They brought her a commode—a dirty, used commode. I took her out of there within 24 hours.

When her mother needed skilled nursing care, she transported her to a nearby facility, where Joanne could supervise her care. It was a long, arduous ordeal, interspersed with a few sweet moments.

[Once she was ill] *she couldn't come live with us. My husband was not very supportive. I had to make all the decisions alone. I feel some anger and resentment about that.*

For seven years, I spent 31 to 40 hours a week transporting my mother to appointments, calling or interacting with medical providers, dressing and walking her, dealing with financial arrangements, constantly filling out forms, taking care of her little room in the nursing home. The food was atrocious, so I took her out for dinner.

The most physically or emotionally demanding were things that involved paperwork. Conversations with my mother and the medical details with the dentist and the skin doctor took so much time. I took her over to our "secret garden" and walked around the apartments. I got her a child's sleeping bag to keep her warm. I took her for drives—so she could talk. That didn't work. She couldn't hear a thing. She didn't enjoy errands and things.

I mostly didn't express my feelings in front of my mother. She was so fragile. I never had a conversation with her. She avoided conversations. I dropped out of all social and professional clubs; dropped most of my friends, too. Eventually, I talked to a counselor.

I do feel sorry for my mother, because of her life. My emotions always go to my children. I owe my mother something. There was the conflict of caring for a mother I didn't know—yet I knew her better than she knew me. There were things she gave me. Still, I had so much trouble picking out Mother's Day cards.

My greatest gain was time spent with my mother. It was an unusual situation—the first time we lived in the same state. She loved hymns, so I sang her favorite songs. During the holidays, I brought her a little gift every day.

I felt overwhelmed one time when I took my mother to the Fountain [drug store]. She had an episode, probably a stroke, and then she looked dead. She loved parades and horses. I always took her to the fair on the bus with other nursing home residents. At the end, she missed the parade.

Death finally resolved Joanne's emotional turmoil, and gave her peace. She had kept the "covenant."

Before caregiving, my relationship with my mother was distant. I took care of her like I was her mother. I learned to keep her routine in the seven years I cared for her. I was able to sit with her all day while she died. And when she died, I had [a] strong feeling that I kept my covenant. 'I took care of you.' It was very satisfying. It was very hard, but I saw it to the end.

Exploring the Meaning of "Caregiving"

From an impartial viewpoint, caregiving is not a singular experience: all burden or all opportunity—insufferable versus transforming. Caregiving is multi-dimensional, involving both physical and emotional care, instrumental and mechanical services. The caregiver can dress and feed her loved one and console the agitated elder. She can also be helpful in providing more subtle services, such as encouraging exercise, bringing little gifts, or taking a loved one to a special event. Caregiving is more than service, though, as Joanne has shown us, because it touches our most primal feelings: confusion, love, hate, anger, pain, pleasure, joy and sorrow—sometimes multiple emotions at the same time.

Let's explore more about what "caring" involves. *Caring* is a relationship that involves at least one caregiver and one care receiver. Although caregivers ostensibly have greater power, the "success" of the endeavor may depend upon the care receiver's reactions. Rubbing the feet of an ailing husband, encouraging a reluctant mother in a nursing home to eat her meal and assisting a feeble family member to the toilet appear to be minuscule tasks, but once achieved, these accomplishments provide mutual gratification. What happens if the care receiver can't provide the "reward" or simply doesn't have the capacity for mutuality? I didn't receive my personal "reward" from Jim. I gained my benefits from my children, my sense of duty, my task-centered way of life. I reveled in the opportunity to make Jim's care as good an experience as I could— one that he would have sought if he had been able to choose it himself (given the dreadful limits of institutional care as we know it).

Caregivers and care receivers are locked into a delicate dance, regardless of the cooperation or lack of it from the care receiver. Under an optimal balanced order, caregivers intuitively know when to press forward with an activity, and when to back down. Care receivers, wishing to please their benefactor within their comfort level, willingly accept the caring assistance, or gently modify it to fit their needs.

We have all known cases in which this intricately patterned juggling act works. The relationship between giver and receiver deepens over time, and each understands and accepts the limitations of their situation. Both are spiritually informed, have a sense of humor and validate one another in myriad ways—for example, with displays of love, support and gratitude. Even within difficult caring relationships, moments may arise that make all the effort of both giving and receiving worthwhile. The equilibrium is restored, if only momentarily. Still, a caregiver knows she will have to repeat the same exercise over and over again.

In matters of caregiving, there can be no impartiality, no neutral position, nor even a resting place. If you ask any caregiver about "what's it like..." the answer will change by the day or the hour. As our caregivers demonstrate, the act of giving care is fraught with deep losses, insecurities and concerns, particularly as the loved one's illness progresses. Caregivers face ambivalence about their own capacity for benevolence. They also confront physical and emotional exhaustion as they wrestle with family baggage. Caregivers must strive to overcome the cultural ethic of individualism, which wreaks such havoc because the act of giving care is genuinely a selfless endeavor.

Levels of care vary greatly in terms of time, special demands on the caregiver, her personal resources and the quantity and quality of care required. Regardless of how much care was given, all caregivers reported they experienced a variety of physical, mental, emotional and other challenges that caused excessive stress. Problems include conflicts with family members over the type of care, medical indifference or neglect, the excessive financial costs of care, as well as the loss of friends and family for daily support. If the caregiver pushes too hard, the loved one may resist—or refuse outright to cooperate. Under pressure, the care receiver can easily regress—exhibit childish behavior and otherwise act irrationally.

Sometimes, the difficulty of care has to do with the nature of the loved one's response to their illness. Care receivers may be less than cooperative as they sink deeply into physical and emotional pain. Difficult behaviors may manifest as obstinacy, rejection, hostility, overly demanding, and even violence, among other reactions.

According to medical persons I spoke with, many physical and emotional conditions (such as depression) associated with terminal illness prove resistant to intervention. A caregiver must develop different strategies, such as seeking outside help. When a loved one becomes a danger to self or others—a condition afflicting nearly 40 percent of these care receivers—tough legal, medical and social challenges arise for caregivers. Such circumstances contribute to hopelessness among both caregivers and care receivers. For caregivers, not being able to help their loved one was a major source of psychological and emotional distress.

In many circumstances, then, care becomes burdensome, an unwanted, even despised obligation. Part of the burden resides in its inevitability—the lack of choice involved—because of moral and emotional ties to family members. Certainly, another part of the burden of caregiving is its apparent all-consuming nature. Robin West writes in *The Subject of Care* that caregiving, by its nature, essentially impoverishes or diminishes the opportunities of those who engage in it, whether freely chosen or not.

Unlike other "chosen" paths of life, caregivers cannot simply leave their charge. Because they are emotionally and ethically committed to the work of caring for their dependents, family caregivers, unlike employees, enjoy no autonomy, cannot walk off the job, unionize or strike for better working conditions, nor even anticipate an ending time. West states: "Consequently, caregivers receive all the vulnerability but none of the solace and certainly none of the security from the 'at will' aspect of their employment."

To appreciate the burdensome aspect of caregiving, we must acknowledge both the special quality of care and the sheer number and complexity of tasks involved. Sometimes called the "36-hour day," the providing of care to a frail elder has no equal. To demonstrate the especially demanding nature of family caregiving, I collected testimony from women who confronted the grueling effort of caregiving for their loved one for months and, for most, many years.

Losses and Imbalances

The sense of loss seems pervasive, at least during earlier stages of caregiving. Not only does the caregiver recognize her own life as undergoing radical change, but also, she perceives the monumental losses assaulting her loved one. I mention a few hardships that profoundly affect both caregivers and care receivers: loss of independence, self-control, financial security, predictability, future dreams, physical and mental health, normal role relationships with one another and other family members, leisure time, preferred lifestyles and a sense of personal balance. At the same time, an overwhelming sense of responsibility hovers over the giving of care. Role relationships are especially fragile. Illness evokes frustration and anger and the care receiver often lashes out.

Anne was a 61-year-old caregiver looking after her 70-year-old spouse, Mike, who had been recently diagnosed with Parkinson's disease. At an earlier stage of Mike's disease, she became the object of his wrath—he blamed her for everything that was going wrong.

> *'It's your fault. If you didn't have that job, I wouldn't be sick. If you would be nicer to my children, I wouldn't be sick. If you'd just behave differently, I wouldn't feel sick. If you weren't so hard on me, I could stand up straighter, speak in public without being nervous and write a legible sentence.'*

Kali's experience was wholly different. At 28 years of age, she became the "designated caregiver" looking after both her grandparents at the same time, one diagnosed with a stroke condition and the other with Parkinson's disease. Her burden was not only the loss of her young, carefree life, but also her inability to communicate with this older generation, and the feeling that she simply could not meet their needs.

> *It was such a dark time for us. I tried to work with them to make life decisions, but problem-solving was very difficult. Trying to explain why things are the way they are* [about their age and life situation] *was truly impossible. I wish I could have done more to help them during that time.*

Jean's experience echoes that of Kali's in that other family members failed to come to her aid, and her sense of futility about the situation undermined her sense of competence. Jean, a 50-year-old married woman, suffered deeply over the course of her caregiving career, including the death of a supportive friend, her mother's nearly total dependence upon her—even living in her home for three years—and her belief that she has sacrificed one dream after another without adequate compensation for the years of providing care. Jean said:

> *While I was taking care of Mother, I was in a car accident, I suffered the loss of a loved one, I was exhausted, and the year Mother moved here from Spokane, I had pneumonia. She moved in with us for a while. I was afraid I would have a heart attack.* [But] *I felt duty-bound. No one else in the family helped. My mother's been ill for eight years. She's 90 years old.*
>
> *Mother had dementia, osteoporosis and Parkinson's disease. I was really taken aback by the Parkinson's. She was incontinent, confused, sometimes unable to communicate, sad and depressed, suffering from eating and memory problems, feeling worthless and easily distracted.*

Jean felt the full weight of moral and emotional commitment. At the same time, her husband and children had to take a backseat once her mother went into care.

[Although] she's very polite, she expected I would provide care. I spent 11 to 20 hours a week providing shopping, housework, transporting [her] to medical appointments, bathing [her], cooking, calling medical providers, personal care, dressing [her], [making] financial arrangements, encouraging her to participate in activities. I try to encourage her independence.

I've tried to prioritize between my mother and my daughter. I've had to abandon my dream of going back to school. I see myself getting older and older as she gets older and older.

My greatest loss is the opportunity to engage in this stage of my life. I've been doing this since I was 44. I didn't realize how great the flexibility was before I began caregiving. I miss the time alone and with my children. I felt relief when my mother left to go back to her house [assisted living]. I was tired and resigned. I have a parent who has lived long and I couldn't imagine she could live this long. Now, I no longer feel this is a stage of my life—it is my life. I don't see an end to it.

My main support comes from my husband. When my friend was alive, she provided so much comfort. She was also my walking partner. I miss my friend so much. She died in a car accident. Mother would have liked me to be her friend. I tried, but I didn't feel that. She didn't have many friends.

I felt better about myself [after] I asked my mother to try assisted living. [Now] I visit her every day and when I get home I know my time is my own. It's difficult and frustrating just to have to go—repeatedly.

Jean's recommendation to others in her shoes:

My advice to caregivers: Start immediately reminding yourself [to] hold onto the dreams of what you want to do with your life, so you don't lose that—especially with the elderly living longer and longer. We need to take care of ourselves.

Many daughters, reluctant to give care, feel imposed upon by family and/or the sick elder. They may resist, but with a perception of having no choice, ultimately become the "designated caregiver," as one caregiver explains it. At the same time, daughters may feel burdened with a deep sense of obligation and responsibility.

Cindy, who commuted between the West Coast and the Midwest for years to supervise her mother's care, observed:

> *I was responsible for taking care of my mother because I'm the oldest daughter. I'm the medical professional—that qualifies me. It was an obligation, but one person should not have to shoulder such a responsibility.*

Inability to Define Moral Boundaries

Caregivers tend to react against—rather than respond to—the feelings and losses of their loved one. Without a strong sense of "I can do this, but *not* this," they often take on any and all family care responsibilities, regardless of their age or capacity. Carrie, now 39 and a student at the local university, has been caring for her blind father and his companion over the last few years. However, as a small girl, her earliest "training" was nurturing her mother. A few years ago she took on the care of her stepchildren while meeting the needs of her sister, who eventually died of cancer. In a significant sense, Carrie qualifies as a "progressive caregiver"—an expert, but without pay or public recognition.

In a written statement she sent to me about her multiple caregiving roles from childhood to the present, she said,

> *When I was born in 1965, my mother had already been diagnosed with M.S. (Multiple Sclerosis). Pregnancy and delivery escalated her symptomatology. By the time I could walk, I was caregiving for my mother. We did have some neighbors, who would stop by and check on us, but basically, I would retrieve or reach for things for my mother (lunch, etc.) and assist her in getting to the bathroom on time. She was wheelchair-bound at this time, and was progressively worsening, so by the time I started attending school full-time (first grade), no one was home anymore to care for her (with the needs that she had), so she moved into a nursing home. From then on, I would ride my bike to the nursing home every day after school to see her… then I would get home by 5:00 p.m. to cook dinner for my father, who was*

returning from work... During the time Mom was in the nursing home, I would read to her, fix her sheets and blankets, give her water, help her eat, and there would be many times I would communicate her needs to the staff at the nursing home. She would get upset, needing something, and I would go get them, and communicate her wishes and follow-up with them [staff] *to make sure they were carried out.*

Because of her continuous caregiving responsibilities since childhood, Carrie said that "part of me feels as if I've never known anything else [except caregiving]."

Now in her sixties, Faith's early life was colored by her mother's alcoholism, and the sense that caregiving defines one's entire existence. Faith said: "Caregiving is a life imprint" that began early and continued throughout her life.

I was the designated caregiver. Some of us are programmed for this. You don't make a choice. I was responsible for all of the five older generations and one of my uncles had Alzheimer's. For three years while I was in high school, I was the enabler [for my mother's alcoholism], *then for two people in my extended family, cousins and others. When I was nine, I contracted polio, and was in a wheelchair, even on crutches, but that didn't seem to matter. I was sent to my grandmother to look after her. On crutches! Later, I took care of the father of my cousin.*

Now, as an adult she faced caring for her mother, who never acknowledged her.

When she was 87, I took direct care of her for 18 months. She had congestive heart failure, dementia, Parkinson's disease and paranoia. She called the sheriff once to protect herself against taking a shower. I was so relieved to get a diagnosis of Parkinson's: relieved that symptoms were not related to alcoholism. Mother was always able to talk—verbally aggressive.

Faith was notified that her mother had been hit by a nursing home aide. The incident caused her to lose an eye. So Faith brought her back to live with her in a four-room cottage. Faith said: "She was supposed to die over the weekend, but she lived for 18 months." The relationship had never been a healthy one, but her sense of responsibility was paramount over any other considerations. Faith pointed out:

> *I really felt devalued when she said, 'You've never been any good,' or 'I should have never had you.' She was alcoholic. I'd heard all that before. Yet I felt a strong commitment to my mother's care… a lifetime commitment. I felt responsible for every bite she took.*
>
> *I had been a professional woman, intellectually growing and providing for my security. After a few months of caregiving, I was tired and confused about the future—no closure happening. I was responsible for so much. My terrible concern is that I left her in a nursing home where she was hit* [by an attendant]. *So I owed her this* [care].

Caring for Someone Who Will Never Get Better

Since long-term elder care is most typically resolved with the death of the care receiver, caregivers must, early on, incorporate the death and dying of their loved one into their everyday thinking and planning. This means that for caregivers, "letting go" early in the caregiving stage serves as the most effective strategy for coping with the declining health of their loved one. Sadly though, we live in a death-denying culture, which strenuously rejects death as a natural process, seeing it only as a failure. As a result, most caregivers woefully fall short at maintaining the necessary distance. They often allow whatever is happening to the loved one to unfold, without processing the experience, and then blame themselves for both their own bad feelings and any negative outcomes.

After Fran received her husband's medical diagnosis of Crohn's disease, she flew into a rage. Matters only worsened. After he became partially paralyzed, he suffered from immobility, incontinence and impotence. Months later, she was still trying to deal with his death. She reflected:

> *I was pretty angry. I still deal with it* [his dying]. *He was numb from the waist down. I was losing my husband, and changing from wife to caregiver. I knew he would never get better. I was so disappointed in myself in terms of giving good care, because of my own medical problems* [chronic back ache, anxiety, stress].

Carla, a 50-year-old mother of two, who cared for a friend during her terminal illness with cancer, admitted that she was frustrated and discouraged. Not only did she need to deal with her own emotional crisis over her friend's dying, but also her friend's daughters refused to acknowledge the reality of their mother's death.

> *I felt overwhelmed when her cancer came back. When people die on you, you lose part of yourself. You give so much of yourself. It's hard to see them get relapses. I worried about her. Was she really going to be OK? Was she ready to die? Had she made her peace with every-one? I felt overwhelmed with* [my friend's] *daughters. I tried not to say harshly, 'your mom's dying. She doesn't want to eat, I can't force her to eat.' I tried to give them information, but her daughters denied their mother's illness.*

Lack of experience also contributes to the caregivers' sense of confusion and inability to process or even ask sensible questions about what is happening medically to their loved one. In my own case:

> *I overreacted to every sign and symptom. I had the feeling from Jim's second heart attack on that he was at death's door. I was actually sur-prised each morning to wake up and find him still here, looking sad, but sometimes just a bit hopeful. Once he began having the mini-strokes, and his medication was upped, his condition ran the gamut from extreme dementia (after multiple doses of oxycodone) to fairly normal cognitive periods, although clouded by deep depression and debilitation. Throughout the ordeal, I never expected to endure four long years of this slow-lingering illness.*

The Balance between Freedom and Attachment

Caregivers frequently have deep ambivalence about achieving a balance between freedom and attachment. In giving herself too freely to another, a caregiver tends to lose herself, contributing to feelings of exploitation or even abandonment by the loved one. This is particularly true when the sick elder has dementia or has lost the capacity for ration-al thinking.

Rosanne, a consulting editor, brought her ailing mother to live with her and her husband in their large house. Initially, she had no idea how taxing this caregiving project would be. She sums up the time she devoted to her mother, and concluded that it interfered immensely with her work.

> *The caregiving role is so draining, [that] you don't have the energy to read the usual books. But the lighter literature doesn't give you what you need! You read mystery stories, preferably ones with lots of humor. Mom would have good and bad days, but she never was herself. I could see the [deteriorating] process going on.*

Rosanne's mother had vertigo, dementia, congestive heart failure and was subject to mini-stokes. As a result, she needed constant supervision. At first, caring for her mother was a joyous, loving experience, but over time her mother's sense of entitlement and self-centeredness wore Rosanne's material and emotional reserves down. Another solution needed to be found.

> *We lived in this neighborhood for 10 years. Taking care of Mother was easier because I lived in a very large house. My husband was very supportive. We had no children, and my father paid most of Mother's expenses. When we realized Mother was not receiving adequate care in her assisted living facility, we brought her to our home, where she stayed for 10 months.*
>
> *I had always had in mind that there was room in the house if we needed to. I thought we could manage with in-home care.*

Rosanne was delighted she could offer her mother a home with benefits.

> *The best part was seeing Mother have a good time; seeing her appearance come back—like a duchess again. We hugged her and smiled at her. We indulged her and made sure she looked like a million bucks!*

Caregiving requirements were more than she had bargained for, though.

> *I provided shopping, housework, transporting [her] to appointments, bathing assistance, cooking, cutting up her food, calling and*

interacting with medical providers, versatile care, transferring (from bed to chair or toilet), walking her, financial arrangements, giving medications. We did a great job! [However] *there's a big price to pay. I had no time to myself. Trying to show her a good time 51 to 60 hours a week, even with 30 hours of help per week left me dragging. We wanted the best care for her. We even used a baby monitor. I was happy to do the caregiving and so was my husband.*

A good chunk of our monthly expenses was for Adult Day Health (ADH). Once I took her to ADH, [and] *I figured things out, it got a lot easier.*

During the time we were caregiving, I lost work, so I lost money. I couldn't concentrate. I lost freedom—that's the thing. Even if someone was there, I was on a short leash—a caregiver continuum. My relationship with my mother had always been good, but that relationship changed as the dementia progressed. With dementia came entitlement feelings.

Her mother acted as though Roseanne "owed" her. The situation eventually became unbearable. With a heavy heart, Roseanne notified her father that her mother needed more care than she could offer.

A difficult decision for me was to send my mother back to Eastern Washington. She had had a devastating Transient Ischemic Attack (TIA). I thought she was going to die or be a vegetable. I told my dad she needed to go home. We found an opening at the nursing home. On Wednesday, he picked her up, and she looked like death. I continue to visit her in Eastern Washington. I'm not happy with the nursing home. They let her eat anything and now she's overweight.

Roseanne simply could not summon up the emotional reserves necessary to sustain herself through the caregiving. When I asked her what caregivers needed to survive the hardships of caregiving, she said:

If I could wave a magic wand, I would wish for a big house and deep pockets for all caregivers. That's what I would do. Take care of yourself. Just sit down. Go outside. Unless you have that time [for yourself] *even a book won't recharge you.*

For Kendra, a young teenager when she took over the care of her father, freedom of choice evaporated when she felt "forced" to replace her caregiving mother, who "deserted" the family to look after her own father. Kendra's optimism carried her through the earliest sacrificial period. However, it did not allow Kendra to heal her mother's continuous grieving over the loss of both her father and her husband, or put an end to the animosity her mother had for her.

> *Before I started caregiving, I was young, with the world at my feet. I'm in high school—a busy student athlete. And after a year, I'm wanting to change my life. I'm wanting for this to end.*
>
> *I didn't choose it, but was more or less forced into the situation when Mom left to care for her father. I took care of Dad 31 to 40 hours a week for six years, [including] high school. He took 25 medications for heart disease, kidney failure and lung problems. The most physically and emotionally demanding was transporting him to appointments and calling or interacting face-to-face with medical providers. I didn't mind at all—he was there and needed me. I did feel hopeless and wished there was something more that I could do.*
>
> *I had a dream of playing softball in college and I was accepted to my first choice school, but I turned it down to stay closer to my father. I lived with him and he had given me all he could, so I gave him all I could when he needed me. The best part was that I could change things for him. I was helping someone and he showed his appreciation. I loved making him happy. He was my mother and my father. We had a stronger relationship and an unspeakable trust as a result of my caregiving.*

I asked Kendra to summarize what part of caregiving turned out to be most of a burden. She said:

> *The burdens I carry involve an impossible relationship with my mother. She is very resentful, blames me for making my dad love me more than her; thinks I get between her and her men.*

Kendra ultimately views her caregiving as "blessed."

> *On the whole though, taking care of my father was an accomplishment. I felt more mature than my peers and more knowledgeable.*

I value integrity and I try to do the 'right' thing. I did a 'good deed,' I guess. I felt blessed for sacrificing some things I cared about.

For seven years, Roberta cared for her 85-year-old husband. She has worked through her loss of freedom by having a strong faith in God and deep forgiveness, but clearly recognizes the severe constraints of her life.

You have to let go of the things you had in the past. If there are things [that need resolving] *in your marital history, you'd better get into the business of forgiveness, or it will eat you alive.*

My husband suffered from dementia, Alzheimer's-like symptoms, hallucinations, Parkinson's-like symptoms and incontinence. He experienced confusion, [an] *inability to communicate—using the wrong word. He was also in denial about his health problems, had memory problems and* [was] *prone to moments of despondency.*

This meant that Roberta needed to take over all the responsibility of the household, prop him up emotionally, as well as structure her husband's time to give him a sense of feeling *useful*. She likened it to looking after a small child. Regretfully, she has had to abandon any sense of independence or personal choice.

I do everything: 80 or more hours a week. This is my life. There's really little Raymond can do. He can vacuum (Oreck) and do the dishes. I try to find any little job to help him feel useful—folding napkins, sweeping. He can't dust or determine what needs dusting. The most physically demanding is cleaning the bathrooms—the times he's incontinent.

He takes my arm when we walk in the wind. I tell him, 'We'll get through this. It will be okay.'

I do feel overwhelmed sometimes. I need to work on patience. It's answering the same questions over and over. Our relationship has changed. I have to do everything—make all of the decisions—no shared decisions or activities. There's a lack of initiative on his part.

My greatest loss is my freedom to do things in the evening. I can't just say, 'I'm going to a concert or a lecture. I'll see you in a couple of hours.' During the daytime, Raymond goes to Adult Day Health

(ADH), otherwise I take him everywhere I go. I have no independence.

Raymond was home for four days. ADH was closed. Those conditions presented a difficult pattern. There's a lot of pressure to keep him occupied and structure the day to keep him busy. I have to deal with my own understanding that he really doesn't know how to do something anymore. I tell myself, he does not know how to do that. He can't remember. My own work is learning those behaviors so I can respond to him in the most Godly way.

I've lost touch with my family and friends. It's like taking care of a toddler. I'm grieving that. It's okay. I have [a] strong desire to serve my husband. I made a clear and conscious choice to be Raymond's primary caregiver. Yes, I could have divorced him, but that would not be compatible with my calling in Christ. Part of serving God is to serve Raymond. I want my life to be a reflection of God.

Roberta still carries a foreboding sense of anguish over the costs of care. She rightly points to the failure of both the medical system and the government for ignoring the vast number of people caught up in the family crisis of extended care for elderly loved ones with dementia.

The most unfair experience I had over the course of caregiving is [that] the whole medical care system is out of whack. I think the rich don't have to care, but for the lower-middle class the costs are exorbitant. There's a lack of attention by the political community of the magnitude of dementia and the care that's going to be involved.

Gender and Caregiving

Women bear the brunt of caregiving, a task seriously devalued in American society, and one accorded little respect. This fact has to do with an array of social conditions—historical legacies, traditional gender arrangements, expectations of "feminine" behavior, cultural conventions and arbitrary definitions of reality—not with biology or human nature. In addition, gender stress exacerbates the caregiver burden. Whereas men are more likely to focus on task orientation, women emphasize emotional relationships. The dark side of caregiving for women involves the limitless obligations and positive emotions they are expected to express. Affinity, sympathy, compassion and affection are presumed to be natural properties of the female gender. Instead, these tender qualities are cultivated social-spiritual practices.

As a result, women are likely to suppress their true feelings, eventually to be overcome by the volatility and persistence of their negative emotions. They are also likely to succumb to chronic health problems, depression and unrelenting feelings of futility and worthlessness, topics I later explore. Additionally, early mortality haunts elder caregivers. Dr. Andrew Weil warns in "Caring for the Caregiver" that 63 percent of caregivers die within a four-year period after taking on the caregiving role.

Wives may be especially prone to gender-related expectations and conflicts.

Mary Beth, married for 47 years, took loving care of her much older husband for 10 years. Despite having a stroke, and for a period unable to read or write, she prepared herself for the worst. Until the final stages of Alzheimer's, her husband proved to be an intrusive, obstinate, if not an impossible, patient. Mary Beth recognized that it was the disease causing the problems, but that hardly erased the day-to-day difficulty of managing their lives.

> *I didn't have much time for relaxation. He became absolutely attached to me. I didn't have a minute to myself, totally, totally. He would talk and talk and talk. Every evening at six or seven, he wanted to go to bed. He wanted me to go to bed. He would pester me for two hours until nine when I went to bed. I did everything for him except transferring. The most difficult physically was bathing and coping with his not knowing what was going on. Early on, he went to a lawyer to get a divorce. He thought I made him sick. I took over the finances. He was a money freak, and I had Power of Attorney. It was important to get his signature while he could sign. Four weeks later, he couldn't. It was awful, awful, awful... When he had bright moments* [of lucidity], *his desperation took over.*

After wives, daughters are next in line for stepping up to the caregiving task. In the midst of a busy college career training to be an X-ray technician, Clarice, a single mom, received a phone call from Florida, thousands of miles away. A relative informed her that her father had deteriorated significantly. She immediately left college, and was forced to sell her home and two cars to make ends meet. Now, she serves as a full-time custodian for her 79-year-old father, afflicted with heart disease. Clarice feels *trapped* with the full-time job of looking after her dad.

Because she was unable to care for her dying mother, Clarice feels especially obligated to take care of her father. "Besides, I'm the only one who is going to do it; there's no one else in the family who can." I asked her what activities of daily living or special needs she carried out for her father, and which of these was the most difficult.

> [I do all] *the shopping, housework, transporting him to appointments, cooking, calling and interacting with medical providers, financial arrangements, giving him medications and walking with him.*
>
> [The most difficult was] *transporting him to medical appointments and calling/interacting with* [medical] *providers. He insists nothing is wrong with him, but hides behind my apron. He's too scared to go to his medical appointments alone.*

Parenting her parent, Clarice expresses her concern for her father, even while admitting, "I have no choices left—caregiving has taken over my life." Still, when she feels cranky and overworked, Clarice manages to be kind and thoughtful. "I tell him I love him every night when I tuck him in and give him medications."

Overall, how does she feel about her caregiving experience? Clarice said of her loving burden:

> *You know, I quit school to care for my father. During the time I've taken care of him I've suffered from multiple chronic problems—low back problems, high blood pressure, always, always exhausted. I buy TV dinners and plan meals ahead when I know I'm going to crash.*
>
> *I have always been an advocate* [for the elderly]. *I like disruptions—find them refreshing. I'm so in the hole financially—don't have anything—lost my house, sold two cars. If he gets much sicker, I'm screwed, but so far nothing's been shut off.*
>
> *No one wants to visit me with my father here. He can be positive, appreciative—also sometimes negative and unappreciative—that's when I say you're more than welcome to do it yourself and he does.*

If I hadn't brought him here, he would be dead. Sometimes I think people look at Dad's weight and think I'm starving him. I'm restoring order in my life with Valium. I did advocate for myself once. A Christmas tree really helped. I put it by the window.

Kathy, a vibrant athlete in her 60s, recognized her parents were aging, so she sold her house and moved into their home. Surprisingly vigorous for their ages, Kathy's mother is 92 and her father is 102. Kathy planned an efficient regime, doling out their medications, and generally keeping track of their lives. Setting up housekeeping for herself in the lower level of their comfortable home, though, did not resolve the problem of the 24/7 schedule. Kathy has become a child again in her newly formed relationships with her ailing, elderly parents. "I was just the one—the designated caregiver."

Who else would do it? I never told my parents about my problems. I keep them at low key, but sometimes I feel overwhelmed when I come home and mother yells at me because I didn't call. I feel like I want to run away. What am I doing? I need to get a life—this is dreadful. I guess I've given up freedom; [I] never go anywhere without telling them. As long as my parents are alive, I don't believe I have choices.

Distinctions Between Child Care and Elder Care

The uninformed public and caregivers who have been mothers often assume that child care and elder care run on parallel tracks. But is this necessarily the case? I believe that elder care offers a distinctive care syndrome that varies greatly from that of well-baby or child care. For elders, illness episodes vary and chronic disease, likely to be very serious, implies no remission or ending. Children's illnesses are typically of short duration.

As adults, elder care recipients have experienced high levels of autonomy, initiating choices and decisions, as compared to children's dependency. As well, community services for elders differ from those for children, requiring a range of agencies for the specific, ever-changing needs of the sick and aging elder. Schools serve as central repositories of services and referrals for most children. Elders lack a similar institutional framework.

Additionally, the caregiver has a far more multi-faceted relationship with her spouse, parents or other sick loved ones than a mother caring for her young child. At the same time, caregivers often equate their efforts with child care, because most women have deep familiarity with that stage of life. It is as though the aged mother or husband is childlike—dependent, helpless and non-rational.

Certainly, the level of sacrifice that one makes to one's own child is not comparable to the care and concern in other relationships. Unfortunately, treating the sick elder as one's child simply muddies the emotional waters, and drives the elder into deeper dependency and mental confusion. Finally, there is a downward spiral in elder care—"things only get worse." This phenomenon is unmatched in the typical illnesses of children, as caregivers sadly come to realize.

Seventy-nine-year-old Helen, married for 62 years, has been caregiving her husband for an extended period of time. Despite the fact that he has seriously deteriorated, she remembers him when he had all his faculties. Now, she ministers to his countless needs. I asked Helen what activities she carried out for her husband during the 10 years she has provided care.

> *Shopping; housework; transporting him to appointments; bathing assistance; cooking; feeding; calling and interacting face-to-face with medical providers; personal-care; transferring; dressing; financial arrangements; giving medications—he couldn't do anything. He didn't understand me the last six months. He was in a wheelchair for seven years—he wouldn't push himself. He lost his volition—he was very accepting—accepted life in a wheelchair, me taking care of him, the kids visiting him—he lost that edge in the 1980s. He said he didn't want to drive anywhere in 1985. We were still square dancing—he got so that there were three beats he was off—he had a lack of connection with everything.*

Helen did *not* identify her husband as a child, an awareness that allowed her to take a more balanced view of the situation, although some women felt they were dealing with small children. Instead, her husband served as a role model for her decision-making about his care.

When Roy died, I had been caring for him for so long I wanted to put it behind me. But people kept coming around with a long face, and it was hard to stop thinking about it. But I've adjusted—I've prepared for this for seven years. As he deteriorated I got more and more technology—handicapped van, hydraulic chair, sling. Roy was very successful, he was a money man; went after his goals with energy and zest. My goal in life in taking care of him was just to keep him out of a nursing home.

The caregivers led me to conclude that the more information the caregiver has about her loved one's disease, the more aware she becomes of the futility of her efforts to make him better. What appears to be counter intuitive makes sense when you consider the harsh reality of many chronic diseases. Mary Ellen's angry reaction to her husband's decline with Alzheimer's disease was not untypical of caregivers I spoke with. She lamented:

I was angry. I fought with my husband and yelled. It was so frustrating answering the same questions over and over. He opened and closed the refrigerator constantly. I cried a lot—depression, frustration and anger. I don't feel I've gained anything. The knowledge of that disease—it's depressing.

When is Caregiving Not a Burden?

We easily recognize full-time caregiving as a terrible, and often unanticipated, weight. But when is caregiving *not* a burden? Among these caregivers, I discovered certain conditions that appear to reduce the burdensome aspects of providing care. Among them, sharing the caregiving load with other family members and having only a short commute to the care receiver living in a residential facility. Looking after a neighbor or any person for whom the caregiver does not feel deep attachment can minimize the time and effort involved. And, a fortunate few have a sense of commitment that is so deep, the word "burden" simply does not enter the caregiver's mind.

Betty is a retired elementary teacher, married with one stepchild, who shared care for her 88-year-old mother with her sister over a five-year period. Because this older sister lived near her mother, Betty handled most of the organizational tasks. She also filled in a few week-ends a month for around-the-clock care. She said she was pleased to be "able to assist, comfort and love my mother during her aging years and death." While Betty was furious with her two brothers, who refused to get involved, she focused on the positive aspects of her loving care.

> *The needs of my mother determined my involvement. Some week-ends, I spent 11 to 20 hours; other weekends, less time. My husband supported and encouraged me to be involved. I enjoyed doing it and felt it was my role as a caring daughter to help my mother. Yes, some-times I felt overwhelmed because of her failing health, but I always empathized with my mother and tried to suggest options that would help her. I've always tried to be sympathetic, helpful and caring. So, I've had no loss at all because of my caregiving. The best part of care-giving my mother? I loved spending time with her, talking about literature, movies, theater. She had a great sense of humor.*

Betty's strategy for dealing with her sadness over her mother's poor health was to live as full and joyous life as she could.

> *I've tried to spend time with special friends and continued doing what I love—read, walk, cook, volunteer, entertain friends and at-tend cultural events with my husband. I try to get through the rough times by enjoying myself. I guess you could say I laugh, laugh, laugh and spend time with friends!*

Joyce, a retired teacher and family-oriented person, exemplifies a caregiver who shares her caregiving load. She lives in close proximity to her 96-year-old mother, who is in assisted living, and is able to get assis-tance from her three sisters when they visit. Joyce's life remains normal, and visiting her mother is an event she anticipates. She takes into ac-count that she has much less personal time, a situation she accepts.

> *Mother and Father moved to* [their facility] *December of 1999. Dad died February 28, 2000. Mom was very arthritic, and that, com-bined with her grief and loneliness, led naturally into* [her] *spending time with me. Mostly, I am privileged to have quality time with Mom, and to hear stories from her childhood. I tell her I love her of-ten. In sum, I feel positive, privileged, lucky.*

In instances where caregiving is perceived as a part-time commitment, or caregivers subjectively minimize their involvement, feelings of being overwhelmed are rarely expressed. Lenora takes care of her 90-year-old husband. She also has temporary Power of Attorney for her neighbor with Alzheimer's, Lilly, for whom she serves as financial manager. Lenora's help enables Lilly to live in her own home, her avowed wish. Lenora enjoys feeling "useful," adding, "When I'm needed, I go over and see what has to be done."

While Lenora admits to feeling obligated at times—running errands, buying groceries and accompanying Lilly to the doctor—she also has a fall-back position, in that she can call Michael, Lilly's nephew, if the situation becomes too difficult. Part of the ease that Lenora expresses ("it's okay doing this") can be attributed to the many years she dedicated herself to community service, working in a volunteer capacity with the American Cancer Society, local hospital and university. Lenora further described her caregiving involvement:

> Lilly had her stroke, and her nephew came over here to ask for my help. Then, Lilly approached me too. She was definitely urgent about staying in her own home. She's had spells when we all thought that she should be in care. But she's adamant about that [staying home]. I wanted to help just to see that she was adequately taken care of: that people wouldn't take advantage of her. I think I'm helping her to the degree I can. I try to practice patience, and after all, things aren't as bad as they seem.

Finally, caregiving is not perceived as burdensome when the caregiver has dedicated herself—heart and soul—to a dearly beloved person, and simply cannot imagine doing anything other than giving care. For the past 50 years, Sharon has been happily married to Carl, a university professor. She has enjoyed a rich life as the co-owner of a gift store, occasionally interviewing job-seekers and making crafts. But her heart was always at home with her husband and their daughter. Sharon believes she has been "truly blessed... and fortunate all my life," feeling especially grateful that she and Carl were able to "celebrate our 50th anniversary with our daughter and son-in-law [with] over 100 people."

Shortly after that event, Carl was admitted to the University of

Washington hospital for surgery, where he was put on a feeding tube for the last nine months of his life. Sharon confided to Carl's brother her greatest fear: "That something would happen to me. What if I couldn't take care of him?" His brother responded: "You can't fall apart. Everything is up to you." And, Sharon rose to the occasion, fully determined to do her best. She described herself as a "competent and caring" caregiver.

> *I guess I coped all right. I managed to take care of him. He wanted to die at home, and I was able to do that for him. I was right proud of myself for being able to do it—the daily care, the wound cleaning, the feeding tube. I guess the worst thing was the wound care—it was terrible to look at. It was very sad, but necessary* [and] *I didn't object to doing it.*

Death was not something either Sharon or Carl feared. They both belonged to Compassion & Choices, and would have chosen the organization's assistance with dying, but the feeding tube prevented that option. A matter-of-factness characterized Sharon's discussion of death and dying, as well as her willingness to let him go.

> *When we found out he was terminal, he would have ended it then if we had* [legal] *physician assisted suicide. Carl got pneumonia at the end. Hospice asked if he should have antibiotics.* [But] *I saw no point in prolonging his life.*

Lessons Learned

After reading these stories, few could deny that caregiving can test the mettle of even the most dedicated caregiver. But consider this. Despite the unpredictability and constraints of giving care to an elderly loved one as their physical and mental health declines, we discover our own strengths—and weaknesses, too. Certainly, life has shifted from a normal working and family self with a set of reasonable routines and relationships.

Instead, we confront a heightened reality, where selflessness and vigilance must take over to meet the ever-changing and complex needs of the loved one. At the same time, the caregiver burden is not absolute. Rather, it is softened and given significance by love, commitment and a sense of duty. In finding the *gifts* and *opportunities* in caregiving, caregivers learned to reshape their lives in positive and life-affirming ways.

Above all, successful caregivers kept their connection with self. Here's an exercise that helps the helper stay grounded. Ask the question: *What is keeping me from feeling totally alive right now?* Write down your responses. Your answers may change with the situation. Then consider what makes you feel vibrantly alive.

In one of the lowest periods of my caregiving, I wrote down these alive-making experiences in the form of a prayer. We live in a beautiful part of the world, so I have much to be grateful for.

May I love my life, and pass it on.
May I be free from confusion.
May I continue to enjoy the natural beauty that surrounds me—sunshine, air, sky, water and mountains.
May I continue to make appropriate choices for my life, regarding Jim, my home and job.
May I enjoy my inner and outer life to the fullest measure possible.
May I remember to pray for Jim daily, as well as all my loved ones. Amen.

And, don't forget that old standard from the 1940s, which reminds us to focus on the positive, eliminate the negative and stay away from the in-between.

Chapter 3

Identity: Who Am I, Anyway?

As I get older I am turning into myself. Job gone, children grown and living far away, parents dead. Can't backpack, can't do hip hop. Who am I, really? Now I get to find out.

— Susan Moon, *This is Getting Old:*
Zen Thoughts on Aging with Dignity and Humor

Who Am I, Really?

Before I could transition into a proficient and confident caregiver, I asked myself the question every day: "Who am I?" Nothing that was happening appeared "normal" or "ordinary." As Jim deteriorated, my sense of self appeared to be unwinding until it threatened to fly away. I took his lack of response and indifference to his life as a personal affront. Nothing I had done in my academic career, nor my past experience gave me a handle on what was happening. I could only hold on to one constant. Even while carrying out basic tasks, I had a sense of the tragic; indeed, the "tragic heroine" seemed to fit me best: "Woe is me; why did this have to happen," and of course, the all-familiar, "Why me?"

Certainly, I knew I had no power to resolve my husband's precipitous decline. Nor could I avoid the utter necessity of restructuring my life around his illness. During a period of medical crises, when Jim faced a series of hospitalizations and nursing home rehabilitation, I began to reflect on just exactly who was I NOW? As I pondered my evaporating sense of self, I reflected on my past and present identities, and how they had transformed over time. My musings went something like this:

Before caregiving began, I am a married woman with children. I have a strong identity as a professional woman, actively teaching, researching and writing. I am an optimistic, take-charge person, a fun-loving person, a feminist, a politically aware person with strong family values. My values were ordered very highly, and I worked hard to implement them in my daily life.

After a few months of caregiving, I am a frightened, disorganized, panicky, out-of-control, reluctant caregiver, which was fast becoming my primary sense of who I was. I couldn't keep up with my research and writing; friends were dropping by the wayside; I felt at loose ends. But I continued teaching full-time because of financial pressures. My biggest hurdle was putting my husband in care. I couldn't believe I could put my dearly beloved in a nursing home, and walk out the door.

When "Who I Am" Slips and Slides

What happens to the identity and sense of self over the course of caregiving, and then, after the death of the loved one? I knew these events dramatically altered my sense of who I was—competent, organized, take charge type—at least, who I thought I was. Suddenly, I could no longer summon up the energy to keep all my social and emotional balls in the air. I frequently succumbed to mental confusion and emotional distress, and even broke down, when I felt overcome by panic.

Losses are expected, but without previous experience with an ill or dying loved one, how does anyone know this? For example, a caregiver might say, "I was a competent mother and nurse, but now I'm nothing since my kids left and my husband died." Such a statement (which I heard numerous times) demonstrates not merely a loss of roles, but more important, a loss of selfhood: an empty identity. Some caregivers believed this emptiness was inevitable, and gave up the struggle. They became ill or just turned over the tasks to others. For a few, the responsibility was simply too much. Surprisingly, most caregivers I spoke with did not collapse in the face of the caregiving burden. They learned how to provide care—and not in a day or even in a week. It takes months to feel yourself coming together again as a self-aware person once you take on the caregiving role. In the meantime, the person you thought you were seems to have disappeared, maybe for good.

The Transitional Self

Until recently, caregiving used to be seen as a short-term commitment, a transitional role. In 1952, when my father-in-law was diagnosed with heart failure at 70 years old, he was still working and carrying on his regular routines. A few weeks after the bad news, he began feeling weak and took to his bed. Within three months, he was gone, easily and quietly, although he was deeply mourned. Yet, his passing was neither unexpected nor dramatic. My mother-in-law resumed her life in the small North Dakota community, no longer a wife, but now a widow, joined with dozens of others in her age group in a time-honored role.

Medical advances have changed many chronic illnesses. Whether heart disease, cancer, diabetes, dementia or the host of other ailments besetting elders, older people can be treated and life may be prolonged, although the treatment is rarely curative or has so many side effects that the affected person develops other chronic conditions. Sometimes, it even seems that death can be postponed indefinitely.

Certain diseases place very heavy demands on caregivers. Tasks seem endless. Old routines must be shed to accommodate new demands. Such is the case with Alzheimer's disease, a neurological malady I explore in Chapter 8. Learning to live with a progressive dementia patient is a vast challenge. How can one maintain a sense of oneself as a competent, independent decision maker and partner under conditions of constant shifts in the loved one's mental capacity? One strategy is to simply "go with the flow" and balance out the confusion and disturbing behavior of the loved one with memories of formerly stabilizing experiences, such as raising children. Another is to accept the shift from the role of wife to that of companion or nurse. Yet, another is simply to endure the sometimes unendurable until the care receiver passes on. These caregiver stories embody different transitional experiences.

Perhaps the most tragic situation for many caregivers, as with Martha, involves the cognitive loss of a highly intelligent spouse. Martha talks about how she adjusted to her husband's gradual decline, accepting ruefully the new circumstances.

I don't know if it was my intention to be my husband's caregiver. You say, 'for better or worse.' We've been married 50 years. We always did things together, but we also had separate lives. We shared all the re-sponsibilities. Now the hard part is getting some private time. I need to get him out of the house, but I can't imagine getting him ready for the morning Adult Day Care. He has a Ph.D. in physiology re-search—and he has Alzheimer's.

For me, the shift of roles came gradually. I had just retired and was enjoying being a crone; having free time and the sense that I had done the things I really enjoyed in my life.

After a year of caretaking, I realized my freedom would be lim-ited. Remember when you had toddlers and they interrupted every five seconds? That's the way it is—the interruptions. I haven't figured out a good way to ignore them. I've abandoned the idea of control and that helps. I had to let go of standards—so he sleeps in a sweater, that's okay. As he's less and less able to do things, I have to do more and more. There's no one else to be responsible. I had to stop him from driving the car. I supervise when he dresses and simplify the feeding— food on his plate not served on the table. He sometimes thinks I'm taking over everything. I'd like to see my grandchildren more often, but Alzheimer's and toddlers don't mix.

After his death, Martha had an opportunity to review her life, and to grasp the wholeness she had lost while caregiving.

Today, I'm back to the crone. I had no escape while he was alive. I'm incredibly grateful I could arrange respite care. I think I should move to a place that doesn't take so much of my time [large home]. *It's wonderful to have kids and grandkids. It's also wonderful to have friends who seek you out for discussion. I read a lot. That keeps me young.*

In the next story, Gloria traces the shifts in her marriage, beginning with the period before her husband's illness to the present day, where interdependence and a companionable relationship have replaced her former roles as an independent, professional woman, in a moderately conflict-oriented marriage.

I retired to have more time with him. I'd always thought indepen-dence was important. My life was disrupted by caregiving. It made me less independent and less able to do what I want to do without thinking of the consequences. Our futures lie out differently now. Before he became ill, we were more independent from one another. We had some shared interests, but we disagreed fairly frequently over things—a little pushy interaction and shouting, but only one major fight in our 37 years of marriage.

I remember the first time I heard, 'You are his caregiver.' I am his voice. After a couple of years of caretaking, I grappled with my changing role. I am more of a companion to my husband. We are closer as a result of caregiving. There's a sense of less independent activity. He doesn't attempt to curtail my activities, but he needs more attention. He is taking 15 to 17 medications for heart disease and a stroke, and I need to supervise this.

I wish it weren't happening. Sometimes I feel low, but I need to stay okay—sometimes it's hard to stay optimistic. It's not that I am uncomfortable, but I'm aware that the role itself will change. I'm learning to be grateful for what we have, rather than what we've lost.

We're closer now that we're interdependent. He's happier now than he's ever been. He enjoys spending more time together. It's a plus— we've adjusted to the new lifestyle. The greatest gain has been more communication and sharing of interests. I think it's made me a much more patient person. I'm a better person than I used to be. It's taught me to be more accepting about things I cannot change.

I know this situation will progress. I don't know how I'll take care of him when I'm not physically able.

Gloria's narrative demonstrates how one can change one's identity— from independent to interdependent. Even an intimate relationship can change—from a conflict marriage to a companionable one without sacrificing the self. Instead, Gloria gained a greater measure of personal integrity and a stronger sense of herself. As her primary relationship flourished, she actually developed renewed strength and vigor. At the same time, she remains haunted by an unknown future of her own possible inability to continue care indefinitely, a frequent theme among older caregivers.

When a friend steps in to give care to a long-time companion, the obligation feels not much different than when a sister or brother requires care. And when the friend's family fails to respond to the call of their family members' decline from Alzheimer disease—much less show up and take over care management—the sense of responsibility can be overwhelming. When confronted with the unwelcome intrusion of her dearest friend's illness, Carmen, a highly successful professional, realized she needed to act. Under the pressure of uncertainty about her decision-making role, Carmen's sense of who she was shifted over time.

> *Before caregiving began, I am a friend of Mary, a single woman. I am an educator. After a few months of caregiving, well, the disease was so gradual, I didn't really notice stuff happening. Once I realized what was wrong, I felt so much dismay and sadness that something can happen to someone with a brain like that—her family died early.*
>
> *After one year or more of caregiving, I became an apprehensive person. I was feeling more trapped. I had a continuous sense of danger. I didn't know how to cope. I thought: I shouldn't have to give up my friends to look after Mary. Today [after her death] I am relieved. I feel sadness because part of my life was no longer there. But now I've retired, and I have my life back.*

Once Carmen learned "to set priorities, and just deal with it," she could work as an advocate for her friend. Later, she was able to locate an excellent care setting for Mary. This decision reduced Carmen's 30 or more hours of caregiving a week to a reasonable number of visits and interventions with the nursing staff. After six years of looking after her friend, Carmen offered a wise approach to preserving oneself through the caregiving process:

> *Just take the situation as it comes. There are more options for you than you think. But the more you think of yourself, the worse it gets. Think of the other person's needs and comforts. Don't lose your identity, but recognize this person's life isn't going to last much longer, and you have time to do other things.*

Young women are particularly tested when they leap generations to care for grandparents. In her early thirties, Teri took on the six-year task of supervising home care and very frequent hospital visits for her grandmother, and after her death, her ailing grandfather. Deeply attached to both, she endured almost 40 hours a week of caregiving along with a full-time job. She alone carried out the myriad of tasks required to keep them going: shopping, housework, dressing, financial arrangements, interacting with medical providers and making day-to-day decisions about their lives. She felt she owed them "love and time." How did these care functions impact her over the years? Teri replied:

> *Before caregiving began, I could describe myself as fun-loving, newly into a relationship and self-centered. I am a lot of fun. After a few months of caregiving I am getting more concerned; I am a worried person. I am a strong activist. I am responsible for them.*
>
> *After one year or more of caregiving, I am stressed. I am deeply concerned. I am short on time—never enough time for me or anybody. My biggest loss was lack of personal time.*

Teri faced not only the care of two deeply ailing elders, but also the failure of other family members to get involved. Yet, she moved beyond the call of duty to provide daily care for her elderly relatives, persisting through the most challenging situations.

> *They both needed assurance that they were okay. I would advocate for them. Sometimes everything was too much, especially when Grandpa got combative.*
>
> *Then I just broke down. I was angry for so long, especially about his medical care. They were negligent with his [grandfather] care at [the nursing home]. They didn't give him enough morphine for his pain. He was screaming into death.*

Now that her grandparents have both died, how does Teri define herself?

> *Today, I am strong. I am appreciative. I try to help others. I try to make a difference. I realize how short your life is. I'm grateful I had the good sense to look after them. I stepped forward at the right time—not a lot of people feel the calling [to be a caregiver]. If I hadn't done this, I wouldn't be as altruistic. I believe it's important to leave the world in a better place for having the opportunity to be here.*

In Teri's case, the transition from a fun-loving self *before* caregiving to a responsible community leader, who advocates for the elderly and other needy people *after* caregiving, involved a steep learning curve. Today, gracious and confident, Teri has emerged as a major political force in her community, overcoming enormous odds, including cancer.

The Turbulent Self

Under the duress of caregiving, women frequently confront the hidden or shadow part of themselves. Emotions and sentiments, normally buried, burst forth under the pressure of daily demands, as well as the loss of a loved one's health, companionship and life. Sandra clarifies how "different" her life became once she took on the caregiving role. I asked Sandra to describe herself in "I am" statements for four time periods: Before caregiving, after a few months of caregiving, after one year of caregiving and today. Here is her response.

> *Before caregiving began, I used to be a different person. I am a married woman. I am a daughter. I am a good friend. I am a lover. I'm an active woman. I am a business owner. I'm the only one left in my family since my brother died, so I had that responsibility, too. I first became a caregiver for my brother, who died of AIDS.*
>
> *After a few months of caregiving, I'm a devoted wife, I'm a loving woman. I'm a business owner.*
>
> *After one year or more of caregiving, I am an emotional wreck. I'm unorganized. I am not a good friend. I'm moody. I felt helpless, frustrated and full of conflict. It's hard to watch someone you love suffer and die and not do anything about it. I was overwhelmed. I'd go on autopilot—do it and think about it later. Only when it stops do you think about it. I broke down a lot.*

When I asked Sandra if she could pinpoint the source of her turmoil, she indicated it was her reaction to circumstances, including frustrations surrounding medical care.

> *At the beginning, I was so committed. But the sicker he got, the angrier he got, and I couldn't deal with his feelings. He was angry at being sick. I wasn't angry at him, but at circumstances. I took things*

out on him; he took things out on me—heat of the moment. And the medical system up here [Canada]*—it's dreadful. That's why he's dead. He died while having kidney dialysis. My husband was in a drug-induced coma. When I asked the doctor what was happening to him, the doctor told me, 'Everything's fine.' I'm so mad that I didn't speak up enough to the doctors about their lack of care, and that I got short and spoke up to my sick husband instead.*

Sandra also complained that her husband's lack of appreciation of her efforts further compounded her sense of incompetence and futility.

He went from an expectation that I would provide care to a totally negative attitude. He was so unappreciative. It got to be overwhelming.

Additionally, Sandra felt guilty about leaving him to go to work. She commented:

I felt terrible about not being with him all the time, but I had to work. No work—no pay.

Clearly, Sandra had over-identified with her personal shortcomings and succumbed to anger and helplessness about the quality of medical care. Her former self-image—competent, energetic and in-charge—had deteriorated over the course of caregiving and had given way to one imbedded in anger, guilt and remorse. Only after her husband died could she reconstruct an integrated self. This time, the "who am I?" question yielded a highly positive response. Sandra said:

Today, I'm a loving wife [remarried]. *I'm a business owner. I am a spiritual person. I'm a good friend. I am an independent woman. I'm seeking balance and prioritizing my life. I've learned to 'let go and let God.'*

The Declining Self

Among some caregivers who embraced the caregiving role as a single, focused experience, the post-caregiving experience was less positive. These women report a sense of loneliness (sometimes, years after the death of their loved one), deep depression or emptiness. For a few, once the ordeal was over, they experienced a collapse—a "kind of falling through space," in the words of one caregiver. Disengaging from care-centered activities, the grieving caregiver may believe that life has been lived already.

At the extreme, they die with the loved one's passing. Their state of being may be masked by normality—they clean the house, answer the phone and e-mail, attend social events and participate in family gatherings—but reluctantly and as little as possible. They speak as one who has withdrawn from life. As a result, energies wane; life's possibilities dwindle; the decline seems inevitable; the future appears bleak.

For Sally, the caregiving journey seemed to be interminable. An only child, she assumed full responsibility of both parents after they were diagnosed with terminal diseases. Having recently buried her mother, she now looks back over the last four years, which she describes as "totally" disrupted by the caregiving task of two ailing, and often obstinate, parents. Sally describes her shifting self over the course of her caregiving.

> *Before caregiving began: I would say I am an outgoing person; I am adventurous, involved with community, friends; I am a wife, a mother.*
>
> *After a few months of caregiving: I became stressed, disorganized. Like when I went to their home for Thanksgiving to sell their house. I was devastated at the shambles. Mother was totally argumentative. She wouldn't cooperate. I had to travel with two sick people who needed hospitalization. Dad had respiratory failure. Once we got here [Sally's home], I had to decide whether to put him on life support. We did it for three weeks. Meanwhile, mother needed care, so I put her in a nursing home for two months. I thought she was going to die, but she bounced back.*
>
> *After one year or more of caregiving: I was thoroughly depressed. I didn't find a lot of joy. I was going downhill, as they got sicker and sicker. It's so debilitating. I just couldn't cope with it. But I felt it was my moral obligation. I was an only child… my mother lived vicariously through me. My whole life was confused by it all.*

Sally is currently trying to re-establish herself after the rigors of caregiving.

Today, it's been a few months and I'm just now beginning to snap out of it. I've had to deal with it: selling the house, supervising their medical care, organizing their finances, sorting out their personal effects, taking care of everything. The entire thing [caregiving] took so long. I'm still in process. It feels real funny... sometimes I feel I'm going to the nursing home again to visit Mom everyday.

Finally, I'm glad I don't have to do it again. I'm sorry that it's over, but I'm sure glad it's done. It's kind of hard when your loved ones pass away. It's kind of hard to visualize what your life is going to be. It takes a long time to even figure out you have a life. I'm just learning to go back to some of the things I used to do. It always feels like something's just hanging right out there.

Rose never recovered from her husband's death. After he died from a sudden illness, she immediately took on the care of her mother, although seething with resentment. Having experienced a "crash course in dying"—her husband survived three months after diagnosis—Rose remains uncomfortably attached to her 93-year-old mother, who refuses to talk about Rose's beloved husband or her own imminent death.

My husband had brain cancer—three months and he died. I was devastated after Bradley died. I felt lost and I didn't know who I was. Even after years, it's still the same. It never goes away. I'm caring for my mother now; no choice. There's not a day when I don't think about Bradley. I want to walk again and play the piano again. Caring for my mother makes me feel like throwing things sometimes and she doesn't want to talk about Bradley. I get nervous and shaky— it plays on my emotions. I tell myself not to be mouthy; to be kind. I get frustrated. She's my mother, so I can't get unhinged with her. She's controlling and makes me feel like a little kid. She has always pulled my strings and I'm aware of it, so I can't express sympathy. I've just learned not to blow my own temper.

I sometimes feel like a failure at what I'm doing; I can't deal with it, but I know I have to. It's difficult to maintain your sense of self when you're caregiving. It's tough to be told by my mother that I treat her like I don't want her, that I have "mud in my eye," that I don't care about her. It's a real tough one. I can't talk death with her.

If I hadn't taken on the role of caring for Mother, I would have gotten my individuality back. It wouldn't always be "we."

Like Rose, Mary Ellen has lost her purpose in life. Caregiving her husband with Alzheimer's disease over a decade has drained her both physically and emotionally. Even sadder, she has no perception that anything could be different than it is. She lacks any prospect of hope or of creating a different life.

Among other things, I watch the fish tank for relaxation. I'm depressed, frustrated and angry. Ron has had Alzheimer's disease for nine years. I watched him go downhill; I'm answering the same questions over and over again. I went from being happy, loving, employed, married and a good companion to quitting my job and living on food stamps. My main concern was medical testing.

Now, I'm lonely and uncomfortable most of the time. Basically, I don't have a life since caregiving. I'd never marry again. I just want a corner to be alone and play an online game for escape.

Cindy, a well-educated occupational therapist and nurse, has a family background that significantly contributes to her role as solo caregiver for both parents. Childless, Cindy's parental commitment undermined the relationship with her husband. Eventually, they parted on negative terms, and Cindy lost her stake in their jointly owned family farm. Cindy struggles to make sense of her five years of caregiving for her alcoholic father, whom she remorsefully put in care. Now, she dreads the future. She will need to convince her sister to take over the duties of her aging mother's care or it will again fall to her. Cindy's story illustrates the special problems of caring for an elderly alcoholic.

All my brothers and two sisters are alcoholic. I cared for my father as a child. My morning wake-up was my father vomiting. Do I have the right to make choices for myself? Yes, yes, I have the right, but will I have the strength to do it? My dad was alcoholic for 25 years. He is very small-minded; he has a tiny little world; he is so immature. It began a long time before because of his long-standing alcoholism— on the wagon, off the wagon. When does the fight begin? Always the dread; always the dread.

He went into alcohol recovery in 1973 and five more times after that. I was the eldest child; my obligation was to care for him. He was an incapable caregiver for my mother, who had Lupus and strokes. I cared for both him and my mother, who developed an ulceric stomach. Both of them had dumping syndrome [a spastic bowel condition].

I have the niggling guilt about not seeing him enough. I'm not looking forward to Mom—she's 75. All my brothers are alcoholic. It's my sober sister's turn. This has really tested my values. Am I an ongoing server—tending to every need? A stronger Christian would be more involved than just maintenance and it ain't much. Caregiving has taxed my spare time, taxed my relationship with my husband, no time to heal—healing did not happen.

Cindy regards the personal changes she has experienced over those years.

When I first began caregiving, I was a married woman, employed. I am the eldest daughter and responsible. I am a friend and highly active, exploring the world around me. After a few months of caregiving, I am confused and frustrated struggling with multiple decisions every single day. My Dad used alcohol on top of his dementia, then he insisted on driving (which was his hobby).

His behavior was so bizarre; he just left his disabled wife behind.

After a year or more, I'm failing to have a significant level of control and comfort in the decisions that I need to make on a day-by-day basis. So I said to myself: 'I know you can't dance, and it's too late to plow...' It just needs to be done [placing her father in care]. *After three years, he's in assisted living. I think I lost a great deal of compassion. It was a task-oriented project. I didn't have any emotions after that.*

Today, I am a woman whose husband is 'out of the way.' I have some remorse and lack of contact with my father—big guilt. I am guilty.

Kali moved into the basement of her grandparents' home for two years so she could care for them. Her 81-year-old grandmother had Parkinson's disease. Her grandfather, a taciturn and competitive character, had a notoriously bad attitude. She describes two vignettes of their intergenerational relationship.

> *It was Grandfather whom I had problems with. My Grandmother was my support.*
>
> *When Grandfather thought I was cheating at cards, Grandma said: 'Just let him win.'*
>
> *When I was there I kept sweaters on Grandma to keep her warm. But when I wasn't there, Grandma was always cold. It was so hard to see her so uncomfortable. Grandfather didn't want her to have a lot of clothes on. He insisted it would be too hard to dress and undress her. Everything with him was an argument. It was too hard to make both grandparents happy.*

How can I describe Kali's life before caregiving began? How did she turn out at 28 years old, the designated caregiver for the older generation?

> *Before caregiving, I was single, living at home with my parents; I was worried about my direction in life. I was a residential care aide. What am I going to do with my life? I try to please everyone—make everyone love me. The care of other people always came first. I felt like no one noticed me or knew I existed.*
>
> *Because of Grandma's illness, I took the RCA* [residential care aide] *courses, when what I really wanted to do was to take human resource classes working with the* [disabled]. *The RCA work seemed the right thing to do. But now I'm still paying for my student loans for those courses.*
>
> *A few months after caregiving, I am lonely and bored. At the same time, now people are praising me, happy for me, proud of me for being there for Grandma.*
>
> *My patience is being tested time and time again. I guess I managed.*
>
> *But, after a year, I was trying to get away; trying to get my own space. I made excuses not to be at home with my grandparents. At the end, I am lost, lost fulfillment. I don't know if this is the right direction.*

Kali clearly has second thoughts about whether she should continue caring for her grandparents, but feels trapped, as well as lacking job options. She had been fired from her nursing job shortly after she assumed full-time care of her grandparents.

> *Maybe this is not what I should be doing. Maybe I don't have enough patience to deal with certain situations. I need a break. I feel like a bad person saying this, but I was there 24 hours a day. It wasn't like I had an 8-hour job and went home.*
>
> *I knew it was either a stranger or me to care for Grandma. I knew I could give her proper care and once I started, she didn't want anyone else. I didn't know her before, but during the process of caretaking, we bonded. She became more like a mother to me, but Grandpa made my job very difficult. It was hard to make both grandparents equally happy.*
>
> *Dealing with death and seeing her sick, seeing her on her down days is my greatest emotional burden. I've been tested too many times. Even though I'm a loving, caring person, I need a break.*

Kali invested all she had emotionally and financially to care for her grandmother. The nearly impossible task of grandmother's care was further complicated by her grandfather's distracting interference. Kali's spirit is broken, and her premature involvement with the death and dying of someone she loves deeply keeps her in a suspended state. Jumping the generations for caregiving could backfire on the family. Who will care for Kali's parents when their time comes, as their daughter remains weary and disillusioned from her earlier caregiving experience?

Getting a Grip on Caregiving

As these stories show, normalizing the caregiving role entails treating the additional duties, issues and problems as ordinary—part of a day's work, a problem-solving task, nothing too special, once a strategy has been devised or help could be summoned. Despite years of selfless devotion, some women pulled off the courageous feat of adapting to changing conditions in ways that can only be described as unflappable. You hear this in the following stories. Ina talks about her life before, during and after caregiving, following her husband's death.

Before caregiving, I always challenged myself to do something new and different. I was a retired teacher, traveling with my husband and actively involved with my children and grandchildren. I had an attentive family—two daughters, both nurses. We had good medical coverage; lived in the same house forty-one years. I'm a reader. I never felt confined.

It was a year before doctors could pinpoint the reason for [his] chest pain. After my husband's diagnosis of mesothelioma and subsequent surgery, he became anxious and started feeling too sorry for himself. My son took him off and they had a good discussion about how important it was to face this and not pull everyone else down. My son is a bright, calm man; I rarely see him react.

I took intense physical care of my husband for a year and then it was 80 or more hours a week. He was physically exhausted and I was emotionally exhausted. I had to sleep, so I slept on the davenport. I tried to maintain a normal lifestyle—birthday parties, grandchildren, videos, Fourth of July and ice cream cones when he went to the doctor.

We skirted the issue of death. We never talked about the end until the very end.

I fed him his food only once—the day he died, once and only once. We were just setting up for Hospice and he died two days later.

It's been nine years since he died and I know caregiving was hard, really hard. Our future was not a topic. You just stop in your tracks about all the things you were going to do. I ate over the kitchen sink the first year after he died—couldn't sit down at the table. The best thing I did was keep up with a normal life.

Today, I try to challenge myself with new interests and new friends—take a class, do something different. I want to stick around for my grandchildren and my children—son, daughters, sons-in-law and daughter-in-law.

A stable self is actually a state of mind, as Evelyn, our next caregiver shows. Regardless of how objectively difficult living with a husband who had Alzheimer's disease was, Evelyn made it work for both of them, even if "normal" was anything but.

I gradually realized Scott's diagnosis of Alzheimer's disease—it wasn't dramatic at all. We continued living a normal life for ten years. I'd sit beside him while he paid the bills to see that it was done right. He's happiest in the kitchen. He's still conscious about being polite, and he is so grateful for everything. His character came through.

I don't feel I've had a change in my identity. I am content with my situation and I don't struggle with problems. I'm not aware of stress, but my daughter sees it in me. I know I'm doing what's right. I don't ponder it at all. I go on with my normal day's activities, and never feel tied down. Caregiving hasn't compromised my values; it's reinforced them.

What would my life be like if I had never taken on the caregiving role? It would be nice if he were active and mentally alert. I would enjoy it. But I owe him my best. He'd given me so much. I knew he would do the same for me.

The wisdom I can offer is the peace you receive from taking care of your loved one. It's reinforced every time Scott says 'thank you' or 'the food is delicious.' Sure, I missed being with other couples. He couldn't interact normally with other people. But no loss around sociability. So many women have husbands with Alzheimer's. I see other women at Alzheimer's support groups, and they tell me that they sleep in separate beds. But I couldn't sleep without Scott.

Sylvia, a former college professor, now retired, has a long history of caregiving. Like Ina and Evelyn, she rationalized caregiving in terms of living a "normal life."

I've always been a high-energy, optimistic, focused and liberal person. I got along well with my family. When Mother moved from Wisconsin to live with me, I was fifty years old. She was 85 and in good health. She stayed for ten years; never complained. I kept my schedule—teaching management. Mother and I went to professional meetings together. My sister called Mother and wrote frequently. One of my friends spoke Norwegian with Mother, which she dearly loved.

I had to change some of the ways I did things—I was willing to make changes, but mostly I just interwove caregiving into my life with my job—the weaving of threads—your life goes together to form a pattern. Her pattern is one of beauty.

Mother decided to move to a nursing home and lived another year and a half. I was there every Saturday and Sunday. I slept in the same room with her and helped with personal care. One day while I was feeding her, I said to myself, 'I wonder how long I can keep this up?' She died a week later.

The process was gradual. I kept up a normal life in spite of caregiving. My life was not disrupted. My life management and high energy, my creativity and optimism gave me coping skills then and now. The only difference in my life now is that I am a retired person.

My grandmother and older aunt were role models—very strict, but they gave me a great deal of stability. Caregiving is a gift if you look at it in a positive way. It enables you to do something for another human being—especially one you love.

Not all older caregivers who exhibit stability express noble emotions about their contribution. Sarah, our oldest subject at 90 and a former actress and singer, has been married for 65 years. Despite her husband's decline, she realistically faces the caregiving responsibilities without remorse or guilt. When asked how she felt about herself before caregiving began, during the caregiving experience, and after her husband's death, she replied:

Before it began, I felt free to do what I wanted. It wasn't a good marriage... still, we had a good relationship just the same. After a few months, I never thought of that word [caregiving] for what I was doing—it's just something one has to do. After one year or so, I just got used to it... doing for Jack.

To maintain a strong sense of who you are, you must be honest with yourself and your loved one. Sarah, who suffers from heart disease, confronted her husband about her limited capacity to manage caregiving. Combining humor with psychological know-how learned from her psychologist daughter, Sarah often "faked" her good feelings. On crucial issues, though, she let her husband know that caregiving was not a forever thing.

Now, Jack, I will do this as long as I know I can do it. When the day comes that I'm too old and too sick to do it, you will have to go to the veteran's hospital. I'm not forcing you. I'm just telling you that I could be struck down... I could have a heart attack any old time... Be aware and alert that something could happen to me. It happens every day in anybody's home.

Sarah retained a sense of being in the moment, a useful tool for maintaining the self during difficult periods. She recognized being a caregiver or helping others may have few or no immediate rewards and many headaches. Her greatest fear remained her own loss of capacity before her husband's death: "I was terribly nervous that something was going to happen to me." A philosophical attitude helped her through the process of learning that caregiving does not involve paybacks.

And it doesn't mean that because you did the right thing, you're going to get paid back. It means that life has a way of altering every situation. But fortunately, it didn't happen. He died just before it could happen to me... I was lucky because I still had some time left. Today, I'm free... totally free. I'm so looking forward to visiting Tuscany. I'm young at heart, you see.

Not everyone has the inner resources to keep themselves level, however. Caregivers play out helping roles learned in childhood and reinforced by family members in the here and now. Claudia provides us with a glimpse of how a group of siblings could rally around their afflicted mother over a six-year period without major loss of self or shifts in identity. Instead, in recognizing their strengths and limitations, they learned mutual tolerance and acceptance. Essentially, mom was still running the show despite her repeated strokes. Claudia clarified how the "team" worked.

I shared the caretaking role with my siblings. We each had a part to play with the roles partly determined by Mom. For example, one sister handled the financial part, one sister was responsible for the medical, one brother visits regularly and offers emotional support to everybody and another brother [disabled and living with mother]

*reads the paper to her. I read to her, too, and fixed her hair and gig-
gled with her.*

*After her first stroke she was in a wheelchair. Then we jockeyed
around in our positions to figure out where to fit into the changed
patterns of her life. My siblings and I found each others' weaknesses,
both glaring and sometimes hard to deal with. But I know we each
did what we could. After all, Mom raised children willing to do what
needed to be done. If we hadn't taken care of her as we did, I would
have regretted it.*

Some caregivers normalize their caregiving commitment by assimi-
lating the activity into their everyday life, and "feel good" about the
responsibility. Antonia, who has been on a life-long caregiving journey, considers herself a heart-centered person. Currently working as
an administrator in a skilled Alzheimer's unit, as well as caring for
her stepfather, Antonia depicts the "ideal" caregiver: positive attitude,
sense of humor, strong values and a desire to serve. When I asked her
how she first became involved with caregiving, she replied:

*Since I was two, my mom said I would place a pillow under her head
and a blanket over her when she came home from work—she was a
single mom. I was a nursing home caregiver at 16 and Red Cross volunteer in high school at the Geriatric Psychology Unit at Northern
State Hospital. My car accident at 12 made me feel I survived for a
reason. How do I cope with caregiving? Well, I understand and value
the need for family, the need for respect and dignity during this passage in life.*

Lessons Learned

Caregiving teaches us obvious lessons: our lives are impermanent,
our circumstances can change abruptly, and who we are often depends
on what happens to aging loved ones in our family or social circle. And
most distressing, our identities shift according to conditions outside
our control.

What isn't so obvious is the most significant lesson we can possibly learn in the process of caregiving a loved one: self-acceptance. It is
an essential part of *giving care* and requires *taking care*. The transitions

in identity caregivers go through are, without a doubt, disruptive, disturbing and painful. We can be emptied out of our old selves. We can feel bereft of a solid sense of our own being—a mere stick figure. Yet, there's an authentic self within each of us that emerges once the obscuring layers we think of as "self" are removed.

What are these layers? They include all the taken for granted, but limited, pieces of ourselves—our roles, relationships, conditioned responses, fears, responsibilities and identities. Once we are free of these identifications, we can acknowledge that something more profound exists within us: the authentic self. It remains steadfast throughout all the turmoil of transitions. It is like the bedrock of our being—totally reliable, unshakeable, always present, never disturbed and indestructible.

Try this: You can shift out of your limiting identifications by going to your heart center—where you live wholly in the here and now—the Divine Present—letting past roles, selves and identities fall by the wayside. Simply look at what has fallen away: if you're caring for your husband, the wife role—well, it just disappeared after a certain point of his disease. Others will appear—friend, companion, nurse, advocate. If you need labels for who you are, I'm sure you can come up with a number of relevant ones. I certainly did. But is that really important?

Alternatively, you are caring for a mother with Alzheimer's disease, who sometimes recognizes you as her daughter, but often thinks you're her sister or maybe the neighbor next door when she was growing up. Now, you can continue to grieve for the loss of your "mother" as you knew her, and feel powerless about helping her in her present condition. Or you can accept this new person in your life, and see beyond the cognitive decline to the authentic self that lives inside her. In that place you can meet and embrace one another for fleeting moments or for a long-term relationship.

Try saying this question when you feel uprooted. *What if I deeply and completely accepted myself just as I am right now?* If you can repeat this question throughout the day, and quietly wait for the response, you may find it life changing. Certainly, you may feel greater ease and comfort living in the here and now.

So, here's a baseline choice you will need to make: Shall I live by the judgments of others or by my own sense of well-being? If you follow your own sense of well-being, the first change you'll make is to let go of external expectations—what others think of you. Other people's rating systems—regardless who they are, living or dead—simply do not matter when we engage in complete and honest self-acceptance. Because self-acceptance is a core piece of our well-being, you can put aside the self-criticism, put-downs and negative thinking that used to make you feel inadequate or limited. You can embrace yourself and recognize that you are doing the best you can in the situation. Free up that energy you spent on feeling bad because you can't control your loved one's disease or reactions. Instead, use your capacities to be *creative*, even *ingenious* in your caring role. The persons you will please the most will be *you*—all your duties become lighter—and your *loved one*—as he settles into *your* more relaxed and energized state of being.

As a caregiver, who are you, really? Now you can find out.

Chapter 4

What Shall We Do?
She's Lost Herself

One of the problems that we workaholics and careaholics have is that we overextend ourselves and believe that we can and should be able to fulfill the promises we make. We want to be nice. We want to be seen as competent and dependable... [but] who I am is what I have to give. Quite simply, I must remember that's enough.

— Anne Wilson Schaef,
Meditations for Women Who Do Too Much

A Starting Point

Your brother John calls you Monday from California and tells you that Mom fell down and broke her hip. He explains that she's recuperating nicely in the hospital, but will need extensive time to get back on her feet. After you recover from the shock, you ask: "What can I do to help?" You had in mind sending a card, or maybe paying a visit to the hospital or recovery center. Your job has just kicked into high gear, and you won't have much time to devote to Mom. But John makes it clear: "Mom needs to be in a safe and comfortable environment. You know how she hates hospitals and other confining places. I can't take her in because I just signed a contract for a new job, and will be leaving town within the month. I'll be driving her up to Washington State next weekend, so you'd better get ready for her."

John couldn't hear you gasp at the unwelcome news, as you said, "Umm, sure, I'll do what I can. See you soon. Give my love to Mom." Now, I'm in for it, you thought. Where do we go from here, Mom and I? We've never gotten along. She's always preferred my brother. What will I do about my job? What about the financial costs? What will this do to my marriage? How will my children react to taking in their often difficult grandmother? What kind of space can I find in the house that will fit "her majesty?" How can I pull this off?

These questions haunt a soon-to-be caregiver, who confronts an unknown situation—one fraught with fear, anxiety and a sinking sense that one's life is about to become undone. Such a situation sets the stage for a condition, popularly known in the recovery literature as "co-dependency."

Co-dependency describes a relationship that begins when one person, the care receiver, relies upon or is sustained by another, the caregiver, and who adopts a subordinate role, simply by virtue of her physical, mental and emotional needs. The "co" in dependency occurs when the facilitating partner—in this care, the caregiver, loses herself in the process. Her identity, her very sense of self, becomes wrapped up in the elder's survival ("He'd be dead without me"), not for an episode or for a day, but often for years.

Whereas society extols specific kinds of human dependencies, such as infants and young children on their parents, or traditional wives on their husbands, the reverse is not the case. Society frowns upon parents becoming dependent upon their children, or husbands losing their independence and leaning on their wives. Yet, this is precisely what happens in most of the caregiving cases we studied, and was certainly true for me.

Caregivers become the operative adult, making executive decisions for their dependent parents or spouses—but not without a struggle by both caregiver and care receiver. The most unpredictable part of this role will be to create a set of routines that will let the caregiver enjoy the interaction with as much grace and humor as possible.

In theory, illness and dying cancel the old rules. After all, we owe a huge debt to our parents, and the marriage vows explicitly dictate, "For better or for worse." Yet, the culture of care remains exceedingly poorly developed in Western societies. No one knows for certain how to create new rules to guide you through the maze of long-term care. And whatever advice is sometimes given—"just act like his 'wife' or ('daughter') and everything will be all right"—doesn't work when normal roles have been turned inside out. The strong, assertive husband, the independent, competent parent are no more. Instead, they have been replaced by a different being; more dark shadow than substance.

The next three sections explore the unforeseen consequences for some women who have taken on the caregiver's task and exhibit signs of co-dependent patterns. Unfortunate childhood experiences with parents may set the stage for co-dependency, which then undermines or negates the adult child's efforts to negotiate difficult interactions successfully.

Typically, long-term caregiving generates vulnerabilities, a sense of being overwhelmed and lacking adequate resources, a loss of confidence, and in the extreme, one's integrity. First, we explore the "devalued self," linked to a consciousness of "never being good enough," or "failing at the task," a condition characterizing a fairly large proportion of our caregivers (more than one-third) at least some of the time. Next, we examine the loss of self—a sense of being rudderless and even emptied out. Finally, we take up the broader issues of co-dependency and how these limit effective and loving caregiving.

The Devalued Self

In the social psychological process of taking on the caregiver role, the newly vulnerable acquires a host of new duties and activities. Many of these require special knowledge and training—for example, timely doses of medications, wound care or regular massage for the bedridden. Perhaps the most demanding response is to the potentially unlimited time commitment, including sleepless nights.

Even more trying is the requirement that the caregiver adapt to deep losses—both her own and those of her loved one, as she continually adjusts her world to ever-changing circumstances of care. In the process an entirely new set of "experts" dictate how the elder must be managed to promote survivability. To cope with the day-to-day necessities she must adopt an attitude that denies her own fears and limitations. Sometimes, this effort produces a muddled reaction, that teeters restlessly between "selfless helper" and "selfish child"—or "why does it have to be me?"

For more vulnerable, ill or overwhelmed women, this process sets the stage for redefining herself as morally unworthy—"I'm no good at this, because I make too many mistakes." "I want to do the best for him, but I'm not sure what I'm supposed to do." "I can never remember all the instructions Dr. Jones gave me for handling his outbursts—so why should I bother? Nothing does any good."

In many instances, a flawed relationship with the loved one in the past now re-emerges as a daunting obstacle to caring effectively for that person. Especially discouraging is the continuous emotional bombardment against the caregiver by both family members and the sick elder. Jill experienced this situation after she moved into her dying mother's home. Although a highly competent university professor in her "other life," she discovered how little she was cherished.

I think I did a good job, although I felt overwhelmed when my brother came.

He didn't want to be there. He came in and started bossing me around. No compassion there at all. But my mother's insults and lack of appreciation were the hardest. Every chance she had she told me I was too fat. She didn't like my [care] work either... I got to a place where I felt that I couldn't do a good job—it was my mother knocking me.

Even where a parent appreciates the caregiver's efforts, and many do, the seemingly unending responsibility of looking after another person undermines the sense of self. Jean admits to feeling devalued by the demands of caregiving required for her 90-year-old mother over the last eight years. Rather than question the non-stop demands, Jean focuses on what she perceives are her own physical and mental shortcomings.

She said:

I'm duty-bound. That's the pattern in my family, and I'm tired of the fact that it's [caregiving] gone on as long as it has. I'm just not smart enough to work out the financial. Financial things make me feel desperate. I do worry about my level of intelligence.

Jean's main worry is that she cannot confront her mother about what is on her mind—to have an honest and open relationship.

I feel guilt and angry. I need to work on my procrastination. I'm trying not to beat myself up too much…but I can't help it.

Eva, an Hispanic woman, now disabled because of a car accident, had always sought her mother's approval. Even with very limited means, she brought her mother into her home, pleasing her with small gifts and clothes, as well as total care. Yet, her mother and brothers had regularly abused her as a child. She commented:

> I used to have nightmares about her. My mother and two brothers— all abusive. I was punished daily. I was fearful of being killed by my mother and two big brothers. I was so overwhelmed [interacting with mother]. I shook and cried all the time. My mother played so many head trips. I spent my whole life trying to please her. I wish my mother would die. The sicker she gets, the happier she is.

Eva feels she owes her mother for bringing her into the world, but also feels guilty about not spending enough personal time with her. "I feel I can't do enough, and I can't express it." Her inability to communicate with her rapidly deteriorating mother causes her daily grief. I asked her how she could resolve this. She said: "Only when one of us dies—that's the only resolution I know."

Loss of Self

Although some caregivers admit to being unable to make choices and prefer to leave decisions to others, many faced a more significant problem. Some women literally lose themselves in the caregiving process. Caring for another begins in the context of a multi-dimensional self. Over time, however, that self gets engulfed—all of their time, energy and social contacts become focused on their caregiving duties. A young woman talked about the two years she provided care for her grandmother, who had Parkinson's disease.

> I tried to have a social life; tried to have a life of my own. It was hard to break strings—going out to get a job, and needing something instead of being here 24/7.

As the demands of the caregiving role expand, a few women realize that something is not right. Their entire life has been thrown out of balance. Most women are able to recognize this before they lose their capacity for self-care. Others abandon nearly everything else to serve the elder. For this caregiver, giving her all to her stepfather left little energy for her own family.

> I promised my stepdad he could die in his home. I understand the need for respect and dignity during this passage in life. I moved into my stepfather's home during the week, then back to my family on weekends—there was no balance. I had to miss my son's baseball games.
>
> For six months, I minimized my own medical crises, and made it clear to my stepdad that he was calling the shots.

For many women, caregiving duties arise at an inappropriate time—when other priorities take center stage. For newly married Natalie, the caregiving of both parents was nearly heartbreaking.

> Right after I got married, by father became ill, then my mother had a stroke. I took care of them for ten years. For six months I lived with them. I did the best I could. I felt overwhelmed at times—dealing with the insurance companies and all the health issues. I missed the time with my husband and put off dealing with my problems. I felt lost and guilty. When I started [caregiving], I was a newly married homemaker with a job; after a year of caregiving, I was a married woman and a daughter. [Now] I had become the parent, handling everything for my parents—financial, health—everything. I put my mom first in everything, causing problems with other relationships in my life.
>
> My husband listened while I ranted and raved.

At the outset of caregiving, women often report a strong sense of rising to the challenge, combined with commitment to the care of their loved one. As the difficulties of giving care accumulate, the caregiver discovers her inability to deal with the situation beyond an obligatory response. In her sixties, Joyce took on a commuter role of caregiver to her mother, who was in her eighties and suffering from heart disease, deafness and arthritis. For 14 years, she traveled 150 miles round trip each month or more to look after a steadily declining loved one. Joyce commented:

I'm always involved since I'm her daughter. I guess since Dad died (1976), she's been alone, but she's totally independent. She's very gullible, lost every penny to a nephew, who ripped her off for thousands of dollars [he was on drugs]. *She was totally in denial.*

Conditions of care went from bad to worse.

Mother had a house fire one week before Christmas. Unfortunately, it was winter. She had an oil stove and flames were up to the ceiling. It was terrible smoke damage. After this, she became so angry. She had no judgment. She was out of control, and that was the issue. My mother took it out on me, blaming me for things I shouldn't be blamed for.

Perhaps the greatest indignity was her mother's lack of affection toward her.

She hugs and kisses her friends, but not me. She doesn't show her feelings.
    She was hard-hearted to me. She doesn't believe in sympathy. It makes it worse she was hurt so badly. My biological father left when we were little. She never showed me love when I was growing up.

Anne, who left her home, family, job and social network to care for her husband, described her fighting spirit when he received the diagnosis of Parkinson's disease. She refers to the diagnosis as her own, stating that in a very real sense she has Parkinson's too, because her thoughts, reactions, and decisions are considered and measured in the context of what a Parkinson's disease patient can handle and absorb. The "I" merges into the "we."

Carrie is a wife and mother who is caring for her elderly father after a recent return to college. As she explains it, she doesn't know where her father "ends" and she begins.

His habits have become part of my habits. Part of me feels as if I've never known anything else. Part of me hopes for a time that I can concentrate on my own life.

Some women were surprised to discover, along the way, their diminishing selves. Jean felt "duty-bound" to care for her 90-year-old mother, who suffered from dementia, osteoporosis and Parkinson's disease.

> *I have been doing this since I was 44—I need to focus, but can't. I finally abandoned the dream of going back to school. I quit looking for opportunities. It's just easier to do what you're doing. After all these years, I am resigned. She has lived so long and I no longer feel this is a stage of my life, but this is my life. I don't see an end to it.*

Sociologists refer to this condition as "role engulfment" or "role entrenchment." This occurs when one role predominately encompasses a person's time and energy. Women who have lost themselves to the caregiving process describe themselves as "sinking into an ocean," "falling into space" or having the sensation that their bodies are disintegrating. The loss of self can be highly problematic, as it can contribute to disassociation and breakdown of physical and emotional maintenance for both caregiver and care receiver.

When individual identity is swallowed up, what can replace it? For a few women, the loss was irreparable, leading to severe depression and an inability to cope with even the most mundane household tasks.

Renae's entire life was thrown completely out of balance when she faced the demands of caring for three loved ones. Her only child, born with Down syndrome, still needed her close attention. Her 90-year-old mother, suffering from Alzheimer's disease, was rapidly deteriorating. David, her 61-year-old male companion, had been diagnosed with pancreatic cancer. Rather than taking charge of the situation, she "gave up" and collapsed into passivity. Renae's story clarifies the caregiver's reality of sacrificing too much for the sick beloved, and abandoning others who needed her, as well as life sustaining activities.

> *I haven't kept in touch with neighbors. I used to play in a music group, but I had to drop that and nearly everything else. When David got sick, he didn't want me out of his sight. He didn't want me gardening. It made me kind of give up any kind of life I might have had.*
>
> *While I was caring for David, I suffered from mental health*

problems. There you go, losing it. I had a hysterectomy. I got lazy. I never had that problem before. I just got fat and lazy. David wanted to eat all the high calorie foods he could. I kept him company sitting around watching TV. I think my health deteriorated because of age, worse diet, [being] more sedentary and depression.

I don't think my health problems affected my caregiving. He wanted me there all the time. He had been a very independent person. He didn't want to be a burden. He was in charge of the bills until the last three months. He was never bedridden—trying to keep up his morale and spirits. I helped him with that. We shared the costs. I should have moved into his house. He had a number of properties.

I told him, 'Just because you're sick, I'm not going to take you out [to a hospital]. You can stay here' [her home].

When I met David, I tried rescuing him, but I fell into the pattern. Once he got sick, I never had confidence in myself. I just always wanted to help him. He felt bad that he caused me all this trouble.

David wasn't anxious to have Hospice. He had chemotherapy and developed cataracts. He was going to beat his cancer. No other family members helped with David's care. His kids were grieving the death of their mother, who had died of cancer. The kid thing gets sticky. It muddies things up. For care, I was pretty much it. I felt overwhelmed toward the end. I started not being able to sleep. I felt guilty because I wasn't seeing my son enough. I said I needed to get out, but he didn't like that very much.

I started out as an independent woman, enthusiastic, [a] workaholic, good friend to David and a good mother. I became more concerned about him and became a person who dealt only with sickness and death every day. I think doing that 24 hours a day, seven days a week is just too much: treatments and sickness all the time—also death, death, death. It gets you down.

I lost myself in this experience... I didn't take care of myself. I forgot to value myself. I feel I could have done better. I gave up things I shouldn't have. Those things would have made me feel better about taking care of him.... I felt I owed him. The most difficult part was trying to always be there for him—always, always, always.

Renae is re-evaluating her main source of self-respect, which comes from taking care of others.

> [I] *don't know anymore—changing in this area. I felt like I owed him. I wanted him to stay here, just because I would feel awful if I had nowhere to go.*
>
> *My life was disrupted. I gained weight. I forgot to value myself. I lost myself and I gave up friends and family... After he died, I paint-ed my toenails.*

Demoralization takes a toll. For caregivers, it stems from a combination of the lack of outside activities, isolation, inability to relate to family members, failure to reach out to supportive persons, the absence of a religious community and a feeling that "nothing really matters." These circumstances contribute to a chronic sense of doom. All of one's consciousness becomes wrapped up in giving care. At the extreme, this is part of a co-dependency pattern in which the self has collapsed into a "blended system," not an interdependent relationship, but one in which caregiver and care receiver merge into a single psychological unit.

Certainly, this merging experience may be more pronounced for a highly traditional woman, whose sense of self is completely bound up with giving to others. Additionally, the feeling of not having control, either over the loved one's disease or one's own life, further contributes to a sense of fatalism and sorrow.

Patricia, an Hispanic woman who fully embraced her cultural and religious values, emphasized how important it was to focus on her sick husband, whose multiple heart attacks required her total attention and devotion. At the same time, she was unable to assume household management and bill paying, because "my husband takes care of the money, and now he's too sick." Patricia commented:

> *I want my husband to be happy and have good health, but he's stub-born (smiles).*
>
> *I want to give* [him] *my breath to get well. I never thought before that in my life I was going to have this experience* [caregiving]. *God gave this to me to prove my love for Him and all humans.*

Patricia admitted to the difficulty of receiving sustained family support, because of traditional arrangements—women look after their male family members first, and only after this duty is accomplished can they consider the needs of their female relatives. With her mother gone, her surviving aunts and sisters are busy with their own families, and could not help her out with her husband.

> *All of my family take care of our brothers down to the last minute [of death]—that's our commitment in our culture for humans—it doesn't matter who they are.*

Patricia expresses a sense of ongoing anguish and grief. Not only did her mother recently pass away, leaving her alone to cope with her husband, but also her work in a nursing home leaves her saddened when patients die—"it was a struggle for me because I loved them." Above all, Patricia wishes to be reunited with her family in Mexico City, an impossible dream because of her full-time caregiving commitment at home.

Co-Dependency

Most caregivers exhibit some elements of co-dependency. Melody Beattie, author of *Co-dependent No More*, clarifies this condition, as: "One who has let another person's behavior affect him or her, and who is obsessed with controlling that person's behavior." Beattie says that some women have been taught that co-dependent behaviors are desirable feminine attributes. Beattie proposes that the loss of self and the accompanying dysfunctional behaviors arise out of necessity to "protect ourselves and meet our needs." In an effort to cope, the individual performs, feels and thinks in erroneous ways, believing that survival itself is at stake.

Originally the word **co-dependency** referred to people whose lives had become unmanageable as a result of living in a committed relationship with an alcoholic. However, the concept of co-dependency also describes relationships with people who are chronically ill and emotionally or mentally disturbed, those who are adult children of alcoholics or those who are engaged in other types of distorted psychosocial relationships.

Two common denominators of co-dependency are having a relationship with troubled, needy or dependent people, and strictly following a number of unwritten, silent rules. These rules include:

- **No** discussion of problems or open expression of feelings.

- **No** direct, honest communication with oneself or the care receiver.

- **No** realistic expectations of self, such as being human, vulnerable or imperfect. **No displays** of selfishness or trust in oneself and other people.

- **No** playing and having fun.

- **Never** rocking the delicately balanced family canoe through growth and change.

For many caregivers we spoke with, it is the inability to speak out that is most difficult.

In the later stages of codependency, a caregiver may feel lethargic, depressed, withdrawn, hopeless and isolated, and may not be able to maintain even the most basic of routines. They may also become violent or ill—emotionally, mentally or physically.

Mary Beth described her relationship with her husband of nearly 50 years before and during the early stages of her caregiving.

> *Before caretaking, we were both independent. After a few months of caregiving I was just unhappy. I felt tied to my husband in an unhealthy way. I was his wife. I was his wife. I was his wife (emphasis). He wouldn't accept respite care. He became totally attached to me. I got tired, impatient and nothing I could do would change the situation. I lived the 36-hour day.*

The National Mental Health Association (NMHA) describes co-dependency as a learned behavior, which can be passed down from one generation to another. Like any addiction, it can profoundly affect an individual's ability to have a healthy, mutually satisfying relationship. NMHA lists some typical attributes of co-dependent persons, such as an exaggerated sense of responsibility, taking on more than their share, lack of trust in self and others. Many co-dependents have special difficulty in adjusting to change, along with problems setting boundaries, chronic anger, poor communication skills and difficulty making decisions. For a co-dependent caregiver, providing care is no longer a matter of choice, but has taken over her life. This is a reality for almost all of us along the caregiving journey—at some point. Women, in particular, are socialized to always place others before ourselves, and may not realize when they have crossed the line from caregiver to *careaholic*. The following statements might typify how a careaholic thinks and feels.

- My good feelings about who I am stem from receiving approval from you and others—our children, my siblings, relatives, friends, employer, or others.

- My struggle affects my serenity.

- My mental attention is focused on you.

- My fear of your anger, disappointment and regret determines what I say or do.

- My social circle diminishes as I involve myself with you.

- My self-esteem is bolstered by relieving your pain.

- My own hobbies/interests are put to one side. My time is spent sharing your hobbies/interests.

- I am not aware of how I feel. I am only aware of how you feel.

- I am not aware of what I want. I ask what you want.

- The dreams I have for my future are linked to you.

- The quality of my life is in relation to the quality of yours.

For some women, the increased reliance on the caregiving role develops a sense of reward and satisfaction simply from being needed. Some have expressed the fear of "losing their job." Kathy, 61, cared for both her very aged parents in their home. "I worry about the time when they will not be here. What will I do? I'm so nurturing."

My personal chronicle of co-dependency presented me with a

shocking reality—but only after the fact. I woke up to the terrible truth that I had become the caregiver for all seasons.

Coming at the end of the fourth year of caregiving, I had my eyes suddenly opened to the realities of co-dependency. Giving care for all those years had become such an integrated part of my life, I stopped agonizing—and even reflecting on it. Instead, I tried to simply work out tasks as practical activities requiring little or no special attention. I managed to stay conscious about my boundaries in the nursing home; leaving time in the evening after visiting Jim for eating and sleeping. My work life was pretty much routine, and I was careful to eat well and exercise daily. My finances were in order; our children played their visitation roles as planned, and I know Jim felt surrounded by family love each day. At the same time, I also sensed that Jim was edging closer to dying; it looked only weeks away. I felt nervous and apprehensive about leaving him, but I also knew I needed a break.

In June, at the end of the quarter, I decided to take a well-deserved respite and fly down by myself for a week to Bucerias, Mexico, a village north of Puerto Vallarta. I had had no breaks all year, and was beginning to feel very weary. Mexico seemed the perfect place. While I was on the airport bus to the resort, an older gentleman sat down next to me, and promptly engaged me in conversation. Randall was charming and informative, having taken this trip a number of times. He was also a widower, I found out, and happy to meet a 'lady' with whom to share meals and sunny afternoons. So far, so good.

That first evening Randall happened to be placed at the same dining table as I, so we continued our conversation throughout the meal. I thought to myself: 'what good fortune' to find a lively conversationalist to take my mind off my situation back home. Once we departed from dinner, we found the area poorly lit, so I took Randall's arm to help guide him to his room. He had expressed a minor complaint about his night vision. As we approached the room, he took out his key and stepping forward, fell from a two-step drop that he had failed to see. Randall was bleeding profusely from the head, with injuries on his right shoulder, arm and leg. Clearly, he needed assistance.

The remainder of the evening was a blur. After we located a doctor some buildings away, and Randall was eventually dispatched with wounds attended to, I managed to walk him back to his apartment. From that moment on, I became his caregiver. He came to rely on me for a variety of activities: namely, shopping, wound care, friendship, and a kind of all-around-the-clock elder sitter. Not until I boarded the airplane after saying our warm 'goodbyes' did I begin to feel squeamish. 'What have I gotten myself into?' I thought. And as Jim entered his final two months of decline and death after my return, I became seriously ill with pneumonia that stopped my life and my caregiving—at least for some weeks.

NMHA clarifies the problem of how the rescue attempts of the co-dependent actually undermine the self-reliance of the needy person, exactly my short-term situation with Randall. Over time, the rescue attempt can result in a dysfunctional course of passivity in which the care receiver becomes ever more dependent on the unhealthy caregiving of the "benefactor." As this reliance increases, the co-dependent feels that *she alone* can carry out the necessary physical, emotional and medical tasks required. Caregiving becomes who the person is, but not without ambivalence and a sense of powerlessness.

Carrie, a 39-year-old university student, has been a caregiver since preschool and now looks after her blind father. She reflects on the caregiver role as one without an end.

Although most of the time I feel grateful that I can 'be there' for the various people I have been able to assist, there is a part of me that sometimes wishes that I had a 'break.' Perhaps, at some point in my life, there will be a time that no one around me will need me to be a caregiver. I do not see that happening. Part of me sees others in my family needing assistance as soon as my father no longer needs me. I suppose I will step up, again and again.

Burn-out characterizes many caregivers at this stage, despite their assertion of being happy. Carrie goes on to say:

It is sometimes difficult to cope after I am done with a 'session' of helping. I sometimes 'crash' when I go home. I'll stay 'up' when I'm with my dad, then later I am mentally, emotionally and physically exhausted. Again, at the same time, I have gotten to spend much more time with my dad than I probably would have…I see him much more often now. I am happy that I can be there for my dad.

When caretaking becomes compulsive, the co-dependent feels powerless and out of control in the relationship, but remains unable to break away from the cycle of behavior that causes it. Faith, whom we met earlier, describes her adolescent years taking care of her alcoholic mother as a role reversal. Even though her mother told her frequently that she was no good, Faith felt a lifetime commitment to her mother's care.

I was the designated caregiver. I was nine years old; on crutches from polio and was sent to take care of my grandmother. From childhood, I knew I would be responsible for my mother. I didn't look for any other way.

Co-dependents view themselves as victims and are attracted to that same weakness in their love and friendship relationships—they do not know when or how to stop. Sandra lamented:

My husband was negative and unappreciative and expected I would provide care, regardless. I was the only one he had.

Over the one year plus, the situation got to be overwhelming. I guess it was my intention to be his caretaker—for better or worse; sickness and health—but I didn't know what it would be like—intentions are there, but it takes a lot out of you. He had a bag and needed help with [his] colostomy.

The most difficult was the financial stuff. I didn't know about any of it till it happened. I was overwhelmed and helpless. I broke down and cried a lot in private; went on autopilot—do it (now) and think about it later. I lost my husband and I felt guilty about feeling bad.

I was really committed in the beginning, but the sicker he got, I couldn't deal with his feelings. Instead of speaking up to the doctors about their lack of care, I got short with my sick husband instead. We took things out on each other—heat of the moment. He's dead because of the medical system. After one year of giving care I'm an emotional wreck; disorganized; not a good friend and I'm moody.

Co-dependency becomes a familiar pattern for women who have been abused or neglected in childhood, and been forced to perform as a parent to their parents. When they move into adulthood, they continue the pattern, assuming the role of caretaker for the abusive parent. Additionally, childhood abuse often generates *post-traumatic stress disorder*. This condition occurs when a person, who has suffered deep trauma, may continue to experience the same disordered emotions and thinking years later. They may feel as though they are still in the midst of the abuse.

As a child, Jane had been abused by her father and mother. Now, an adult, Jane has been diagnosed with bipolar disorder, depression, post-traumatic stress syndrome and anxiety, as well as stomach and intestinal problems. Additionally, Jane's two sons both have chronic medical conditions, and require close supervision and care. Yet, when Jane's mother was ill, Jane left her husband and children, and flew across the country to take care of her mother. After her mother's death, she felt obligated to act as caregiver for her father, who had Alzheimer's disease. Prior to caretaking, their relationship was "stressed and tense."

To facilitate care, she transported her father across the country to be closer to her home. Once her father was located at a nearby nursing home, Jane reported feeling very stressed and out of control, finding it difficult to divide herself between two sick boys and a demanding, mentally incompetent father. During the entire 18 months of caregiving her dad, Jane saw a doctor for depression, but apparently did not respond to treatment. She described herself as her father's lifeline.

> *I moved my father cross-country to be in a home near me. The job of caregiver was stressful. My life was out of control. I found it difficult to divide myself between two sick children and a father dying with Alzheimer's.*
>
> *But my method of operation has always been to address the immediate concern. I'm good at rescuing. I felt helpless on the plane—they need to make adult diapers available in airports. I had a stressed relationship with my dad, and in the end I made choices for him that he was unable to disapprove of. I wanted him to be happy with the choices I made.*

After one year of caregiving, Jane described herself as simply "a very tired daughter." After her father died—without warning—she left her husband and children, and moved away to care for a man who had cancer. The bizarre fact is that she only had known him for four months. Caregiving situations like Jane's—of sinking into the role and excluding all other options—are certainly not common, although I, too, was briefly submerged in the role with a virtual stranger. But hers is a story of co-dependency, perhaps at its most obsessive, in that she abandoned all her family relationships in one fell swoop.

Lessons Learned

Caregivers, if you followed my recommendations for self-acceptance in the last chapter, you are ready to deal with the next issue: depression. Depression is a common problem among those who sacrifice everything for the caregiving role. Andrew Weil, a holistic physician, recommends a cutting edge treatment for depression that involves a *therapeutic lifestyle change.* Following this lifestyle change, it's possible to overcome depressive symptoms and recognize that *you* simply cannot do it all. Above all, you *must make time* to allow new choices in your life.

"When the student is ready, the teacher will appear"—has an Eastern ring to it. The following **lifestyle changes** can be *your* teachers out of the darkness of depression and obsessive concern for your loved one.

Omega-3s. Take 1,000 milligrams of Omega-3s, the fatty acid EPA each day. Weil says this is the most studied dose for combating depression, plus a multivitamin. Restoring your energy levels is a basic start for addressing the challenges of caregiving.

Aerobic exercise. The next most basic thing after meeting your nutritional deficits is aerobic exercise. Weil emphasizes 30 minutes a day three times a week as a minimum. I recommend walking, biking, swimming, jogging or other vigorous exercise *daily*.

Light Exposure. For those of us in the Pacific Northwest, where rain and clouds dominate the landscape for months on end, we know the advantages for getting our sunshine when we can.

Sunshine helps regulate the circadian rhythms that govern sleep, energy and hormone levels. Alternatively, sit in front of a special light box that simulates natural sunlight. Whatever you do, remember that sunshine is a must. Take your chores outside, if necessary, but let yourself soak in sunshine for a good 30 minutes. Avoid getting sunburn, though. Sunscreen helps here.

Social Connection. Social support is crucial for the caregiver to overcome the isolation of caregiving. It's usually a good idea to schedule at least two social activities a week (even if you don't feel like it when you do the scheduling). Leave behind or limit time with the people who bring you down. You have taken on enough responsibility with caregiving. Enjoy your free time with people who make you feel *good*.

Adequate Sleep. Chronic sleep deprivation increases the risk for depression and for falling into the careaholic mindset. Aim for seven or eight hours of rest a night. Weil recommends dimming lights about an hour before your bedtime, and go to sleep and wake up at the same time each day. This lifestyle change will probably be the hardest to achieve if you have night duty. If sleep shortages are unavoidable, take regular naps to refresh your energies.

Anti-Rumination Strategies. Rumination is a tendency to dwell on negative thoughts in a non-productive way. This is most likely to happen when you spend time alone, so avoid extended periods by yourself. If you find yourself ruminating, Weil reminds us to pick up the phone and call a friend or do something enjoyable.

I am adding two more lifestyle changes.

Seek Professional Help. Consult a holistic physician or naturopath to work with you on any physical changes you may be experiencing. Menopause results in sharp fluctuations in estrogen levels, which can create mood changes. Thyroid depletion often occurs after menopause, and can contribute to a host of symptoms, including exhaustion. Blood sugar irregularities can signal more serious medical problems, such as diabetes.

Locate Respite Care. When you need a break—and you surely will—locate a nearby nursing home or assisted living facility that has *respite care* openings for your loved one. A few days or weeks may be all you need to recharge your batteries. Working with your medical provider and local nursing facilities makes complete sense, because you certainly cannot sustain long-term caregiving without maintaining your health and well-being. The life you save may be your own!

Chapter 5

Whatever Happened to the Family Doctor Who Cared?

When it comes to the healing professions, wisdom means knowing what it takes, and understanding all the factors that are involved in the healing process. It is not limited to making the correct diagnosis and applying the proper medication or surgical procedure. Wisdom incorporates the attitude of caring along with all of one's training, experience and knowledge of disease. It is the combination of all these factors that we can call wisdom.

– Chokyi Nyima Rinpoche and David R. Shlim, M.D.,
Medicine and Compassion

The soaring cost of health care is the greatest threat to the country's long-term solvency, and the terminally ill account for a lot of it. Twenty-five percent of all Medicare spending is for the five percent of patients who are in their final year of life, and most of that money goes for care in their last couple of months which is of little apparent benefit.

– Atul Gawande, "Letting Go:
What should medicine do when it can't
save your life?" *The New Yorker Magazine*

A Caregiver's Lament

Teri's story of caregiving her grandparents reflects every caregiver's grievance. Widespread complaints about end-of-life care are complicated by a medical system that appears to lack the basics: prudent medication, effective communication with patients and a tender heart for the old and dying. Her grandparents, along with 1.5 million other reported Americans, experienced a worst case scenario: the ills of mis-managed medication. Add to this, the difficulty—and for Teri, the impossibility—of finding good home health care, or any decent care, anywhere, for that matter.

Teri reflected:

> *Grandma had Parkinson's disease and dementia. The doctors didn't talk to each other and consequently, she was over medicated. She suffered from dopamine-induced schizoid behavior because of the over-medication. I had five gals handling Grandma around-the-clock. One of them was using [dirty] needles under the sink. When I had to move her, I found the facility was a horrendous experience: no bed, Grandma was sleeping on the floor. The rooms were hot, hot.*

Nursing homes and hospital stays were tortuous for her elderly relatives.

> *Grandma fell a lot and was sad and depressed. She had trouble keeping all those medications going—just too much. She was always so positive and appreciative. I was amazed at how she was treated by the hospital. She had arrhythmia and they released her at 3 a.m.*
>
> *In the nursing home, my grandfather rejected the feeding tube. He was combative and boycotted his pills and in the end, they didn't give him enough morphine. He was screaming into death.*
>
> *The most unfair experience I had in the 6 years—31 to 40 hours a week—of caregiving for my grandparents was dealing with the medical professionals and how they handled it… keeping my grandma in a room for one hour and then misdiagnosing and sending us on our way. It really made me distrust doctors.*

Despite such agonizing setbacks, Teri, like so many of these care-givers, expresses gratitude for the opportunity to care for her beloved grandparents.

> *I was pretty much alone in their care and grateful that I had the good sense to step forward at the right time; put myself out for them. I am appreciative of the opportunity to care for them. I try to make a difference and I realize how short life is. It felt good to give back to people who were good to me—instead of taking from them.*

Health Care: A Broken System

Elders and their families confronting terminal illness turn to their medical providers as lifelines in a shattered world. They seek not only medical "treatment," but compassion and understanding as well. Hope and inexperience fuel their efforts to locate the most effective and caring treatment for what appears to be an unknown medical problem—one, most seekers assume, that is easily remedied by the multitude of new medical technologies spawned over the last thirty years. Their belief is that medical support comes in tidy packages, or at least a reassuring safety net. Included would be the necessary providers and their professional acumen and wisdom—personal physician, medical specialists, nurses, hospital, recovery center, followed by home care. Above all, these seekers believe that the physician plays an enlightened, indeed critical, role guiding and facilitating the patient and his/her family through the health care labyrinth.

"Today, the medical care system resembles more of a tightrope than a safety net," says Nicholas D. Kristof in a 2005 *New York Times* editorial, "Medicine's Sticker Shock." In a sign of the growing disenchantment with our health system, Kristof says, 13,000 doctors have joined Physicians for a National Health Program, an organization that lobbies for a single-payer government-financed health program. It is not merely the exorbitant and growing costs of our existing system—we have the most expensive in the world—but 45 million Americans also go without medical care. This translates into higher mortality rates: Americans' life expectancy has been steadily slipping and now ranks lower than Costa Rica's. Additionally, Kristof writes, the entire system is grossly inefficient. The emphasis on curative medicine, rather than public health and prevention, further contributes to runaway costs.

Other critics support Kristof's assessment of the costs of America's medical system. Defibrillators, which jump-start the heart if it enters an arrhythmic pattern, cost about $1,800 to $2,000 each. Institutional models fetch even more. "Miracle" drugs to treat cancer are so expensive consumers often must weigh the value of extending their life for a few months for a lifetime of debt for their survivors. And often, they do not work. *Avastin*, the best-selling drug in the world, can add an average of 20 months to the life of a colon cancer patient, but costs more than $4,000 a month. When the same drug is used for non-metastatic breast cancer, the costs are $8,000 a month. Does the drug work for metastatic breast cancer? Apparently not. Avastin has been rejected by the Food and Drug Administration as "ineffective" for that disease. And, Bristol-Meyer-Squibb's new colorectal cancer drug, *Erbitux*, which was recently approved for treating head and neck cancer, will cost $16,800 to $26,400 for one course of therapy lasting from seven to 11 weeks. In contrast, many popular, brand name drugs can be purchased for 30 to 80 percent less in Canada, because government price controls aim to protect consumers.

What's more, medical providers must confront patients about end-of-life care as "reasonable assistance" and *not* heroic interventions that circumvent the course of nature. Hospice, a program for the dying, focuses on palliative or comfort care and comes replete with compassionate and supportive medical staff to assist the patient and family in easing the coming death and ensuring a smooth transition. The best news: Hospice provides a better alternative than risky treatments for prolonging life. People not only live longer, but they also have a higher **quality of life**—more awareness of themselves and their surroundings, an opportunity for saying "goodbye" to family and friends, and the ability to complete unfinished business before dying.

Long-Term Care

Unlike death and dying in an earlier age when a patient lingered only a few weeks or months, today's terminally ill elder is likely to languish for years, too weak and listless to undertake a normal life, yet too wedded to the idea of living to envision stopping the medicines and moving toward an intentional and deliberate death. A protracted dying process, with no end in sight, challenges even the most well-intentioned caregiver. As Anne told me in a moment of frustration:

> No matter what I do, how much positive or up-ness I conjure, squeeze or drag from within, these diseases absolutely will not get better tomorrow or next week—or ever. There will be no reversal. This thought occurs frequently to some caregivers, once in a surprising while to

others, but can never be allowed to escape in the presence of the person who is really suffering.

Long-term or chronic care taking place over years is wholly unlike acute care. Childhood illnesses, adult colds and flus may interfere with life's routines, but they don't stop the flow of normal life. Long-term care turns our deepest expectations and sense of personal and domestic order inside out. Many caregivers observed that once Hospice stepped into the picture, care became both more predictable and humane. The turmoil until that point can be extraordinarily challenging. I carefully tracked my husband's medical encounters, from first heart attack until we needed to make a life or death decision.

Jim returned from the hospital after treatment for his first heart attack. I made sure I could help with medications at home—follow-up care. Four months later, he had the second heart attack—more heavy care. I fully intended to take care of Jim, but with a cardiologist, a personal physician and a psychiatrist, I found the medical structure confusing. I simply could not find a single doctor to treat him as a whole person. Certainly, of all the activities I performed as a caregiver, the most demanding was interacting face-to-face with medical providers. I had the sense that they had no clue as to my feelings or Jim's needs; they never seemed to answer my questions. Quality of life was not their bailiwick.

My deepest values are independence, self-management, a spiritual component to personality, being kind, family and friendships, but after a few months of caregiving, I was frightened, disorganized, panicky, out-of-control and a reluctant caregiver. I felt hopeless and overwhelmed. I couldn't see that what I was doing had any point. It seemed he was just getting worse, as he ingested more and more different medicines.

The medical professionals were dodging my questions and patronizing. I experienced a cavalier, and in some cases abusive, treatment by physicians and medical people, even facility administrators. After a period of frequent episodes of hospitalizations, Jim's personal physician was on target. He said to my husband, 'You're not dying right now, but you will need a lot of care. You have a choice—live or die.'

He couldn't walk and could barely speak, because he was so weak, and the doctor knew this. So if Jim chose to die, the doctor carefully pointed out, he would need to stop his medication and stop eating. But if he chose to live—and the doctor emphasized this was his choice—he would need round-the-clock care. Jim chose to continue his struggle for life.

The most difficult decision, the one I worried about most, was keeping Jim in institutional care. In one of the many nursing homes Jim was in over a three-year period, the staff shouting made us both cringe. No one was on the floor to supervise the workers. It was utterly frustrating. I was devastated—tormented by a place that couldn't provide proper care or enough staff. I wondered about the honesty of the word 'skilled' in skilled nursing facility—that was not my experience most of the time. Thankfully, the Hospice volunteer stepped in for the last 18 months.

But segmented medical care for Jim made his choice to live incredibly difficult, as I indicated in the interview I had with Traci Harpine, the student who interviewed me for the study. I said:

The medical system is fragmented and many of its practitioners are incompetent. I suggest that caregivers find physicians/medical people with whom they feel comfortable and leave behind practices that don't work.

Those who must cope with institutional placement of their loved ones confront equally formidable problems, as described by Sally, who had two parents who required supervised care. According to Sally, her father's Crohn's disease led to episodes where he could no longer leave his home, while her mother's Alzheimer's required a special unit in the facility. She recounts her difficulties in coping with their care.

My father had progressed to the point where his bowels were completely out of control and he was almost a skeleton, really. He had all his mental faculties, but couldn't leave the house. So I felt that they needed to come to assisted living. They were admitted to assisted living here, only on the basis of my father, because my mother's confusion was so great by that point, that she absolutely needed a full-time caregiving facility.

Once Sally located the facility, she thought her problems were over. But this was not the case.

> *The facility was very lovely, a new facility, but I felt that the staff was not satisfactory. They didn't hire the higher level professionals and the Alzheimer's unit was absolutely a nightmare. They were absolutely incompetent. They hired people who had no training and no skills and who would work at the lowest wage possible, and the people in that unit did not receive any of the type of care that was necessary... even to the point that they had one LPN for the whole building and the only way that they could control many of the patients was to over-medicate them.*
>
> *My mother had three very serious accidents because of being overly medicated and trying to walk. One time she fell into the nurse's station and just bashed in one side of her head...They didn't even keep her clean. Every time I picked her up in the ER, she was soaked up to her armpits in urine, because they couldn't even diaper her correctly or keep her clean...or wouldn't do it.*

Sally regrets she never reported these incidents. However, the precarious state of her own health from the stress of caring for her parents created impossible obstacles for follow-up of the systemic abuse and neglect. At least her doctor's intervention made it possible to place her mother in a safe, if far less attractive, environment, which was uncarpeted and extremely noisy.

> *They [accidents] probably should have been reported. I shouldn't have blown it off. The doctor recommended I take her to another [less] pretentious facility—but with more expansive service. Once I did that, she got the care. They kept her clean and they kept her dry and they fed her well.*

Sally was fortunate in having medical assistance in locating a different facility, even if the environment was less than ideal. She was also fortunate in being on-site to supervise her parent's care, and intervene before the situation became disastrous. Sally felt she had triumphed over the situation. In the end, her mother "lived three-and-a-half years there [different facility] with lots of social contact and lots of stimulation."

When the Burden of Care is Magnified

We intuitively know that the problem of treating elderly patients depends upon the nature of medical knowledge, the organization of services and the medical profession itself, as well as the type of diseases—many of them incurable and untreatable. Above all, the medical profession, as currently organized, contributes to patients' dissatisfaction. Negative encounters with impersonal medical and institutional staff and unhelpful hospital experiences contribute heavily to the burden of care. Caregivers articulated widespread frustration with the treatment they received. Some complained that their doctor failed to take charge or clearly avoided direct contact. Others were deeply upset over the hostile nursing home staff they encountered. Here are a few statements that summarize these caregivers' more frequently expressed concerns:

My medical background [registered nurse] *made me feel very positive. Even so, when it was time for my husband to quit driving, we went to a very good neurologist, but he wouldn't say 'no' to his driving.*

My husband had mesothelioma, a cancer that attaches to the nerves in the chest. The most difficult part of caring for him was having to take charge of medications and not knowing anything about it— doctor's appointments, day-to-day care, writing everything down. [There were] *too few answers from medical professionals, especially in the year-and-a-half before he was misdiagnosed. They weren't persistent enough to get the right diagnosis.*

I took my dad to his neurologist. They did an MRI that showed spinal cancer. The doctor never said a word. I read it off the chart.

We experienced four different doctors, four different evaluations before they could tell her she had cancer. They were very evasive.

My mother had mini-strokes, heart problems and osteoporosis... she really was not receiving adequate care. I didn't think the medical professionals were forthcoming about my mother's condition. Doctors and nurses were vague [about pain management]—*morphine was too high a dose.*

I was sorry that the primary doctor couldn't visit in our home, where I provided round-the-clock care. Doctor didn't visit in the hospital, either.

I didn't know. The doctors didn't know either. I got a lot from reading—the doctor never explained anything to me.

I felt great apprehension after Jim had his second heart attack. He needed so much care—hospital visit followed hospital visit with frequent stopovers at various nursing homes. I felt stymied by the sheer lack of care or caring—or of anyone telling me what was going on.

Failing to inform the patient of a terminal diagnosis was another leading complaint among caregivers. Another major issue was a lack of communication with hospital and institutional staff. As a result, a sense of frustration and powerlessness typically dominated caregivers' interactions with doctors and medical personnel in hospitals and nursing homes.

Over-reliance on the medical system and on the "correct" medical diagnosis reduces patients and their families to a state of childlike dependency. Their entire sense of reality becomes centered around the doctor's understanding of their loved one's symptoms and his or her ability to reduce or eliminate them. In many cases, they are disappointed. In an interview, Anne, who is featured in "The Human Face of Parkinson's Disease" (Chapter 7) expressed her profound frustration around the lack of knowledge and caring she confronted in her efforts to find a physician. Initially, Mike self-diagnosed his symptoms. Anne said her husband noted his changing and stooped posture, his stiffness and inability to smile and his dark moods. But finally he knew he had Parkinson's when his handwriting went to a flat undecipherable line.

Still, he wanted to have a medical confirmation of his suspicions. Their first encounter shocked them both.

In the spring of 1993 we made an appointment to see a neurologist to either verify Mike's own diagnosis or worse, to determine whether his symptoms were something more frightening: a brain tumor. The first time my husband was examined, the doctor asked him to do a few simple finger and hand coordination exercises. Mike tried to repeat what the doctor had demonstrated but couldn't quite match the coordination. The doctor slapped his hand. 'No, that's not right. Do it this way.' We were stunned and saddened and immediately left the doctor's office to request a transfer to a different neurologist. Our first response was to leave the clinic and look elsewhere for a neurologist.

This couple concluded that the problem was not the physician's off-putting behavior, but rather their treatment, which was beyond impersonal.

The expertise is, without question, at the [distinguished] clinic, but the assembly line process of morning registration; conveyer-belt to next waiting room; more waiting; conveyer-belt and waiting, and finally being called for an afternoon appointment was dehumanizing and the doctor's brusque and impatient treatment added something sour to our already wrenching situation. In spite of our disappointment, we decided to stay with the experts and had to wait another two months for the clinic machine to reach a diagnosis of Parkinson's disease.

Although the clinic doctors' visits improved, Anne and her husband needed much more.

Our future visits to the clinic were more pleasant, but too short. Mike and I would prepare our lists of questions to ask the doctor, but after a half-hour of interview and hand exercises, the doctor had no time for questions. He explained his expertise or specialty in neurology. 'My work is really in the area of Parkinson's disease research.' And while it seems a common practice for doctors to tape record the present condition of the patient after the check-up, this doctor taped his observations in front of us, referring to Mike as a number and summarizing his current physical appearance and condition on a machine rather than talking directly to us. There are too many machines in medicine! We found an independent neurologist, whose manner was compassionate and kind. He gave us the time we needed to vent our worries. However, he admitted his lack of expertise in the area of Parkinson's disease. 'That's really not my specialty and everyone is so specialized today. You're better off doing your own research.'

I shared with Anne the exasperation of getting the facts or of understanding the process of my husband's disease.

During our family's efforts to get a diagnosis for Jim, I experienced a similar sense of futility dealing with specialists. At one point, during my most agonizing experience as a caregiver, I confronted the cardiologist's resident nurse practitioner about Jim's prognosis and asked: 'What can we expect?' 'What can I do to ease the pain?' 'What does the future hold for Jim?' Other patients must have asked these same questions innumerable times, because his answer was short and glib. As he patted me on the back, he murmured, 'Don't worry, dear. In a year it will all be over.' I wanted information and consolation. I received only a death sentence for my loved one.

We returned home to resume the difficult and lonely path of congestive heart disease patient and overwrought caregiver. My feelings ran the gamut from helplessness to rage.

I remained deeply angry for months. I was furious with what I perceived to be an indifferent medical system, upset over Jim's apparent passivity and concerned about the spiraling costs and bungling of home care. Above all, I was disappointed with myself for lacking the knowledge to know the 'right' course of action and for succumbing to anger and a sense of futility, instead of following my normal pattern of taking a clear, positive course of action. In the meantime, my personal and social life began to shrink and eventually disappear. There seemed little time for anything, aside from teaching and caregiving. I felt trapped and helpless—and incredibly alone.

True of most caregivers in the midst of providing care, I eventually had to confront the reality that my husband's disease would never get better, and the best course of action was to accept this fact and muddle through the medical system as well as I could.

Years later I had a vivid dream that helped me understand the source of my anger and sense of futility.

> *I am in a hospital waiting for Jim's diagnosis. The halls are a-flutter with white coats, rushing in and out of rooms. Something seems to be wrong. No one will talk to me—I keep trying to get the attention of one of the white coats to answer my questions. My children and grandchildren are physically with me, but they, too, seem to be spinning and unapproachable. I am filled with consternation. I feel so vulnerable—who cares about me or Jim? I weep with helplessness. One of the white coats feels sorry for me. She says, 'I need to tell you this with my deepest apologies. We cannot find Jim's head. We have looked everywhere, but it is nowhere to be found. Perhaps you and your family would have better luck searching for it. We've done all we could.' Despite the family's frantic efforts, we could never find it again.*

I was flooded with awareness—Jim had indeed lost his head. His deep intelligence, profound knowledge, bookish, but sweet personality, loving presence—all gone. We were blaming outsiders—doctors, nurses, attendants, anyone near at hand—for our sorrow and loss. Jim was beyond medical or family help now.

Costs of Care

Adding insult to injury, the cost of care for many Americans is out of reach. Certainly, we've all benefited from technological and pharmaceutical innovations. I heartily agree these have improved people's health and extended their lives—but at horrendous costs to individual consumers, their families and society. The rising tide of spending stems from demographic and health trends, as well as from medical technologies that older Americans need and demand. According to the RAND Corporation, if half of the patients who had recently suffered a heart attack or been diagnosed with heart failure were to get defibrillators (automatically correcting the heart beat), health care spending on the elderly would increase $14 billion, or four percent, over the next ten years. Add to this the ever-rising expense of health insurance and we quickly see how health care costs are spiraling out of control. Most of our caregivers were managing fairly well with their current health insurance policies. However, for a significant minority, financial costs for self and care receiver were overwhelming.

While in her fifties, Laura assumed care of both parents located in two different settings. Her mother was living in a nursing home and her dad was in his own home some distance away. While her parents were thankfully able to pay for their health insurance, many of their incidental costs fell to her. Between her own personal difficulties—health insurance costs, living expenses, cancer relapses, death of a beloved parent—it is no wonder that Laura experienced deep exhaustion and inability to cope.

My yearly income was $28,000. I didn't balance my checkbook for a couple of years—just do the necessities and keep going—that's about it. I [relocated in order] to care, for ten years, for my mother who had Alzheimer's, diabetes and dementia, and my father, who had a stroke, depression, arthritis, lung problems and chronic problems with asbestos poisoning. The most frustrating time was getting them through the initial part of their illnesses—just getting the diagnoses.

For ten years, I ran back and forth between Mom's care facility and Dad at home. Go see Mom, then Dad, drive home, do errands, then cook and take meals to Dad, then visit Mom again. Dad had an eating disorder; he called two or three times a day. Mom tried to feed me and fix my clothes; very physically and emotionally draining. I didn't know how pooped I was till it was all over. The most difficult decision I made was at the end [of life] with Dad. They didn't want feeding tubes [for him] and he was saying, 'I'm starving.' But I didn't give him food.

The largest item in my budget was medical insurance, plus eight to nine times a year [with] the chiropractors. During the time I cared for my parent, I was diagnosed with colon cancer one year and ovarian cancer the next. It was a horrendous time! Sad, but not tragic. Financially, we had some pretty tough months—mainly paying for health insurance. And still, I felt the medical professionals were being evasive. Not once did we talk to the doctor regarding Alzheimer's— we need to clue the doctor in, but he doesn't listen anyway.

I checked in recently with one of the caregivers I initially interviewed. Following a stroke, she is now in a wheelchair and is unable to drive, cook, dress or toilet herself. She depends on a local agency for help around the clock at an astronomic $480 per day. She relies on her three generous children to sustain her financially. Although she bought long-term care insurance years ago, the policy pays only $100 per day, hardly sufficient for the momentous cost of staying in her own home.

The middle class are not alone in their concern over elder care costs or medical competence. Billie Mae, a wealthy caregiver in her eighties, reflects on the frustrations of hiring competent help to provide home care during the last months of her 95-year-old husband, John. Agency trained staff did not appear to have adequate patient training, insight or compassion.

> I had a 24-hour care force, six caregivers from the agency, and four caregivers from Hospice over the course of the day-night shift. And all this help costs us a total of $12,000 a month. But the agency help just stood by, physically and emotionally. They kept misplacing our things. I could do a better job without training. As it was, I was caring for him over 80 hours a week. I just got tired of being captive [to the professional caregivers]. I had to supervise everything. I even had to cook for the work force. Six persons coming in and out, all day, every day, was just too much.

Billie Mae's greatest concern was a lack of patient drug monitoring on the part of the staff, which contributed significantly to her husband's cognitive decline.

> When I reviewed the care force notes, I realized that John experienced medicine-induced confusion and restlessness. There were very few notes from home care workers. This meant they weren't keeping score of what they were doing: no indication of tasks completed. I think they must have been talking to each other and neglecting John.

Reasons Why Our Medical System Fails Elders

Why can't the medical profession deliver efficient, low cost and effective long-term care to elders? Let us count the ways why our American medical system fails to measure up to our expectations for top quality care. Caregivers are not alone in their frustration with the "system." A significant number of professional groups have offered critical assessments of medical care for the elderly, including the American Academy of Medical Colleges, American Geriatric Society, American Medical Student Association, American College of Osteopathic Family Physicians and American College of Emergency Physicians (See **Health Care Facts**).

These physician groups emphasize that managed care by insurance companies complicates treatment for the elderly, and most poor elderly patients do worse in this system than do younger and more affluent individuals. Certainly, the most serious concern of all—the medical model has only a truncated idea of the social good. Cut, cure and drug is the shorthand recipe for intervention. For elders facing terminal disease and death, the system appears wholly out of sync.

Lessons Learned: How to Talk to Your Doctor

Times have changed. Caregivers and their elderly charges can no longer depend upon the intimate environment of the old-fashioned doctor's style—the home visits, the doctor's wife bringing over cookies or calling you at home about your vitamins and diet, even bringing over a used bassinet—experiences I cherish from my first pregnancy. How can we deal with this new reality of a precarious, bewildering, often indifferent medical order? Will the overwhelming number of frail and infirm elderly patients be whittled down by sheer neglect? Will these elderly patients in peril simply give up and wait for death? Not on your life. Boomers are not the generation that plans to sit idly by and allow themselves to be cast off as surplus product. They're looking for solutions—and looking fast.

So, how do we talk to our care partner's physician (usually more than one) for those interminable doctor visits and procedures? Our culture has set doctors on a pedestal, assuming them to have godlike objectivity, wisdom and emotional intelligence. Of course, they can't deliver. They can provide knowledge of a particular sort—after all, they are highly trained for carrying out *specific* medical or surgical tasks. However, we need to line up our expectations with reality. As a start, we can reduce the agony of the medical encounter and feel more empowered as a caregiver if we plan ahead. I invite you to try some of the following suggestions.

Don't be afraid to **ask questions**. Bring your list of inquiries. What can we expect? **Pain**? How much? Where? **Disability**? Temporary or long term? **Mental health or behavior issues**—mild, moderate or severe? If the doctor is less than forthcoming, ask the nurse or physician's assistant. Sometimes, you'll go away empty handed, but be persistent. It never hurts to ask—but we need to ask the **right** questions. I had little luck inquiring about my late husband's general "prognosis." I had much better results when I asked for specifics: "Is Jim likely to be in a wheelchair six months from now?" And even—"Is my husband dying? How long will he live?"

Be informed. Ask the doctor or attending nurse to provide more detailed information about the disease that threatens your loved one's life and sanity. Go to the Web and seek out resources intended for the general public. Keep in mind that Web-based information can be out of date, based on erroneous or poor research or offer only contradictory and misleading material. You might also find helpful some organizations with monthly newsletters entirely relevant for answering at least some of your questions. I've used Alzheimer's Society of Washington and Northwest Parkinson's Association to give me some specific insights. I've also found my local pharmacist provides the best sources of information about side effects of prescriptions and drug interaction effects. Don't forget your caregiver support groups. Other caregivers may be an outstanding resource that will help you get a grip on your caregiving.

Be in charge of your emotions. Don't overload the doctor with your grievances. He's not likely to have the tools to comfort you. He may even look for ways to avoid you. Use your voice—as we say to our four-year olds. I predict the doctor's response will be a great deal more positive when he isn't required to read your mind or try to console you.

Expect medical miracles. Chokyi Nyima Rinpoche and David R.

Shlim point out that major advances of the past fifty years include antibiotics, anti-inflammatories, sophisticated non-invasive diagnostic capabilities, minimally invasive surgical techniques, immunization against a wide variety of diseases, kidney dialysis, open-heart surgery and organ transplantation. That's just a short list of miraculous medical achievement.

Don't expect miracles with terminal illness. We want so much to hope that this terrible disease will go away. The doctor will pull a magic rabbit out of the hat—an astonishing drug that will completely revive our mother. The medical team will pounce upon an extraordinary (and of course, painless) surgery to restore your husband. The radiologist read the MRI wrong. Your father doesn't have brain tumors after all. Such fantasizing wastes too much time and energy. Stay in the real world of limitations and only too often, bad news. Be guided by the motto: Hope for the best, but be prepared for the worst.

Express an attitude of gratitude. Gratitude works wonders for overworked professional staff. Acknowledging personal services with a smile and "thank you" can smooth the edges of a long, ragged day for everyone. Eye contact with your physician, nurse or receptionist raises the human quotient of the medical encounter 100 percent. Being kind to beleaguered staff can make their day. The best part is not simply getting a more positive response, but how it makes **you** feel—more in charge and a more effective communicator for your loved one.

Recognize that the problem between you and the doctor may be conceptual when confronting terminal illness. For doctors, the main point of a discussion about terminal illness is to determine what people want—whether they want chemo or not, whether they want to be resuscitated or not, whether they want Hospice or not. Their focus is to present the facts and figures that will help you make the right decision.

As a caregiver, your issue is not to focus on medical details, but to deal with your own and your family's crushing fears about your loved one's life. Atul Gawande writes in *The New Yorker*: "A large part of the [doctor's] task is helping people negotiate the overwhelming anxiety—anxiety about death, anxiety about suffering, anxiety about loved ones, anxiety about finances... There are many worries and real terrors."

Gawande recommends that all of us need to arrive at an acceptance of our own mortality, and a clear understanding of the limits and possibilities of medicine. This process may take weeks, and is rarely accomplished in a single conversation with your physician.

Develop a trusting relationship with your primary physician. If you don't have a doctor you can trust, find one, preferably before your situation deteriorates further. You may be harboring complaints about doctors from your past. "They let Granny die without painkillers." "The damn doctor was wrong with my diagnosis, so what's the point?" This antagonistic attitude will net you little satisfaction when you attempt to seek medical assistance for your loved one. Once you've established a doctor-patient relationship you can count on, ask your doctor what **she** would do if her mother or father had terminal cancer—order more chemotherapy? Or for late stage heart failure—endure another surgery? Or silenced in the grip of a diabetic coma—demand resuscitation?

When asked what doctors would request for themselves if diagnosed with a terminal illness, the overwhelming majority of doctors choose to limit or withdraw life-sustaining therapy. At the same time, they are likely to support patients who ask them to withdraw care. In other cases, they may feel obligated to continue treating others for fear of legal repercussion or because other family members urge them to push on for remedies.

Pauline W. Chen writes in *Final Exam: A Surgeon's Reflections on Mortality* that "hope can hurt." When doctors push for greater intervention for older patients, they reflect not only the family's hope to keep their loved one alive, but also the medical belief that dying represents failure. Chen says that a third of attending physicians and almost three quarters of residents felt they had acted against their conscience while caring for the terminally ill.

Admittedly, few people are happy with the way that medicine is practiced—and this includes the doctors. Many of those who manage health care systems throw up their hands at making medicine either affordable or available to all Americans. Additionally, the over-treatment of terminally ill patients both raises costs and severely diminishes quality of life. Ultimately, two components are missing from this picture:

compassion and caring. We must compensate for the absence of these elements by our own inner work—prayer, meditation, lucid dreaming, breath exercises, intuition and preparation for our own dying—and by finding soul-reviving friends to sustain us during the invariably tough times.

In the meantime, don't give up hope for a more enlightened medical system. Reform is in the air, and younger physicians are being exposed to more humane and communicative approaches with end-of-life patients. Not to overstate the case, but palliative care remains an option in some hospitals. Take advantage of it. This care focuses not only on treating the illness, but offers a more compassionate perspective and practice than general medicine. Still, the healing professions have a long way to go before they universally manifest the quality of mercy we call wisdom.

Health Care Facts

- A lack of medical-psychological knowledge of the aging process impacts the care process, as well as failure to train specialists for the geriatric population. Only 10 percent of teaching universities require students to complete at least one course in geriatrics.

- Severe shortages of geriatric physicians exist throughout the country, leading to the assertion that the elderly are "patients in peril" by the American Academy of Medical Colleges.

- Our current health care system cannot respond to the growing numbers of older people and their complex ailments, especially among the very old. Americans 85 years and older are now the fastest growing segment of our population.

- Fifty percent of hospital beds are occupied by patients 65 years and older. This percentage will substantially increase over the next 20 years as Baby Boomers enter retirement age.

- False assumptions about elderly patients as physically and cognitively disabled across the board contributes to physicians' discomfort with primary care of elders.

- The "heroic model" of American medicine emphasizes high technology and skills, appropriate for acute care and younger patients, rather than care and compassion to deal with elderly patients, who have chronic diseases and are facing death.

- The cure orientation of American training runs counter to the reality of sick elderly patients, who often have one or more incurable chronic illnesses, requiring the attention of various medical specialists (who may or may not communicate with one another).

- Many physicians suffer from an ageist bias that contributes to discrimination against elderly patients, resulting in an "elderly care gap"—too few services, especially for minorities and the poor.

- Bureaucratic obstacles to care confound the system, and discourage the elderly from pursuing treatment. In a study of five Boston hospitals by the American Geriatric Society (1996), people 80 or older received less care in hospitals than did patients younger than 50 by as much as $7,000 per patient.

- Poor and unsatisfactory communication between physicians and elderly patients hinders effective health care. In a study of elderly emergency department patients 65 and older, only 15 percent of elderly persons could list all their medications, dosage schedules and indications. No medical provider had ever spelled out this information to them, or they were too cognitively impaired to understand the directives.

- A patchwork system of financing health care for the elderly leads to excessive or inadequate treatment, and invariably higher costs for elders and their families.

- Health care providers are typically between 25 and 60 years old, and show little interest in caring for the frail elderly on an age basis alone.

Chapter 6

Family Support:
True Grit vs. Wash-Outs

Family caregiving, however noble and essential, is an act done largely in private, invisible to the world. Perhaps for that reason, it's a subject often confined to private conversations.

– Marilyn Gardner, *Christian Science Monitor*

The Care Network

If your elderly loved one collapsed today with a heart attack or stroke, or was incapacitated with terminal cancer or a chronic disease, how ready are you and your immediate family to move into a helping role? Can you actually depend upon family members to come forward with social, financial and emotional help? And how sustained would this assistance be? Most people can pull it together to be with you for a few days or weeks. But how about being your back-up for months or years? Is it likely you will be left stranded by your adult children if you're caring for a spouse? What if you're the designated caregiver for a mother or father—or maybe both parents? Who can you count on then? Will your siblings jump into action? How can your family and friendship networks be mobilized to ease the caregiving commitment?

These essential questions are rarely asked *before* a catastrophic event. Only after a medical crisis, do people begin the hard work of assessing the human resources that will pull them through the initial emergency and into the grueling task of the day-to-day caregiving.

Care networks do not spring up spontaneously. I discovered this fact only after much trial and error—but mostly error. I grew up with such a plenitude of beliefs about what the family is and does. "The family is forever." "Children will be by your side in your old age." Or

Jim's favorite—"The family will always be there to take you in"—a belief that explained why we had six boomerang kids over the years.

These reassuring beliefs lulled me into expectations that simply could not be fulfilled. Somehow, I thought all the adult children would be on board from Day One until Jim passed. I totally took for granted that everyone would play the same role, perform similar tasks and serve as my substitute at any time. I also assumed that they would understand how much they were needed, and behave accordingly. How wrong could I be?

Once the crisis was over I was on my own. Our children drifted off to their respective homes, spouses, children and jobs. After a series of hit-and-miss visits it began to sink in that I needed to actually recruit help from them. And I needed to work with their strengths—and limitations.

Tim, our oldest son, was on board from the very beginning until the day Jim died. I could always count on him. Patti was always good for daily visits, and shopping for special goodies and necessities for her Dad. Sue was a faithful, if brief, visitor. But other family members were less disciplined, less compassionate and less in touch. Our family dynamics explained some of the differences. But the children's lives explained the rest. Like most families caught up in long-standing adversity, individual members had their own complicated lives—finishing professional school, exhausting job, poor coping skills, young children, unsympathetic spouses or a combination of these constraints. I had to make do with the resources I had at hand—especially if I wanted them to have a good experience with their Dad.

Even with limited support by family members and trusted friends I felt greatly sustained at first. I was true to form, though, in maintaining my silence. I never discussed my situation with my employer or even fellow workers. Most friends were sympathetic, but early on I found that no one really wanted to hear about the grisly details. Even our willing children who took on some of the care burden did not share with each other their feelings of anger or resentment. For a variety of reasons—embarrassment, pride, disgust, fear, trauma or grief—our caregiving remained out of public view, our labors were ignored, unappreciated or simply taken for granted by the people around us.

Yet, I characterized our family network as strong and durable. Once I accepted our children's individual—and always special—contributions, I let go of my expectations. I felt both grateful and compassionate about their struggles to provide both their Dad and me with emotional support. I knew their hearts were broken. I stopped assigning duties and time frames. I let the process of helping unfold for each person. So, while most of our children showed true grit in the long vigil from initial crisis to death, others, I sadly admit, were washouts, at least part of the time. I suspect most families have a similar story.

What Happens with Ineffectual Care Networks?

Unfortunately, countless caregivers have poorly developed personal networks or highly fragmented family relationships. They may be unaware of outside resources, believing themselves to be alone or completely dependent on family or close friends. Because caregivers are often anxious, fatigued and consumed with grief, they may not feel it's worth the effort to seek out a more extended set of relationships. For caregivers with few financial and personal resources, the very idea of sharing their load appears inconceivable.

In most cases, caregivers expect their family to take on the crucial role of directly supporting their care efforts. Elders turn to sons and daughters, daughters-in-law, female grandchildren and siblings for day-to-day support. Those middle-aged or younger caring for their elderly parents expect spouses, siblings and sometimes friends to come to the rescue. But what do we know about these family care networks?

True, in stable and supportive families, caregiving can produce unexpected rewards, strengthening ties between those who give care and those who receive it. But what happens in troubled families, where relationships are strained and normal bonds of affection are frayed? What about those families where the adult child has been the victim of sexual, physical or emotional abuse, or the wife has been a battering victim of the now-aging husband? This raises an entire series of questions about the nature of relationships in caregiving networks.

How stable and resourceful are family networks during good and bad times, especially when the going gets tough? What kinds of support can family members realistically provide—financial, practical or emotional? Do such persons share the caregivers' values? Are they willing and able to serve the needs of the elder? What expectations does the caregiver have about family and friends' contributions? Do these expectations correspond with the kind of relationships the caregiver has had with individual family members?

How are caregivers expected to "pay back" intimate others when they step into the circle of care? What circumstances contribute to caregivers seeking non-family and paid services, rather than depending on family members? How consciously and cautiously do caregivers construct and maintain their care networks? I will explore these and other issues as I discuss characteristic network patterns among elder caregivers.

The Network Anchor

In most families, the mother or older wife serves as the "network anchor." Her job is to locate people or organizations who can support herself and her charges. Karen Hansen, who writes about networks of care for children, identifies distinct patterns that are loosely correlated with income differences. Hansen offers four network types: (1) "an absorbent safety net;" (2) "a family foundation;" (3) "a loose association of advisors;" and (4) "a warm web of people." I discovered these networks also typify our caregivers' network patterns. In addition, I found two more types among these caregivers: (5) a weak network; and (6) a failed network.

Here's a riveting fact. I inquired of each caregiver the number of *potential* network members who could feasibly provide financial, practical or emotional support. Here, our caregivers' networks included an average of 10.19 persons. These included the people who had the *capacity* (but not necessarily the willingness) to participate. I contrast this with the *real* number of persons, including kin, friends, neighbors, colleagues or others, who actually showed up to provide help. For our caregivers, the average number was 4.24—a significant gap between the potential number and the actual availability of supporters.

Child Care and Elder Care—So What's the Difference?

A distinctive feature of elder care is the widespread belief that because a woman has raised children, she can easily handle caring for her older husband or parent. But this is not necessarily the case. And here's why. Every viable culture promotes procreation, and couples without children are often perceived as deficient or "selfish." By contrast, long-term elder care is a recent phenomenon among developed countries, and is specifically related to technological, communication and medical advances.

Another salient feature of child care and elder care is the primacy of gender. An assumption among the general public is that taking care of anyone—child or adult—is a gender-specific activity, regardless of age. This belief is part of the cultural bias that presumes women to be maternal; therefore, they can handle childrearing or sick elder care as an everyday activity.

Regardless of social circumstances—career, family, vocational, professional or creative commitments—these women were uniformly expected by family members to take on the responsibility of caring for their elderly relative. Because most of our caregivers have raised children or are in the process of doing so, they felt they had the tools to do elder care as well. And they needed to make it simple. Most hit upon the truism early on that *dependency* is *dependency* is *dependency*. No difference between a child or an ailing elder. They left out some very significant distinctions, though.

Like most middle-class and upper income parents, they sought information about child care needs through their pediatrician, or later adolescent medical specialist, as well as through the media, friends, school resources, their children's peer groups and the larger environment. Children are a central focus of most social groups. What parent doesn't delight in sharing information about the "stages," problems, joys and stresses of childhood with friends and strangers alike? When a parent is in doubt about a child's behavior, tune in to Dr. Phil or pick up a favorite self-help book. Knowledge and cultural sharing about children characterize most parents' lives.

But these same adept women who managed to negotiate jobs, family and community activities while raising their children admit to being overwhelmed with elder care. They report finding themselves baffled with the cognitive challenges of their mother's Alzheimer's disease, the gasping breath of their husband's congestive heart failure or the slow, laborious decline of their father's Parkinson's disease.

Another feature of childrearing and family ties involves grandparents' expectations that their adult children will "allow" them to baby sit or help with child care. Many grandparents relish the opportunity to enjoy the children with or without their parents around, rekindling the maternal and paternal warmth and love that sustained them throughout their own children's growing up. Aunts and uncles often get involved too—playing ball with energetic nieces and nephews and going on outings together. Hansen's research emphasized that looking after children was "fun"—allowing adults to be playful and "young again," reliving their own childhoods.

By no stretch of the imagination can we say that most elder care is "fun." Since when can most caregivers turn over elder care to peripheral relatives, casual friends and helpful neighbors? It simply isn't done as a routine matter. The demands of care are either too exacting or difficult. An immobile elder may need assistance using the toilet, while another may need help with the morning routine of washing, dressing, shaving and hair combing. Each may require medications to be dispensed at specific intervals. Clearly, caring for a sick, often confused or depressed elder is fraught with complexity.

Another difference between child care and elder care worth considering is that healthy children follow an upward track—growth and development over time—an inspiring story as it unfolds. Each child has his/her own special destiny, and wise parents promote the best attributes of their offspring: first steps, first words, first day of school, graduation from eighth grade, high school, college or even graduate school, first regular job, and thence into full adulthood with marriage and family. The parent role mainly has a steady and predictable pacing along a well-established cultural groove.

None of these positive conditions prevail for elder care or parents whose children have illnesses like terminal cancer or inoperable brain tumors. Here, the track slopes downward and stops. It is only a matter of time before the loved one is gone.

Networks of Interdependency

Whereas two caregivers in this group had lifestyles that happily can be described as "it takes a village" to care for a sick elder, all other 58 interviews indicated more typical network arrangements. They relied on family, close friends and agency or institutional support. The small village approach has definite advantages available to only a few families living in Western societies. Most of us live in cities, suburbs or larger towns, which have limited access to spontaneous support persons or groups. Work and careers, family obligations and community commitments prevent most of us from the free give-and-take of traditional kin and neighbors. Instead, the majority of us are under continuous pressure to be clock watchers and schedule keepers. At the same time, individual "anchors" can create a strong support network to be mobilized during periods of family crisis. This is the case with Rachel, a vibrant high school teacher and mother of adult children, who, in caring for her ill spouse, developed her own "absorbent safety net."

An Absorbent Safety Net

An *absorbent safety net* is a network that remains in place for times of need, a kind of "rainy-day" social investment. Network members maintain their independence, but can be summoned during critical family episodes. Members are willing and able to absorb the shocks of a family crisis, and even stand in for the caregiver.

Rachel could always count on close family and friends to be there for her. The network could be easily mobilized for crisis periods, because Rachel's relationships with network members—her children and friends—were strong and resilient from the start. These relationships actually strengthened over the months of caregiving. Calling herself a "traffic director," Rachel summoned her children and close friends to assist with the high level of care Philip needed in his valiant struggle with colon cancer, now metastasized to his liver. Rachel admitted she "wasn't up for taking care of Philip myself. But how fortunate I am to have children who insisted on not only being with their dad during his final illness, but also taking over the caregiving reins."

My husband knew I was burned out on caregiving. My mother had been trying to commit suicide since I was five years old. I couldn't go to the prom because she had overdosed. I couldn't sleep at night, afraid my mother wasn't breathing. I just shut down. I was an adult when she finally succeeded. She left a suicide note saying that it was my fault.

Instead of feeling besieged, Rachel turned to her children.

The feeling of incompetence overwhelmed me and when Philip was diagnosed with liver cancer, I asked for help. Our adult children moved in to help with his care. We knew it was going to go fast and I knew I would be a terrible caregiver by myself, just unable to cope. I really was afraid of doing it wrong again. Philip and I went to Europe in July and he died at home in October.

With the family network in place, Rachel continued her active life.

With our children there to help, I was able to keep my job, go for walks every day, keep my husband at home and remain detached enough so I didn't lose it. The children loved him and we shared the load for 80 or more hours a week. The family support was the best part of caretaking. I leaned on everyone I could. My advice is to minimize the impact of caregiving.

Rachel and her husband, both in their sixties, were professionally established in their local university and high school communities. Both had extensive friendships and community connections. Rachel's network structure involved a large number of potential members, and had three levels. The inner circle comprised her two children, a son and daughter, as well as a stepson and his daughter, an "adopted" daughter (her son's best friend), a daughter-in-law and one grandchild. This constituted an immediate practical and emotional support group of seven persons. Within that inner circle, her son emerged as the *anchor*, coordinating practical tasks and providing emotional support to his dad.

In the next circle, long-term friends, teaching associates and a religious mentor offered primarily emotional support. Later, Hospice entered the scene to take over many of the more difficult medical tasks, as well as grief counseling for the family.

And finally, in the outer circle were professional and religious associations—not necessarily individual persons. Still, these organizations served as group sources of knowledge and strength. Such resources proved essential when the family had to confront the myriad of emotions and practical details associated with end-of-life issues.

Rachel's network is among the strongest of the caregivers I interviewed. Part of the reason is that she could let go of the burden. She reserved her strength and energy to devote herself body and soul to her husband. By absolving herself of the practical details of care, and focusing on keeping her life together with her teaching job, community and athletic activities, Rachel had energy left over to fortify the care team by shopping, cooking and leisurely enjoying her family. Rachel felt unburdened because the safety net she had created over her lifetime was a remarkable success. Her husband contributed to this positive outcome by "making it so no one had any feelings of being burdened." After her husband's death, she showed her appreciation for her children's efforts by taking them on a three-month vacation, which included swimming and scuba diving in the Caribbean.

A number of other caregivers created networks that could be described as "safety nets." In Rachel's case, clearly the network members acknowledged specific obligations and responsibilities toward one another, as well as shared the expectation that the assistance they provided would be "repaid" at some time in the future. For Rachel's children, a relaxing vacation followed the rigors of shared caregiving. Among friends, Rachel remains a hospitable, delightful companion.

Loose Association of Advisors

Not all caregivers have the luxury of a well-established and highly supportive network when the need arises. Yet, many manage to meet the demands of caregiving by mobilizing support wherever they can find it. Such a temporary network requires a solid anchor, one who intuitively recognizes that a *loose association of advisors* has a makeshift quality, but can fill in the gap when family bonds are weak.

I earlier introduced Kendra, a 23-year old college student, as an example of an overburdened caregiver, because of her vulnerability as a teenage girl struggling with her father's care without adequate family support. Now, we examine her role as "anchor" in a disrupted family situation. Kendra was raised in a middle-class family where high achievement was a standard expectation—and Kendra had never disappointed. An outstanding athlete and honor student throughout her high school years, Kendra suddenly confronted another challenge—the task of caring for a terminally ill father with lung cancer, heart disease and kidney failure. The task was "almost too much to bear."

I was forced into caregiving. Mom had to take care of her ailing father…. [she] left me with my dad through my high school years.

In her mother's absence, Kendra was responsible for shopping, cooking, running the house, arranging medical appointments, transporting her father to his various doctors and dialysis treatments, even administering his 25-plus medications over the course of the day. An impossible schedule? Somehow, she still managed to keep her head above water as an honor student and competitive athlete in high school basketball, softball and volleyball. Her immediate family could not come to her rescue, leaving Kendra with a sense of desperation. On the one hand, she had an absentee mother, who had moved into her ailing parents' home. On the other hand, she had a younger brother, who limited his contribution to yard work and occasional handyman duties—when he was in the mood. Otherwise, she was bereft of other willing or able relatives. Where was Kendra to turn for help with her dad?

At first, she felt "hopeless," wishing there was "something more I could do." Then, she swung into action. First, she identified a family friend to assist with day-to-day household chores. Next, she succeeded in shifting the dialysis care from hospital to home with a nurse, who could also answer her medical questions, as well as spend time with her father. Lastly, she turned to her school teammates—girls her own age—who came forward with an outpouring of emotional support and practical help with shopping and keeping house. Low family solidarity was balanced with high friendship bonding.

Once Kendra had her "team" assembled, she felt more able to share her feelings with "trusted friends, cry and take alone time at a beach near my house." She also discovered the "gift" of caregiving—loving and sharing with her father.

Not all was drudgery. Their time together evolved into a deep and unspoken level of understanding Kendra described as "unspeakable trust." In this sense, caregiving for Kendra became another accomplishment. "I felt so much more mature than my peers and more knowledgeable." Another plus was that her father was both positive and appreciative, lightening her load considerably.

Certain sources of unresolved tension remained, however. One was her mother's surprisingly negative reaction to the father-daughter bonding during her husband's illness. Another was Kendra's own feelings of loss about the mother-daughter relationship during her adolescence. It seemed damaged beyond repair.

Since her father's death, Kendra has tried to make every effort to appease her mother's anger. Despite being busy with college, she visits regularly. Her mother continues to insist she return home after graduating and "look after her." Kendra expressed both resentment and regrets about her caregiving experience.

> I'm still dealing with my mother's anger and resentment. I continue to go home once a week to assist her around her house and visit. But the majority of the time, she is verbally abusive.

Tragically, Kendra's dreams for an athletic scholarship had to be abandoned.

> I wanted to play softball in college, and planned to go to California [for] college. I was accepted by my first choice school, but turned it down to stay closer to my father. I think if I hadn't taken on the caregiving role I would have a better relationship with my mother, and maybe a better degree.

At this point, Kendra remains caught between family expectations—her mother's pull to remain a faithful caregiver—and her own push into independent adulthood.

A Family Foundation

Affluent and well-connected individuals are most fortunate in tapping into a large pool of financial and human resources for managing caregiving tasks. At the same time, very old age inevitably brings illness and decline, regardless of status. When 85-year-old Billie Mae became the network anchor for her 95-year-old (now deceased) husband John, she was well prepared. Over time John had been afflicted with multiple ailments, including blindness, mental confusion, eating problems, chronic pain and prolonged physical dependency.

Together, they had been a force in their local community. The creation of a family foundation made it possible to support large community projects, such as major reconstruction of the local opera house and various child-centered charities. With a generous disposable income, this "independent woman," as she enjoys calling herself, has maintained her active life over 10 years of caregiving—exercising, reading, listening to books on tape, traveling and dining out. During the period of John's dying, she supervised three shifts of home care workers over a 24-hour period, plus Hospice staff during the last six months of John's life.

Day-to-day help was also provided by Jim, a full-time paid home assistant, and two daughters, one of whom was an executive director at the nearby hospital, and the other, a school psychologist located an hour away. Paid and unpaid family help included her husband's son, Don, from a former marriage, as well as other children and grandchildren—all of whom provided additional assistance. Add to their combined family of seven children, an abundant collection of friends and fellow board members from their various charitable trusts, and you get the picture of an abundant, bustling, well-supported household.

Billie Mae embraced the caregiving role with enthusiasm and profound love. When I asked her if she had made a "conscious choice to be the primary caregiver," she answered, "Yes, I just did it. That was my role; that was my man."

She was very unhappy, though, with the local agency's six person nursing team, who appeared to be less than stellar medical assistants. Billie Mae reported they rarely initiated services and failed to write adequate drug and medical notes—egregious errors which led to John's medicine-induced confusion and restlessness. However, what was most challenging for Billie Mae was providing meals for the workers three times a day. None of the agency workers contributed to household management or domestic tasks, which tended to pile up over the course of the week. And, turnover was high. Over a three-month period during October through December, Billie Mae hired 12 *different* nursing assistants—a dizzying number when you consider she was also juggling a daily housecleaner, weekly chaplain visits and maintaining her presence on various community boards.

Because of her background of owning and managing three successful companies, Billie Mae had high expectations about her professional caregiving staff. But performance-wise, they didn't measure up. Instead of being physically and emotionally supported by their presence, she needed to pay very close attention to John's care: "I was on call every minute." As her husband's medical condition worsened—frequent hospitalizations, and when home, either bedridden or limited to a wheelchair—this highly capable caregiver admitted to struggling with "patience."

What sustained Billie Mae through this ordeal of home care? "It was our long, loving relationship, my husband's appreciative attitude toward my efforts and the fact that John could be in our home." A deeply religious person, Billie Mae now welcomes the peace and tranquility of her life and, despite blindness, has taken up an invigorating schedule again. She has only one regret—"I don't have John to share it."

Warm Web of People

Flourishing non-family networks are also possible. Such networks certainly can supplement support when family members are few and far between. They can also provide a sense that one is not alone in the struggle. Anne is the anchor for her care network. At 61 years old, Anne is a special kind of a caregiver who, first, moved away from her all-embracing family network in the Midwest, and then, had to kick start an entirely new network with few family members in a different state. In Minnesota, Anne managed to raise four children, work full-time at various creative jobs, including head chef at the leading art museum's restaurant, and, later, as an executive director of a nonprofit organization. Once the children were raised, Anne readily made the shift from child care to elder care when her husband was diagnosed with Parkinson's disease. What made it all possible is Anne's extensive network of family, friends, co-workers and community supporters. She had no choice but to begin anew—to create new networks.

My husband was diagnosed in 1993. As the disease progressed, so did my attention to it. In 2001, he felt he had to leave Minnesota [and said], 'or I'll just die.'

As for Anne, losing her network was tantamount to tearing a huge chunk out of her life, requiring her to make a fresh start. She admitted to feeling ambivalent about it.

I left my home state of 55 years, my children and grandchildren, my job, my network and my history. But all of that is also positive! I didn't mind being a caregiver. It seemed a natural part of my life. I was, however, extremely anxious about leaving my family, friends and huge support network.

Anne recounted her list of "misses"—those irrevocable losses in her life.

I gave up a lot when Mike got sick, and we moved. I am missing pieces of my partner, I am missing my friends, I am missing my good job, I am missing my home.

In a real sense, Anne is walking the walk of Parkinson's, as she struggles with adjusting to her 73-year-old husband's deteriorating physical and mental state, a decline that severely limits his life's work as an artist/sculptor.

In a very real sense, I have Parkinson's too. My thoughts, reactions and decisions are considered and measured in the context of what Parkinson's can handle and absorb. My husband's gradual loss of strength and speed have challenged my patience and 'alert' level, as if I had a young child in my care again.

Now more than six years after the move, Anne has a beautiful new home in a park-like setting, and serves as a round-the-clock caregiver, while attending the nearby university as a full-time student. Anne's newly created network continues to expand. Frequent trips to Minnesota allow her to stay connected with children, grandchildren and dear friends. Now that her son and his family have moved nearby, she receives practical help on an almost daily basis. One daughter, a therapist, serves as a constant source of wisdom for weekly phone chats, where Anne can unburden herself and be consoled and restored. Mike's outpouring of appreciation renews her self-confidence to carry on with the tasks at hand. Furthermore, Anne understands the necessity to take care of herself, and treats herself to an energizing regime.

> *I walk fast to keep my brain balanced and I write every day. I read wonderful books, garden and eat good food. I am gradually developing a satisfying routine of daily activities, some with my husband and some alone.*

Anne's capacity for flexibility attracts friends, neighbors and fellow students alike, who are attracted to her positive energy and outgoing manner. As one of her network members said, "To know Anne is to love her."

With ample resources—Mike still sells some of his artwork, receives retirement earnings and Social Security—this well-situated couple has considerable economic advantages over most American families facing long-term illness. Additionally, Anne continues to seek information about the disease to better equip her for dealing with the limitations she must confront in caring for her husband.

Mike is actively involved in both national and local Parkinson's associations, and attends annual conferences as a participant. Anne supports Mike's autonomy, facilitating solo trips to visit his own children, which keeps his family ties strong. As part of self-care, Anne has consciously made a decision to "turn lemons into lemonade" in her struggle with the disease. Anne reviews the ways she benefits from her commitment to caregiving.

> *Today, I am accomplishing a new adventure. I am adjusting to pulling more of the wagon. I am a more patient person as a result of caregiving. I am stronger than I was 12 years ago* [when this began].

Her care burden lifted once her husband recognized her dedication.

> *I feel much better about myself now that Mike admits to me that he needs my assistance. This has empowered me and made my presence valuable and gratifying. Mike now believes that I will take care of him, advocate on his behalf and knows that we have productive and valuable time left.*

Caregiving has ultimately opened her to a new way of being in a relationship.

> *Caregiving has been a healing experience for me, in that I've been forced to slow the pace of my life, and that has been healing. I have the rare opportunity to know my husband as a child. I especially cherish the quiet times with Mike, where he spends sweet moments recollecting and reflecting out loud.*

Change has been a mutually gratifying experience.

> *But the best part about caring for him is living with the evolution of Parkinson's, and the gradual release of Mike's normal 'power over'* [others] *behavior to a gentle acceptance of help.*

Weak Network

Not every caregiver has the strength and persistence of Anne. Some caregivers must operate with only a weak network—the people who logically should help fail to come forward or relationships in a family never developed. The step-parent of adult children may face this situation most acutely. The inability or failure to build a strong support network bedevils many caregivers. So do lack of personal and monetary resources, as well as a limited education. For those with restrictive beliefs about oneself or one's place in the world, building a strong network may be impossible.

Our next story focuses on a caregiver, Fran, who never really had an opportunity to create a new network after her marriage. No sooner did she say "I do," before she was hurled into full-time service as a "worker bee in my husband's business." Not only was she providing care for her long-ailing husband, but also for his mother, who was sickly and required her assistance.

Subordinate to her husband's demands, Fran could not overcome her feelings of unworthiness. Fran believed these feelings came from her limited education and lack of formal training. Her inability to visit friends because of family and work commitments completed the picture of a caregiver who felt bereft and isolated. (These sentiments were underscored by Fran's frequent outbursts of crying during both interviews. Still, she persisted, saying "it's important to tell my story.")

An attractive, but exhausted, 61-year-old caregiver, Fran has been nursing her husband since the beginning of their marriage, more than 15 years ago. Married late in life, Fran knew at the outset that Pete had Crohn's disease, and it would be her "duty" to take care of him— "Doing what I know I have to do for the duration." Now, at 72, Pete moves between care sites: home, hospital and nursing home, with little or no assistance from his two sons from an earlier marriage. Fran's own two sons are unavailable for assisting their mother. One son, who lives in the same state, is "too busy" with his job, while the other son is men- tally ill. Her husband's two sons, both professional pharmacists, "don't do anything to help their dad." Fran often expressed anger and frustra- tion during our conversations.

> *I find it most unfair that his children have no feeling of responsibility to help along the way. I left it up to Pete. We took care of their grand- mother. That's how they grew up—'family takes care of family.' I told them to visit their father now that he's at home.*

When I probed further about Pete's sons' response to their father's illness, she replied:

> *Until the last three months, they didn't respond very well. Both sons are pharmacists. The doctor spoke to his sons. They didn't seem to care—they didn't have any realization of how sick Pete is: his kid- neys, his ileostomy. They seem to be visiting better when he's in the hospital or nursing home. How they'll do once he gets home? I can't say. But it's not with helping* [their dad].

In earlier years, Pete's pharmaceutical skills helped build a flour- ishing drug store. After marrying Fran and appointing her as store assistant, they were able to make sound investments and accrue wealth. But these arrangements rarely favored Fran, whose care assignments seemed endless.

> *I also had his mother, who lived behind the store. Since I married him, I was chosen to take care of Grandma. Living at the lake, I worked all the way through Grandma's illness—made lunches for both Grandma and Pete. His boys said: 'You married him, so you take what you can get.' Eventually, we got to the point where we got*

someone else to cook for Grandma, and then I cooked only dinner. I was constantly working and taking antidepressants. My schedule? I made Grandma's breakfast, then I went to work, went back and made her and Pete's lunch, cleaned up and served, then more work, and then cooked dinner. Pete had his knees replaced—but no one came forward. The sons' attitude was: 'You married our dad, so you married the job.' They called me their 'dad's wife.' They had an 'I don't care' attitude toward me. I've cried myself to sleep many times. I was supposed to prove myself.

Grandma's care proved to be far easier than her husband's.

She was a very appreciative, loving person. Taking care of her was much easier than [taking care of] *her son. Pete can be very demanding. I have a baby monitor, so I thought the situation would improve. But there's just too much work and physical stress.*

"How do you manage all the work," I asked? Fran said:

So, how do I deal with this? Sometimes with anger and complaints, other times with organizing more help for us.

Fran's sister-in-law, once a strong supporter, backed out after Fran ignored her advice not to bring Pete back home, because of the intensity of his medical needs. While Fran's sister could be counted upon for an occasional lunch, friends have worked out best for support. Still, she doesn't have much opportunity to make the 90-mile trip to Seattle to see them in person.

Friends have been better than my relatives. They keep calling me— my dearest friend keeps in touch with me all the time [by phone].

At the time of the interview, Fran was struggling to apply for COPES, a statewide program that provides medical and household support for at-home elderly patients. This has necessitated hiring a lawyer to avoid the worst repercussions of the "spending down" requirement—a condition that would have left them with greatly reduced assets. Fran prides herself on successfully negotiating this process, and indicated that rather than losing $50,000 to the state, they have been able to hold on to the rest of their nest egg of $90,000. Despite a weak network, Fran's community outreach efforts resulted in excellent financial advice. The Northwest Regional Council on Aging also assisted in providing respite care, giving her a few hours off from caregiving. Help from her attorney in negotiating the state system and visits with a counselor have taught her both the virtue and necessity of speaking up for herself.

Fran experiences the all-too-common plight of women who believe they have an obligation to care for others before themselves. "I know I should take care of myself in order to take care of others, but it's hard," she said. At the same time, she faces failing health, especially back problems, and serious questions over whether she will be able to continue her current responsibilities without a great deal more help. With few close friends, none of whom live nearby, and no family allies or neighbors to carry out the day-to-day care and home maintenance, Fran feels incapable of handling the job of caregiving.

Fran says she once "loved her wifely role," and cherished time together with her husband. Now, her strategy involves seeking outside help, turning to state and local agencies, doctors and professional counselors to get her through her days.

Fran treads a lonely and difficult path. As expectations about her stepsons dissolve and she comes to accept their non-involvement, and instead, relies on government and paid assistance, some of the tension of her situation may lessen. Until she releases herself from her overburdened sense of "duty," reclaims former friends and reaches out for new experiences and friendships, her life may continue on a dangerous course—one of exhaustion, illness and despair.

An Empty Network

The sheer absence of day-to-day support plagues a number of caregivers. Having drifted into the task without giving it thoughtful intention, the caregiver has devoted little or no time to building a support network. An *empty network* is more than a lack of people, however. It also involves a state of mind in which "doing it alone" is part of a lifestyle. Such is the case with Toni, a fifty-two-year old, self-employed woman who never married.

Toni has been forced to reinvent herself—admittedly without much success at the time of the interview—after she brought her mother to live in her home. Not only is Toni accustomed to living alone, she cherishes her solitary life. Now, she has been confronted with the full-time care of an 81-year-old mother with multiple maladies: diabetes, peripheral neuropathy, dementia and depression. A highly successful web and book designer, Toni never anticipated taking care of her mother, and expressed her resignation in the face of the failure of other family members to come forward to help ease the burden.

> *She is my mother, and it is my job as her only daughter, I guess. It is very wearing and can be frustrating. I can't seem to come up with a 'best part' in this situation.*

Toni has a brother and an aunt, her mother's sister, who potentially could have helped with the care, if certain conditions had not prevailed. The aunt offered help only if Toni's mother moved in with her, a plan her mother rejected. Her brother was a different story. Toni felt that her childhood memories of her brother's "mean behavior" excluded him as a support person.

> *Mother didn't want to live with my aunt. My brother wouldn't do it. She* [mother] *wants me to make all the decisions. She wants to know where I am every second. I am expected to take care of everything, and I wasn't prepared to be a 'mom.'*

Toni deeply resented losing both her freedom *and* privacy. Parts of her home had to be remodeled to suit her ailing mother's needs. To accommodate Toni's desire for privacy and quiet for her at-home business, she changed some doorways that separated her mother's living area from her own. But that failed to keep out the sounds of the TV. In addition, Toni has experienced a number of health issues. Her multiple symptoms, including mood swings and chronic pain, were somewhat relieved recently by two surgeries—a hysterectomy and hemorrhoidectomy. Although her physical health has improved, the strain of her mother's constant presence provokes her into frequent frustration and simmering anger. Losing control further deepens her sense of failure—and worse—of feeling isolated and overloaded.

> *I expected to help with Mom's care, but I did not expect to be in charge of everything. I am overworked. I have no privacy. I remodeled the*

house to suit her needs, and did a lot of the work myself. I feel trapped and angry. There is twice as much work to do. I have to repeat things over and over because of Mom's dementia.

Aside from a few friends, who once listened to Toni's self-admitted "whining," she had no practical or financial support for four years. Finally, after a medical emergency she placed her mother in a skilled nursing home, and later in an assisted living facility. Toni managed to convince her brother to contribute some money to costs. Still, she had to remind him.

I was very direct about my frustration and anger when I asked him for help. I told him, 'You will have to take care of her if this kills me.'

When her mother demanded to be moved back to Toni's home, the daily irritations resumed. Toni is weary from her mother's non-stop requests. She thinks her mother is quite capable of carrying out ordinary tasks. Toni asks: "Why is she acting reluctant, childish or simply refusing to cooperate?" Toni has little sense of reciprocity with grace. The idea of giving back to her mother for her care during childhood doesn't seem very compelling. Being responsible is an important value for her, but the spirit of giving does not come easily.

Friends have dropped by the wayside because of her unavailability, leaving her even more vulnerable. Toni buries herself in her creative work, but cannot seem to strike a balance between care for the other and care for self. Toni recognizes her predicament only too well.

Having to deal with the frustration, overwork and anger makes me realize it's probably just a character flaw that hadn't surfaced yet, because I never married and had kids. After talking with friends, social worker, doctor, etc., I'm accepting that I'm not really caregiver material.

Perhaps the irony is that Toni—like thousands of other women who feel trapped and angry in their caregiving role—cannot seem to find a satisfactory strategy to resolve the tension of having their lives turned inside-out for years at a time.

When Network Structures Change

Networks are not rigid social arrangements. Instead, they are more likely to undergo profound change over time as caregivers learn new approaches or situations drastically change. I actually experienced *four* distinct network types over my four years of caregiving: safety net, loose association, warm web of people, a weak network and finally, reliance on nursing home and family to reproduce the safety net once again.

> *My adult children and grandchildren provided my initial safety net after Jim's first and second heart attacks, rushing to my aid in the hospital and following through with countless hours spent in emergency rooms and rehabilitation centers. I could always depend on a quorum of family members to show up around Jim's bed, quietly waiting for him to be responsive, and after he improved, to be gratefully present when he was awake.*
>
> *Once Jim was home, four of my six children who lived locally visited daily through that first Christmas season of his illness. I felt completely supported and loved throughout the ordeal.*
>
> *Once the new year rolled around, I realized that everyone had busy lives, and I needed to release my beloved assistants to their jobs, homes and families. I entered a new phase of network building. I first attempted to hire a friend to help me out with Jim during working hours. Although she had prior experience caring for her father who had Alzheimer's disease, after six months she found the caregiving tasks to be onerous—too labor intensive, and too many unhappy memories with her Dad. Additionally, Jim was a reluctant and resistant patient. Under our joint care, Jim refused to eat or take his medicine in a timely manner. Often, he was one or two prescriptions behind, for example, taking his 9:00 a.m. pills at 1:30 in the afternoon or later. I felt desperate, but had little success in turning things around.*
>
> *Yet, Jim had to be supervised around the clock. Because I was still working and needed daily help, I turned to private agencies and professional caregivers to to assist me. First, I was able to persuade Mark, a trained caregiver from the last recovery center Jim had stayed at, to attend Jim from 9 to 5, promising to pay higher wages than the*

facility. Second, I located a trained nursing assistant to give Jim his daily shower and provide personal care. Third, I found a second-year medical student to assist in the evenings from 6:00 to 9:00 p.m. For some months this arrangement flowed evenly. Jim also enjoyed a large group of admiring colleagues who called or visited during this time. I recall my June birthday party where friends and family gathered on two floors, the majority of guests, as it turned out, laughing downstairs with Jim. Life felt almost normal.

But in matters of caregiving, life rarely stands still. First, my medical student had to return to school. Next, Mark, my backup guy, decided he had learned enough on this job, and decided it was time to go. I was also vexed with his self-involvement and neglect of Jim in favor of his beer drinking. Additionally, the agency sent another nursing assistant who was quite inept, and couldn't be trusted showering Jim alone. Her 'medical' information was also wrong, as I discovered, when Jim experienced a bad setback after taking one of her special 'brews.' By the end of the summer, one year after Jim's first heart attack, I faced an empty network. My children assumed throughout this period that I was in charge, their Dad was getting better, and all was well. But life was destined to become even more chaotic as Jim endured a series of medical crises.

Attempting to continue using outside help to maintain my sanity, I called on my friend, Margaret, a trained nurse from Australia. Earlier that spring she had indicated that she planned to return to home care nursing after an absence of a number of years. Perfect, I thought. She is gentle and intuitive and will know how to handle Jim after this most recent medical emergency. So, I invited her over the day Jim returned in a wheelchair from the recovery center.

We had a lovely dinner together, including a couple of the children. I prepared Jim for bed in what was once my study, emphasizing to him that he could ring the bell and either Margaret or I would help him with his night toileting. The house settled down for a good night's sleep. Suddenly, an explosion of sound echoed through the house. Jim had fallen, and thrown his surgically repaired hip out, and could not move. And neither Margaret, a slip of a woman, nor I, could move him. Another emergency call, and back to the recovery center.

The next day Margaret looked deeply at me, and said: 'No one can take care of this man in your home. He needs full-time nursing care in a facility.' With Margaret's departure, I felt a sense of doom. The empty network loomed larger than ever.

How did I reach an equilibrium after this point? I got very tough with myself. I realized my error about proclaiming, 'never a nursing home for Jim,' when it appeared that I didn't really have a choice. Although we tried out the assisted living route, Jim's care eventually required a fully staffed nursing care facility. My next move was to bring back the children for regular visiting or duties when I couldn't be there.

At first, I approached the situation as a zero sum game. I tolerated no exceptions in the schedule. Jim needed his family around him, and that included more than simply my presence. Jim adapted very slowly to living in these facilities, but I always managed to have a private room for him, regardless of cost. It was the least I could do to make his situation bearable. During the last seven months of his life, Jim was in the right setting receiving the best possible care. The nursing staff were warm and embracing. Hospice was in regular attendance, and the family was more or less supportive. I had learned to let go of rigid scheduling. Both children and grandchildren brought what they could to the table. Carrie, our oldest granddaughter, had her first baby in 2001. He took special delight in holding Meghan, his new great grandbaby, in his arms.

Lessons Learned

In my part of the country—Northwest Washington State—the hardy, self-propagating native plants like Douglas fir, Oregon grape and rhododendrons, as well as a host of others, seem to thrive almost anywhere. River banks, mountain tops, meadows and valleys, each have their habitat with distinct flora and fauna. They require no cultivation or special tending.

Social networks are a different species altogether. Although one is born into a family, a life-sustaining circle does not simply happen. As siblings grow up and leave home, they often lose track of one another, or move into adulthood without resolving childhood issues. When the time comes to care for elderly parents, adult children have probably cultivated very distinct interests and lifestyles, far removed from the life their parents lived. Given the constraints of independent lifestyles and heavy work/family loads, a care commitment has *definitely* not been part of the unspoken contract for most contemporary Western people.

Conditions of estrangement are even more likely to occur among married partners. Separations, divorces and staying together "for the sake of the children" mark a high proportion of modern marriages. Care of older parents as a cultural expectation for adult children may still occur, but the likelihood of practical follow-through is poor, unless older couples have explicitly indicated their personal preferences to their children—and their children are willing to comply.

Among caregivers in our study, almost all have made a strong commitment to care, and most have maintained solid, flexible networks that could adapt to life's inevitable changes. At the same time, we have a few cases in which friends or neighbors are the primary caregivers, in the complete absence of family involvement. In other instances, we have very reluctant caregivers who are physically carrying out the job, but are mentally and emotionally distant from the care receiver, and suffering from the effort.

Members of family and friendship networks, then, must have a high level of awareness as to their rights, responsibilities and rewards, as well as the ability to draw boundaries. But the reciprocity issue looms large. The sense of obligation often remains below the threshold of consciousness. We normally do not keep careful records of what we owe someone, or what someone owes us. But reciprocity entails a kind of spiritual indebtedness that may or may not involve material transactions, such as money, gifts or services. It could involve something as simple as *recognition* of the gift of service.

So, what does nurturance of network members involve? Let's place ourselves in the role of caregiver for a moment. It involves a mindset, so that *you*, the caregiver, situate yourself in the fullness of each relationship. Recognize, applaud, acknowledge specific offerings, value each contribution and honor the donor's presence. This level of network cultivation may not be possible for everyone. Some young adults, never-married persons, couples without children, persons isolated by work or excessive family demands, those with few social skills, those handicapped by negative childhood experiences, illness or various deprivations—may have to rely on the charity of others. The "other" may include state agencies for caregiving help. For the rest of us, building and maintaining viable social networks for caring for our elders demand our creativity and persistent attention.

Once you've located respite care, consider connecting with an active organization, where you can meet like-minded people. Every community has a number of these—book clubs, music or song circles, walking groups or any cluster of people who share your deep abiding interest. Or try your local church or temple. Go to the place you "feel the love." Don't hesitate to put out your hand to those around you, and introduce yourself by name. You can start a real friendship in these settings.

Reaching out to neighbors is another route. Seek the ones who are most accessible—the stay-at-home mom or older retiree—and the friendliest. You can jump start any relationship with a plate of cookies or an invitation for coffee and homemade muffins. You could also get involved with a volunteer community group. The need is great, but your reward is priceless: a warm reception by staff and other volunteers and their avowed gratitude.

Whatever course of action you take, you *will* feel more energized and in control when you develop meaningful bonds with supportive people. Sharing with others is the best antidote to feeling isolated.

Chapter 7

The Human Face of Parkinson's Disease

You put your right foot in,
You put your right foot out;
You put your right foot in,
And you shake it all about.
You do the Hokey-Pokey,
You turn yourself around.
That's what it's all about.

– Reinisa MacLeod,
"Tool for Grande Prairie's
Parkinson's Support Group,"
Parkinson's Post (September/October 2011)

What is Parkinson's Disease?

Doing the "Hokey-Pokey" may seem to be a simple child's song from a distant generation, but its use as speech and movement therapy for Parkinson's disease sufferers cannot be equaled. The song teaches breath control, posture corrections, balance and voice control, all of which have sharply declined. "Project a loud voice," says the voice coach, and everything else will become "louder"—thinking clearer, breathing stronger, balancing better and speaking louder. So, what is this malady that affects millions of Americans over the age of 50?

Parkinson's disease is a degenerative nerve disorder of later life that significantly affects both body and mind functioning. The disease is characterized by rhythmic tremor, muscular rigidity and slow movement, masked facial expressions, slurred speech, depression, anxiety and stress—conditions caused by degeneration in the basal ganglia of the brain where dopamine is produced. When this happens, our brain starts to fail in synchronizing its stimuli to the actions of our muscles and body structures. This gives rise to signs and symptoms of early Parkinson's disease, which may also progress as the disease becomes more complicated and full-blown.

Four early indicators of the illness include: **tremors while at rest, slowness of movement, muscle rigidity** and **mask-like facial expression.**

Tremors While at Rest

This is also referred to as "resting tremors," and is a very common early sign of Parkinson's disease. When a person is relaxing or his attention is not directed into any activity, tremors may start to appear. The tremors are usually present in the fingers, hand, lips and even the head. Apart from these physical tremors, the patient with early Parkinson's disease may feel as though his internal organs are trembling, as well. When the person begins to move—getting a glass of water or reaching for a book—these tremors will disappear.

Slowness of Movement

This is medically termed Bradykinesia (*Brady*, which means slow and *kinesia*, which means movement). A person with early Parkinson's disease will exhibit slowness of movement due to the impaired conduction of impulses from the brain to the muscles. The slowness of movement can be dangerous to elders, as it affects their climbing stairs, crossing the street or other actions that require accurate or rapid movement.

Muscle Rigidity

Muscle stiffness and inability to move a specific part of the body occurs with early Parkinson's disease too. The muscle rigidity can strike anytime, anywhere. This symptom is also referred to as "cogwheel rigidity" and affects balance, thereby contributing to stumbling and falling.

Mask-like Facial Expression

A person may exhibit a mask-like expression, or fail to show any expression at all, regardless of circumstances. This is another effect of the inability of the facial muscles to respond to the commands of the brain. Even with extreme emotions, a person may be unable to show his or her true feelings either by frowning, smiling or grinning since Parkinson's disease lessons their ability to carry out these expressions.

Parkinson's disease profoundly impacts the sufferer and his family. Fortunately, early diagnosis through identifying the early signs and symptoms may help reduce their intensity and provide a more stable lifestyle, despite the progressive nature of the malady.

According to the National Parkinson's Foundation, 1.5 million Americans have the disease. About 60,000 are diagnosed with the condition each year. No known cure exists for Parkinson's disease, but various medications can delay or help reduce certain symptoms. Parkinson's disease is a disorder that affects not only the person with the disease, but even the close relatives and people caring for the afflicted person. Without doubt, the caregiver can easily be consumed by the disease and its demands. Or does she have a choice?

Living with Parkinson's Disease

Anne Mikkelsen, whom we featured in Chapter 6, is an active caregiver for her husband Mike, who was diagnosed with Parkinson's disease more than 10 years ago. Her observations about the difficulties of caring for her husband clarify the special problems associated with this type of disease. Other diseases are equally challenging, but in this instance, the difference is that both Anne and Mike have made a pact to mindfully monitor both the disease and each other as they move together through their travail. Mike retains his lively mental ability, but confronts the erosive effects of the disease on a daily basis. Anne's narrative contains elements of many of the stories provided by numerous other caregivers, who found hope even when surrounded by despair.

Let's first begin with Anne. Following Anne's story, we shift to Mike's experience with Parkinson's disease to provide the only extended self-reflection by a care receiver in the book. Although the book focuses on the caregivers' perspective, bear in mind that both parties—caregiver and care receiver alike—must cope with the disease, and for some, old age and ultimately death.

Anne's Story

We've been living with Parkinson's since 1990. Mike and I had been married for ten years, when I first noticed his posture changing. Mike is an artist and always had been a resourceful, brilliant problem-solver. Together, we built our earth-bermed home on 40 acres in the country. We built stone walls and graceful stairways around and through the gardens we planted. Every year, we planted trees to commemorate our anniversaries, our birthdays and to honor people who died. Together we could conquer anything.

Mike began walking from the house to his studio with his head down. Over the months, from my office window at home, I watched as his shoulders gradually slumped forward, his walking becoming more difficult. He looked beaten, wounded and sad. I felt guilty because I was happy with my job, my children and our home in the Minnesota countryside—and he was miserable. Then in 1992, Mike became seriously depressed and angry. We couldn't talk rationally about the problem. But what I didn't know was that for more than a year, Mike had been following his symptoms in [a] patient handbook. In 1993, when his handwriting deteriorated to a flat line, he made an appointment at [a leading clinic]. He self-diagnosed either Parkinson's—or worse—a brain tumor. The neurologist concurred; it was Parkinson's. So, this was our time of celebration—it was not a brain tumor. We could live with Parkinson's. How little we knew then.

Mike asked for a prognosis. The doctor told him that he could go an average of ten years before he'd need serious care. The celebration did not last long and the reality of end-of-life and end-of-identity took center stage for Mike. His depression worsened and he chose not to take medications. As a couple, we were in crisis and not at all mindful of the physical or emotional stages of terminal illness. We were not ready to let go of anything. Yet, simultaneously, we were more than willing and ready to let go of everything to ease our pain. In the meantime, I resigned myself to the seemingly endless rounds of his deterioration and depression.

The positive changes began in 2001, when Mike declared that he could not stay in Minnesota another winter. This was the time when I would have to make some serious changes in my life. I would have to leave my job, my children and grandchildren, sisters and friends to move to a more temperate climate. I was conflicted, angry and anxious. I did not completely trust that our situation would improve even after making such a radical change and another significant commitment on his behalf.

After some soul searching, I decided to view the move as an adventure for myself as well as for Mike, what I termed—'getting down and wrestling in the mud together.' Now, I look out my kitchen window in Bellingham, Washington to our hillside garden. I am constantly thrilled by the accumulating generations of euphorbia, heather, artichoke, rosemary and lavender, as well as the cedar, cypress, fir, ceanothus, Asian pear, Rainier cherry, fig, apple and plum trees we've planted, most of which would not grow in Minnesota. Mike's lyrical sculptures are permanently displayed in our new yard and he is designing and creating more than we ever dreamed was possible or even likely.

In 2005, I made a decision to go to school full-time at Western Washington University's Fairhaven College, where I created my own concentration of study in Creative Writing and the Science of Social Relations. There, I met extraordinarily generous professors, as well as smart and compassionate writing friends. My son, Andy, and his wife, Juliana, moved to Bellingham from California three years ago. They have two children, one-year-old Teddy, born in Bellingham, and three-year-old CharlaAnne. All of these unplanned gifts ease the rough edges of change; they increase my joy and give me hope. I know we did the right thing. I am fully accepting of the path we are on, including my caregiving responsibilities and the traumas brought on by this ever-changing disease. I am inspired by the cultural anthropologist, Angeles Arrien, who described the second half of life as a time to create a legacy, rather than waiting for illness and death. It is, indeed, a time for me to embrace my creativity, make reparations and open up to true intimacy with myself and others.

Less than a year after we made the decision to leave Minnesota, I was walking on the beach in Bahia d'Kino, Mexico. I was alone on the wide, warm sand with the sun on my back and the seagulls gathered in noisy conventions. I focused on Tiburon Island ahead of me and I thought I heard my father talking into my left ear. 'So that's how she turned out.' I knew he must be talking to my mother. He made it clear by his intonation that he'd left early and appreciated the fact that Mother finished the job. Then I heard Mother answer, 'Yes, it is.' I interpreted the encounter as a message from my parents, who would be proud of the decisions I've made.

Along with this vision, I've been uplifted by Mike's ongoing awareness of his own suffering and losses. His experience touches me deeply, because he has managed to transcend the pain and loss by holding on to a double reality—as both the sufferer and the observer of one who suffers. And thus, he has found a measure of salvation.

Mike's Story

I am a lifelong artist. 1956: the ceramics department at Montana State University, where Frances Senska 'gave me legs.' For years, I had no limitations of size or scope or time or endurance. I taught pottery, drawing, painting and jewelry making. I could keep five plates in the air at once and still answer the phone.

After 40 years of wedging and throwing the 25-pound balls of clay into over-sized platters and colossal bowls, decorating, glazing and firing thousands of pieces of pottery, I began to notice the loss of small motor control. Gradually and reluctantly, I accepted that I had to give up clay. With the aid of an assistant, I began a short career of sculpting and welding four by eight-foot sheets of stainless steel into lyrical, life-sized lawn sculptures. But soon my endurance and muscular ability dwindled and I could no longer participate in big or heavy work anymore.

As Parkinson's disease gained ground in my muscles, I explored less physically demanding methods of pursuing my art. After another seven years, I could not lift or move heavy objects. Sometimes, I could not move myself. I could not safely walk to or around my studio without the fear of 'freezing' and falling. I sat on a stool and looked out the window. What can I do now?

My wife and I spent winters in Kino Bay, Mexico, where the seagulls noisily convened in straight lines on the beach or bobbed and rolled on the azure waves of the Sea of Cortez. I sat on my chair and watched them move. Graceful, buoyant and free. Anton Chekov's play, 'The Seagull,' used that bird as a symbol of Konstantin's broken dreams. I thought about that.

My speech deteriorated to the point that I was forced to repeat every statement three times, but I overcame my insecurities and was able to communicate with two Mexican welders in their dusty, rusty, dirt-floored shop in Old Kino. They understood my desire: my need to create the images of the seagulls. We formed the birds of bits and pieces of scrap metal and made them to fly freely over and even through obstacles.

Today: The strength in my legs is almost gone, but I am still an artist—in my mind and in my soul. That is exactly what I have left and I will use my mind the best way I am able.... Big, bold and colossal statements have been replaced in my life with the simplicity and power of symbols. For me, it has become more critical to convey essence and meaning. My yellow seagull symbolizes the freedom that eludes people with Parkinson's disease. There is an adjustable nut on the back of the yellow bird that allows for dependable and graceful movement. The color yellow symbolizes hope, courage and perseverance, all of which have been critical for me in recognizing and embracing the continuing and exciting possibilities for the creation of art in my life.

I am the orange gull—different from the others, but still standing. There is something I can do.

– Eduard Alden (Mike) Mikkelsen

Chapter 8

When Your Care Partner
Has Alzheimer's Disease

This disease robs my life.

– Alzheimer's disease patient

Empathy is like a camera lens. It puts things in perspective.

– Terri Trespicio, "10 Thoughts on Whole Living"

What Caregivers Need to Know

Most of us know that not all diseases are created equal. A number of chronic diseases include dementia as one of the defining symptoms, although it impacts mental and physical functions differently. Parkinson's disease certainly manifests a deterioration of mental functions, but not necessarily in a steadily progressive manner. A husband may be unable to remember his wife's name today, but next week he appears quite cogent—a pattern of in and out. Congestive heart failure shows up as mental confusion, especially after a mini-stroke, but after the brain re-stabilizes, Mom can suddenly remember where she put her list of drugs.

The word *dementia* is a catch-all phrase that indicates a decline in a person's ability to think, remember and reason. It can be caused by a number of brain disorders, such as a stroke—afflicting 795,000 people in the United States each year—and other ailments. People with dementia may lose the ability to solve problems, experience loss of emotional control and undergo personality changes. They usually develop impairments in their ability to perform daily activities, such as dressing or eating. Many, though not all, dementias cause memory loss.

Alzheimer's disease, among the dementias, is progressive, incurable and eventually kills the patient.

According to the Alzheimer's Association, 15 million family members and friends provide unpaid care to people with dementia. Hundreds and thousands of them meet regularly in support groups to exchange information and understanding not available elsewhere. Early warning signs of Alzheimer's disease are especially relevant. Although most Alzheimer cases are not diagnosed until mid-stage, medical recommendations urge patients to begin Alzheimer drugs as early as possible to improve and stabilize thinking, language and behaviors. These drugs treat only symptoms, though, as the disease has no cure, and will continue to advance.

The warning signs include:

- Memory loss for recent or new information—for example, repeats self frequently.

- Difficulty doing familiar, but difficult tasks—managing money, medications, driving.

- Problems with word finding, mis-naming or misunderstanding.

- Becoming confused about time or place—getting lost while driving, missing appointments.

- Worsening judgment—not thinking things through as before.

- Difficulty problem-solving or reasoning.

- Misplacing things—putting them in "odd places"—the ice cream cake into the oven, the coffee cups into the freezer.

- Changes in mood or behavior.

- Alterations in typical personality.

- Loss of initiation—withdraws from the normal pattern of activities and interests.

Many abilities are affected by dementia—thoughts, words, actions, feelings. It is variable, and affects people differently, depending on which specific brain parts have been impacted. If progressive, more of the brain dies over time and key areas get hit. These typically involve the frontal lobes, our intelligence center. Why is cognitive loss considered to be so devastating in our culture? Because our over-rational society has put cognition as the most prized part of human activity. Irrational behavior is treated as pathological—out of control, unreasonable and deviant. Without a doubt, dementia can produce extreme behavior that violates anyone's sense of normal or appropriate. Teepa Snow, a dementia care and training specialist extraordinaire offers some examples of deepening levels of concern: **Annoying**, **Risky** and **Dangerous** behaviors.

Problem Behaviors

Losing important things, getting lost, unsafe task performance, repeated calls and contacts, "bad mouthing" you to others, resisting or refusing care, not following care plans, being rude, making 911 calls repeatedly, undressing in public. These are definitely **annoying** for the caregiver and her family, and become wearing over time. Such behaviors also take time away from other responsibilities. Still other behaviors are **risky,** and unpredictable, and could cause harm to self or others. These can include: using drugs or alcohol to "cope," eloping or wandering, and forcing intimacy or sexuality on another. **Dangerous** behaviors are especially problematic and put the person, care provider or loved ones at immediate risk for injury. Paranoid or delusional thinking, threatening caregivers, striking out at others, falls and injuries, infections and pneumonias, failure to eat or drink all constitute behavior that puts self or others in jeopardy. The secret for caregivers is to have a clear understanding of what level she's dealing with and develop a strategy, rather than simply reacting to difficult behavior.

Susan and Peter Confront Alzheimer's Disease

Take a typical case of Susan and her husband Peter, a composite of a number of interviews. A couple in their late 70s, they were married in the 1960s, managing to stay in love, through sharing mutual interests and delighting in their children and grandchildren. Not that they have escaped sorrow and loss. Instead, they resisted the tendency to get swept away by it. Today, they confront a new battle: the dreaded diagnosis of Alzheimer's disease. Grappling with Peter's strange new behaviors has become a full-time occupation for Susan.

Keep in mind that bizarre or troublesome behaviors do not happen in a vacuum. Let's consider Susan's efforts to cope with Peter's recent tendency to wander late at night. She'll need to consider crucial pieces of information. What type and level of cognitive impairment does he have? What is the history of his personality, habits, preferences and stress behaviors? Does he have other medical impairments? Has his environment changed, and in what way? What about his work and family history? What of his leisure time and spiritual life? What typically sets him off versus offers him comfort? Susan has an eureka moment! She realizes that a proposed visit from their mentally ill son, Johnny, has triggered old fears and resentments. At the same time, his faithful Rover is at the dog hospital with a recurring virus. When upset, Peter used to hop in his car with the dog and drive for hours until he could settle down and resume his routine. Now that he can no longer drive, Peter takes off a different way—walking for hours and invariably losing his way.

Because Peter is in mid-stage Alzheimer's, Susan knows that lecturing him when he's distressed can send him into orbit. Instead, she reaches out for an emotional connection through eye contact, hugging and assuring him that "all is well." When Peter expresses his anger about their "lost" dog, Susan nods sympathetically and agrees with him that the house seems empty without Rover. Together they move into the kitchen, where Susan pulls out a worn scrapbook containing photos of Johnny's early years, before he was afflicted with schizophrenia. Susan also promises that Rover will be back home tomorrow, and then all three can take a long walk in the woods. The next morning she goes to the hardware store and buys secure locks to ensure that Peter cannot open the doors by himself, night or day. Peace is restored.

Changing the Caregiver Perspective

Susan was not born with the ability to handle difficult situations, such as troublesome dementia behaviors. At one time, she could only concentrate on her WOE—she felt chronically *worn-out, overwhelmed* and *enraged*. She was too proud and ashamed to confide in outsiders.

Her focus was on the negative. She recounted the disappearance of old friends, whose discomfort around Peter kept them away. She mourned the loss of his former companionship and their sexual relationship. She guiltily admitted to bouts of irrepressible anger in the face of Peter's intransigence and aggression, which is typical of some dementias. She acknowledged her deep resentment over Peter's three siblings, who have been less than attentive. Their primary involvement has been interfering and critical.

Once she confronted her feelings of anger and shame, she decided to seek help. As a result of attending a local Alzheimer support group, she has undergone a major shift in her thinking and behavior. She no longer feels so powerless and voiceless. Workshops on dementia care, as well as reading medical newsletters and inspirational books, have provided countless ways in which she can develop skills and strategies.

What she has learned are six very basic principles that have transformed the way she provides care. **Empathy** comes first for Susan because it allows her to see the world through Peter's eyes. From this vantage point, his world often appears confusing, lost and disconnected. **Compassion** allows Susan to stay centered with Peter by offering kindness and sympathy, even when his life appears upside down. **Connection** for Susan involved a wide array of visual, verbal, physical, emotional and spiritual cues. For instance, Susan and Peter hold hands as they begin every meal with a familiar blessing of the food, and after eating, they finish with a simple statement of gratitude. Mealtimes, once full of turmoil, have become calmer and far more enjoyable.

Supportive Communication requires not only acknowledging what Peter says, but Susan validates his statements by repeating them or asking for clarification. She also has a detective's intuition for exploring what he really means, what his needs are and what may lie behind the words. She doesn't stop there. She offers new words, a shift in location and a new activity or focus.

Above all, making real changes involves **Self-Acceptance**—of limitations, foibles, past errors of judgment, fatigue, lack of patience and other shortcomings. Susan feels she's a "work in progress" as she struggles to eliminate negative thinking in her relationship with Peter. She understands all too well that Peter does not have control over many of his functions and behaviors, and does not blame herself for Peter's frequent setbacks. If what she is trying is *not* working, professional advice is: she STOPS, backs off, thinks it through, and then re-approaches the situation by trying something different. For instance, if the scrapbook idea simply caused Peter to be agitated, she would put it away, and consider an alternative plan. It might look like this. "How about some delicious hot chocolate, Peter? I even have some leftover marshmallows from last week when the grandkids were over." Who could resist such an offer—surely, not Peter?

Undoubtedly, the most radical idea proposed for successful caregiving is the notion of being a **Care Partner**. For Susan, this took a leap of faith. She quickly rejected the "no-relief-in-sight" formula, because it undermined both her efforts to give care and Peter's attempts to adjust to his illness. Instead, she cast about for an alternative approach. Gratefully, she found that caregiving can be regarded as a special, perhaps unique lifestyle, one that focuses on the *benefits* and *rewards* of being in *partnership*, even while living with a serious disease.

Susan also knows that their **Partnership** is time bound. As Peter increasingly loses mental functions, and can no longer participate in a mutual way, she must shift into being a **Coach.** She remembers her son's football coach, and how his leadership style inspired and encouraged the boys to do their best. He was a hands-on guy who knew the strengths and weaknesses of his players, and always focused on what a player *can* do, rather than push what he can't. In fact, she spent yesterday with their new computer showing Peter how to access his photos, check his email and gain access to the Web. Peter's enthusiasm was infectious, but when Susan left on an errand, he became easily discouraged. Susan will need to be by his side for this activity to be successful.

Focusing on the **Positive Aspects** of caregiving allows Susan to pursue her interests, while at the same time assisting her partner's efforts to live a quality life. The challenges of caregiving have reshaped Susan's idea of giving as she recognizes what her care partner is still able to do. Through sharing dishes, folding laundry, sorting out or writing bills and other tasks, she has become more open to a deeper level of awareness in her day-to-day life. She continues to marvel at how animated and happy Peter can be when they work as a team or enjoy a film at home together. He remains his own person, despite changes, and she finds joy and satisfaction in acknowledging their ongoing relationship.

Building Skills and Strategies

Let's explore in greater detail the idea of communication with a person who has considerable cognitive loss. Peter can no longer grasp overly abstract ideas, and Susan frequently has to reframe *what* she says, *how* she says it and even *when* she says it. She relies deeply on Teepa Snow's basic **Do's** in "just having a conversation." This means she has learned to go with the flow, use supportive communication techniques and rely more on objects or examples to help clarify an idea. Since their married daughter, Janine, has been traveling on a river boat down the Rhine recently, Susan uses their International Atlas to show Peter the couple's daily itinerary.

She often finds herself gesturing and pointing, such as when Peter cannot find the word for his favorite cereal. Instead of trying to say the word, she points from one box to another until the correct one is identified. Once so stoical, Peter now weeps easily when he's both frustrated and happy. Rather than trying to uncover some hidden meaning, Susan simply acknowledges and accepts his shifting emotions by using familiar phrases—"you're fine, darling, it will be OK"—to soothe him. She's also found that if she can engage him in a favorite interest, such as his precious coin collection, she can both respect his values and beliefs, while avoiding the negative.

Teepa Snow's training materials also taught Susan that later in the disease, she will be focusing more on making an *emotional* connection, rather than "having a conversation." She is prepared to use visual cues, such as props or objects in their interactions. To get his attention, she can lift up a book, which serves as a signal for "time to get ready for bed" and "story time." She will talk a great deal less, wait longer to hear him out, take turns to speak and keep it short. She will never confront him if he isn't getting the words, but simply nod in ascent, showing how she is enjoying the exchange. She is likely to start interactions with familiar speech— "How are you?" "Did you sleep well last night?" "Did you know it rained last night?" "Tell me about the new friend you met at Adult Day Health." It makes little sense in late stage dementia to insist on a reality orientation or correcting errors.

Susan understands she must be well connected emotionally before she can distract her husband, when he is on a negative roll. Visual cues work best, she's been told, and they should always be positive. She invariably knows that when she pets the dog, Peter will move forward to stroke his beloved pet.

Susan recognizes from the onset of Peter's diagnosis that she will need a supportive network. Caregiving is not a role for the "lone wolf" or martyr. She begins by contacting her two daughters, who fortunately live only a few hours away. Both have offered to provide respite time for Susan once a month. That makes only six weekends a year for each girl. Both daughters, Janine and Patricia, express delight at spending quality time with their dad. They also intend to step forward for a "social call," when brother Johnny comes marching home for his annual visit. Now that they have their own children, they can appreciate the tough times their folks experienced during their younger brother's defiant adolescence. Both sisters know Johnny's hot spots, and can sidetrack him from verbally attacking his dad by taking him to movies, cooking his favorite dishes and everyone playing a mean game of "Train" with their dad's domino set.

Calling on her retired sister, JoAnn—who, after sympathizing deeply with her, consents to bringing her husband and taking over the caregiving—Susan is able to go on a much-needed yearly two-week vacation. Over the years, Peter has always enjoyed his sister-in-law and finds her husband, Mack, a "regular guy and a great fisherman." Susan plans to continue her annual travels, this time with a daughter or friend. She's excited about re-visiting the Grand Canyon with her new digital camera.

She also lets her favorite neighbors know Peter's diagnosis, and asks for their help in relieving her while she shops or goes to the dentist and even visits friends on occasion. They soon discover how overjoyed Susan can be when they also volunteer to pick up a few groceries on their way home from work. Ben, next door, is especially helpful, keeping watch out his window for any sign that Peter might need a pal. Since he works at home, dropping in for coffee or to share a new guitar CD gives him a well-earned break and allows Susan to complete some household tasks. She may even pick up her latest novel and read in peace and quiet for a few minutes.

As a stay-at-home mom, Susan developed what turned out to be a perfect hobby: scrapbooking. Her kitchen cupboards are bursting with old and new volumes celebrating their family life together. Peter never tires of gazing at the childhood snapshots: there's seven-year-old Janine with a missing front tooth, five-year old Patricia's chopped hair after she took a pair of scissors to her lovely locks. Johnny, the athlete—what a kid! Here he is at 10 in his football outfit showing off after making three touchdowns. Susan has managed to pry loose and remove all of Johnny's photos taken during those "bad" years, until he settled down with a diagnosis and medications. No point in "getting dad started again." Another lifestyle change that suits both Peter and Susan is to alter their eating habits: whole foods, low or no dairy, plenty of fish, and stacks of fruit and vegetables. Susan's found her energy level is so much higher, and Peter's digestion and moods have improved remarkably.

Engaging the Care Partner in Meaningful Ways

Susan joins with other caregivers in recognizing one more essential step she must incorporate into her day: engaging Peter in meaningful ways. First, by reducing distress and, next, by filling the day. She will need to do activities *with* him, not do everything for or to him. She has come over a lifetime with Peter to be sensitive to his personal preferences and values. Who he has been. What he has valued. Who he is now. What he values now. Why it matters to him. She has become skilled at letting Peter have his "say" and set some of the priorities. At the same time, she remains aware of his limitations—reasoning and judgment are often flawed because of ongoing brain function loss. Still, she pursues what it takes to make a day have meaning and joy for him.

She knows she must manage the environment as she did when she had young children—safety first, then health, and after these, structured activities. She figures out that Peter is capable of doing a variety of things: sorting socks, adding herbs or placing cut carrots and tomatoes into the salad or even learning a new exercise. The importance of stress reduction for her Alzheimer's partner has contributed to her own sense of ease.

Early on Susan enrolled Peter in Adult Day Health, a program for Alzheimer and other dementia patients sponsored by their local hospital. This has turned out to be a godsend twice a week, when Peter gets picked up and returned home, and spends about five hours in organized activities he enjoys. Peter especially raves about the guitar and vocal guy who comes in once a month with the old 20s and 30s standards. Susan makes certain that Peter never misses this treat. She's learned to lean back on those days and catch up with her paperwork or attend a volunteer program she's still involved in. Because Peter is beginning to lose his balance, she plans to sign him up for a yoga class for elders. She's already met the teacher, and loves her, and has decided to join Peter "just for fun."

A friend passed this along to Susan from her Alzheimer's support group. She's now learning to live by this "never-never list" in her daily interactions with Peter:

- Never argue, always agree.

- Never reason, instead divert.

- Never shame, instead distract.

- Never lecture, instead reassure.

- Never say "remember," instead reminisce.

- Never say "I told you so," instead repeat, regroup.

- Never say "I can't," instead say "let's do this."

- Never command or demand, instead ask or model.

- Never condescend, instead encourage and praise.

- Never force, instead reinforce.

When a Hospital Visit Becomes a Medical Emergency

When Peter, now aged 78, needed to be hospitalized for a hip replacement, both sailed into the hospital room with daughters in tow. Everything was going well until a complication landed him in the intensive care unit (ICU), where he began behaving oddly. He thought he was in a hotel room, swore that rats were living under the bed, struggled at night against invisible intruders, and complained that the "hotel" staff were trying to poison him. After a psychiatric consult, Peter was given medication to calm him and help him sleep. Mystified, the family stayed with him day and night until he was back in a regular room. Here, with more normal routines, the **delirium** cleared.

Susan soon learned that during illness, hospitalization or recovery from surgery or stroke, many people experience **delirium**, a rapidly developing and severe confusion accompanied by altered consciousness and an inability to focus. It's the most common complication of hospitalization among older people, and almost 80 percent of those treated in ICU's develop it. When this malady isn't recognized, it can hinder recovery. Prolonged delirium is associated with poor long-term outcomes, both mental and physical, and may even lead to death.

Among older people, delirium can be induced by a wide range of conditions: infection, insufficient food and drink, a trauma, such as surgery or injury, uncontrolled pain, medications, or simply the unfamiliar surroundings of a hospital. Susan now understands that people who have dementia are more likely to develop delirium when hospitalized. She does not confuse these two conditions. Delirium usually arises rapidly, fluctuates in severity, involves changes in consciousness and attention. It also clears up within days or weeks. By now she is very familiar with *dementia*, which comes on slowly, is progressive and usually permanent. Until it is severe, consciousness and attention are still possible.

Susan has a list of her own from the *Harvard Women's Health Watch* she subscribes to, and plans to share it with her Alzheimer's support group: essential how-to's for preventing delirium when the patient is hospitalized.

Families. An engaged and attentive family member can help prevent delirum and advocate for the patient so they receive optimal care. Because family members see their loved one through the entire journey from primary care to hospitalization to rehabilitation, they are the logical advocates for their patient.

Consult with a geriatric specialist. Not all surgeons are familiar with delirium. When an older person plans a hip replacement or any other surgery requiring anesthesia or sedation, advice from a geriatric physician can facilitate planning for medication, pain control, postoperative mobility and sleep support.

Bring a full medication list to any new health professional. Many drugs that act on the brain can cause delirium, including narcotic painkillers, sedatives, stimulants, sleeping pills, antidepressants, Parkinson's disease medication and antipsychotics. Even antihistamines and some drugs for digestive problems, allergies and severe asthma can contribute to delirium. Additionally, all medications should be reported because they could interact with drugs given in the hospital.

Make things familiar. Take along a few family photos or comforting objects—a relaxing music CD, a rosary, a favorite blanket—to the hospital. Calm conversations about current events or family activities can be comforting.

Staying close. Family members provide the greatest comfort and reassurance, and are the first to recognize when their family member is behaving inappropriately. Plan to have a family member there night and day while the patient is in a state of delirium.

Don't forget sensory aids. Eyeglasses, hearing aids and dentures are often put away during a hospital stay, but that could leave the patient disoriented and less able to function. Be assertive to hospital staff about their use. If concerned about loss, leave an expensive hearing aid at home, and pick up an inexpensive hearing amplifier at an electronics store.

Promote activity. Help your loved one get up and walk two or three times a day. Exercise their brain with conversation, crosswords, card games or other pastimes, depending on their mental ability.

Be there for meals. With companionship and assistance, the patient is far more likely to eat and drink an adequate amount. Be prepared to bring in some special goodies that you know will help to cheer up the patient.

Participate in discharge planning. Patients are sometimes sent home or to a rehabilitation facility while still delirious. A patient with delirium cannot fully understand discharge instructions, so family members will need to be there to help—and learn about signs that he or she needs if the loved one must return to the hospital. Make certain that nursing staff know your loved one's pre-hospitalization level of

When Your Care Partner Has Alzheimer's Disease   151

functioning, so they won't assume that the current behavior is typical. Ask for a complete medication review. It might be useful to discontinue some drugs (such as sedatives) that were added during hospitalization.

Reclaiming the Self

Susan could easily succumb to despair if she becomes too enmeshed in Peter's frame of reference and his needs. Especially when he's hospitalized, she feels a constant anguish that the illness has taken them both. Despite her awareness of maintaining a level of emotional distance, sometimes, she just loses it—she falls off the pedestal and crashes. Even though she goes for days, even weeks, being the "ideal caregiver," once her feelings get away from her, she simply can't control herself. She weeps for all of her family—herself, Peter and their children. Peter can never be a real husband or father anymore. His "patienthood" has taken over. She rages over her daughters' expressed concerns that perhaps they too could inherit the disease. She surrenders to self- pity and the morose sense that her life is over—she's done with having her own interests, her own space, her own self. At such times, she feels ready to sink beneath the earth—give up and let both die—caregiver and care receiver.

Fortunately, these anxiety-ridden episodes have been fewer over the last year. As a result of taking care of herself, they are far less intense, and don't frighten her as much. Despite Peter's progressively downward spiral, she realizes she has been through the worst of it. She's developed skills that provide a sense of competence. Now, instead of collapsing into hopelessness, she looks for alternative ways to reduce the stress—talking a walk through a nearby park always works wonders. About a year ago, she fixed up the spare bedroom so she could be in her own space from time to time. She's now considering moving in and sleeping there after Peter's last hospitalization. She's found she sleeps sounder and feels more comfortable having a room of her own. At this juncture, she is increasingly turning within to find the strength and courage to see her through Peter's final years. She also plans to propose to her daughters the likelihood that once Peter becomes incontinent and unable to speak because of the last stage of the disease, she plans to place him in a nursing facility. She has determined that she will survive this caregiving experience.

Susan's Pearls of Wisdom

While Peter was recovering in the hospital, Susan once again took up her journaling. She realized that feeling despondent over the turn of events was neither productive nor helpful. What to do? She let her pen do the talking, and came up with her own "pearls of wisdom"—positive and healing ways of being in the care partnership. Susan recommends:

Keep an open heart. Wisdom of the heart brings intuition and love into all phases of my caregiving relationship. Because I am connected to the circle of life, I am assured that I will both give and receive as I move through my journey. I am at peace.

Connect with the generations. I cultivate relationships with my daughters, sister and grandchildren. I make regular telephone contact with Peter's family members to keep them abreast of Peter's condition. I realize that kinship goes beyond our immediate family to extend to all who care to participate. Our family stories, traditions and activities fill our days and provide a wealth of meaning for us. Even friends and neighbors are brought into the fold—some to help Peter, others to help sustain me during difficult times. I remain hopeful.

Expand my coping abilities. When a family or partnership crisis happens, I used to allow things to fall apart and give up. But I have learned more effective and life-renewing strategies. I have learned to accept *what cannot be changed* and let go of *what should be or what can never be.* I know that I must continue to develop new routines that fit the changing conditions of Peter's disease. I continue to *love, appreciate* and *accept* Peter regardless of what physical and mental ailments he has.

I am also learning to be a more effective manager in setting up our daily routine. I am hiring outside help for daytime. I am taking more breaks over the course of the day. I am closing down the house early in the evening so I can spend time with uninterrupted reading. And I am letting so much go—windows, woodwork, clean floors, even supper dishes if I'm tired. I have serenity.

Be willing to experience role reversal. Once Peter was diagnosed I vowed never to take over his role as head of household. I even organized the day so he would feel in charge. After a while this approach made no sense. Peter simply couldn't handle the bills, schedule medical and other appointments, garden, and more recently, the errands. Sanity and well-being won the day. Peter seems relieved he is no longer thrust into activities that confuse him or which make him feel like a failure. I am at ease.

Reinvigorate family relationships. I never realized how Peter's medical crisis could bring family members together to achieve a common goal: giving comfort and aid to Peter and myself. I know everyone can't be on the same page all the time. Sometimes, my daughters weary of hearing about their dad's newest setback. Johnny can't be expected to fit into the family healing circle like his sisters. But what a joy when he does call and inquires about his dad or shows his love with an occasional greeting card. My sister has been my greatest comfort, always open for listening to my sad stories, which she's heard far too many times. I am deeply grateful.

Strengthen bonds with the community. Now that I've learned to be an advocate for Peter, I can reach out in new ways for friends and allies. My Alzheimer's support group sustains me through the difficult days. I'm well over the early point in caregiving, where I was exhausted and joyless. Now I repeat the word HALT frequently throughout the day, reminding me to avoid *hunger, anger, loneliness* and *turmoil.* I manage my eating habits better. I also know I can pick up the phone or connect with email to a wide variety of old and new friends.

I especially find advocating a satisfying experience. I can let Peter speak when he has the ability, and speak up when he cannot. This gives me a sense of purpose and accomplishment, and shows Peter how deeply I care. Once I explained to Dr. Jones that he should speak directly to the patient—instead of to me—Peter was less agitated with the medical exam. I keep notes of everything the doctor says, but Peter feels he, too, has a relationship with Dr. Jones. I am happy.

Give back to others. Being openhearted with Peter reminds me of how I was in my early parenting days. I love being a hero who can put the needs of another before myself. I've even discovered from everyday experience that bringing help and solace to Peter or to one of my support group friends is a "feel-good" experience. It has its own reward: In giving, I receive. I am comforted.

Express my spiritual values. I have admitted to my support group (at last) that the challenges of providing long-term care for Peter are enormous, and watching him deteriorate tears me apart. The road has seemed too long—it feels like a lifetime. I have had to reach inside for my very survival. I have found, though, that by being in charge of the day's structure and closely monitoring Peter's health, abilities, level of functioning and medications, caregiving has turned out to be a transforming experience. I continue to act on my core beliefs that the family comes first and I am providing a legacy for my children. I also have faith in the future. I plan to outlive him so I can care for him to the end. I love the last drama of our life together. I never knew it would be quite so all consuming. All is well.

Persevere with self-care. Taking care of my physical, mental and emotional health is a top priority if I am to be a successful caregiver. No matter how much I throw myself into the daily routine I set up for Peter's well-being, I still must maintain a sense of myself, and to be aware of my own needs. I have no intention of losing myself to the point of health problems. I've seen this happen so frequently among our Alzheimer group members. Of course, I must accept my own limitations, always ask for help when needed and remind myself every day that no one person can do it all. I have trust.

Lessons Learned

Susan and Peter's situation is representative of a number of couples I've encountered in my research. Their story expresses that of millions of caregivers and care receivers in America. The learning curve is steep when we commit to caring for people with dementia. Knowing that dementia is a terminal disease can be daunting, especially as it confronts older care partners. What will become of our loved ones if we die first? How will we manage our own final years as we rapidly exhaust our financial resources? Will our children and grandchildren drift away after years of being attentive and devoted? How can we handle the situation if our care partner loses his power of speech, can no longer feed himself and requires a feeding tube? How can we manage after years of pouring out our love and energy only to find that the brain disease has wiped all memory of our care from the afflicted loved one?

The sandwich generation face a different set of issues than elderly couples. The Parent Trap means they are caught caring for their elderly parents while still in the process of raising children and holding a full-time job. We've all heard about parents in their 80s, who absolutely refuse to move into an apartment/condo or smaller home and are always calling on their adult children for help in the vegetable garden, to tackle the mountain of housework, or worse, cleaning the garage or basement where a lifetime of clutter has collected. Some boomers complain they feel like parents to their children.

This or other calamitous situations with older parents will undoubtedly arise. Roll up your sleeves, because at this stage of life you may have to put your folks at the top of the list. Better medical care is likely to keep your loved ones living longer. Be prepared for the fact that people who live past 85 die slowly and expensively, typically spending an average of two years needing full-time custodial care: feeding, dressing and toileting—and don't expect Medicare to pick up the bill.

Jane Gross, a *New York Times* reporter spent several years looking at the relationship between aging parents and their grown sons and daughters. Gross writes in her compelling memoir, *A Bittersweet Season: Caring for Our Aging Parents—And Ourselves*, how she found herself totally unprepared for her own independent mother's rapid descent into utter reliance on her two adult children. Gross offers a number of significant tips. Face the fact that your time with your parent is limited and make the most of it. This involves maximizing positive shared experiences and healing unresolved wounds. Keep in mind that older people are more than five times as worried about being a *burden* on their children as they are about *dying*. Making your parents as comfortable and content as possible contributes to their ease, and allows you to feel good about their last years after they've gone.

Under ideal circumstances, caregivers can pull the necessary resources together to care for their dementia person at home until the end of life. But conditions are rarely ideal. The primary caregivers may have too many responsibilities—young children at home, a demanding job, other relatives that need care. Or the caregiver is too old or too sick to carry the burden to the end of the journey. Sometimes, the potential caregiver—the person that appears most appropriate for the task—lacks the willingness or capacity to carry the load. These and other circumstances require that long-term care take place outside the home in assisted living, group home or skilled nursing facility.

Moving an ailing parent or spouse to a good skilled nursing home can be an act of kindness, not neglect, says Gross. A good nursing home offers not only physical support to the parent, but also emotional and practical support for the child. Try a non-profit facility. Consulting an elder lawyer, geriatric physician or Area Agency on Aging staff member can best determine a suitable placement that fits the family's pocketbook and the health and safety needs of your loved one with dementia.

Chapter 9

Dealing with Grief the Hard Way

Stress is the scaffolding of the caregiver's world.
— Sandy Stork, M.C., Mental Health Specialist

God will wipe away every tear.
— Revelation 7:17

"A Nice Soup of Chaos"

Sally offers the most compelling caregiver statement about becoming ill as a result of stresses, and the deep grieving often associated with caregiving. A divorced mother of seven children, Sally worked full-time as a housekeeper, and frequently commuted to Los Angeles from Washington State to look after both of her parents, and later, her husband's parents. Today, a sprightly blonde, Sally's story captures the extent of how complicated life can become when juggling too many roles. She describes how illness usurped her caregiving role. An only child, Sally believed that *only* she could handle the caregiving, but illness intervened, and prevented her from managing the role.

> *During the years I was traveling back and forth to help my mother and father in their crisis, I could count the days I was home. If I made it through a whole month not having to fly down, it was a good month. Somewhere in advance of* [moving my parents] *my large intestine ruptured. I had to have major surgery and they had to remove a foot of my intestine. I had a colostomy bag, and then they did another surgery too... what they called a 'take down,' where they re-connected my intestine.*

I had so much pain that I was throwing up and throwing up. I couldn't walk. I was dry heaving. I learned, though, that if you're not spurting blood in the emergency room, you're the last one to go in and it doesn't matter. I had a hard time convincing them that I didn't have some minor problems… they kept sending me home. Finally, they determined that they needed to do surgery. [Doctors] thought it would be a gallbladder surgery—and I did have gallstones—but the major problem was that my intestine had ruptured. So they took out my appendix and some intestine. For a year-and-a-half or so, I was in and out of the hospital with that issue and still not well. Dad did all he could to keep things together there in California, knowing that I was going through my situation, but it all created a nice soup of chaos.

Eventually, Sally moved both parents out of California into nursing homes in her local community, but she recognized that her life remained "oppressive" until her parents died.

Anticipatory Grief

What Sally was experiencing was a classic caregiver grief pattern. The grief spectrum is vast, and can range from twinges of sorrow to full-blown trauma, illness and death. The long-accepted grief model of death by Elizabeth Kubler-Ross describes the process as occurring in discrete categories—denial, anger, bargaining, despair, acceptance. But such a classification rarely describes the long-term caregiver who struggles with the grief process over and over months or years before their loved one has died. We now recognize that caregivers for the elderly observe a distinctly different face of grief, the "new grief" of protracted dying.

My first encounter with grieving happened quite by accident about a year after Jim first had his diagnosis of heart failure.

I had taken my husband to a bi-weekly routine visit to the cardiologist, who once again assured us we were doing the best we could with the medical skills available, and urged us to keep up with his exercise and spirits. I received no information about the progress of his health, but looking at my discouraged husband, whose energy seemed to be waning week by week, I shrugged away the doctor's kindly words while muttering, 'Heck of a lot of good that appointment's doing us.'

Pulling into the driveway after the appointment, I caught a glimpse of our helper's husband running around the side of the house, and wondered, "what's up?" When Jim finally tottered to the top of our split level stairs and into the kitchen, with me close behind, he let out a gasp: the water pipes had burst, and the kitchen, living room, dining room and downstairs were swamped with water. Disaster! And no one could remember where to turn off the water to avert total calamity. In that moment of watching the water gushing from the broken pipe, I realized the truth. Jim was never going to get better, would never feel normal, never have his old energy or spirit back, and what was left of his life would be spent in illness and further decline. I felt as drowned by that reality as my kitchen with its rising water. Once we found the shut-off valve, we could control the water, but none of us had any power to alter the course of Jim's disease. And, as I came to discover throughout those first years of caregiving, I was unable to change my sense of loss and failure.

The ongoing mourning experienced by caregivers involves both an outward expression of grieving and a continuous process of reorientation after suffering one loss after another. Almost all caregivers in my study spoke of their deeply felt losses, even while their care receiver was still alive. Among these is the passing of an idealized image of themselves, and their family, work and life. Another cost entailed the end of emotional, social, and financial control over their lives. They also reluctantly let go of the possibility of "what might have been."

Seeing their cherished dreams die can be painful. For a daughter, returning to school, for a wife, retiring as a couple, saving money for that long-awaited travel after retirement—such wishes have become pipe dreams. Even the hope that wounds between family members will heal seems out of reach.

Some Hospice workers observe that "anticipatory grieving" is an integral part of caregiving, as current and future losses accumulate over time. Caregivers know they must prepare themselves for the death of their loved one. For long-term caregiving, the mourning process seems endless, as their loved one disintegrates from wholeness into increasing disability and cognitive impairment. Our loved one's struggle with disease and impairment provides yet another wellspring of grief.

The caregivers in my book expressed their anticipatory grieving in a variety of ways, but almost always in strong emotional terms: "I am sad... exhausted... depressed... overwhelmed... sick to death... on stress overload... wrung out... collapsing... ill in mind and body... agonized... at the end of my rope." Most caregivers found ways to cope with unending sadness and grief. Yet, some carried their sense of loss and futility to their graves. Certainly, chronic mourning undermines both the capacity for empathy and, ultimately, the commitment to another.

Perhaps the most significant challenge experienced by the caregivers in this study was denial—of one's basic needs, serious medical conditions, simple joys, such as visits with grandchildren, and even the time required to grieve the loss of loved ones. In such instances, the presumed needs of the care receiver assumed dominance over all aspects of life.

When we are deeply connected with a very ill or dying person—spouse, parent, grandparent, sibling, friend—we participate in the slow diminishment of that person, who is so dear to us. Caregivers' feelings, like grief itself, are vast: guilt, frustration, impatience, fear, resentment and anger may come in waves. Often, emotions seem to come out of nowhere. We can't even identify the trigger. As we see our loved one's capacities slowly eroding, it becomes more and more difficult—sometime impossible—to cope. While most of us practice denial, rather than confront our feelings of sadness and loss, this is ill advised. Buried emotions never die—those repressed emotions need to see the light of day.

Stress is the Scaffolding of the Caregiver's World

According to Sandy Stork (December 2010), a mental health specialist working with families with Alzheimer's, "Caregivers experience an ongoing stress state, including low-grade anger, and a host of other dangerous emotions—fear, resentment, frustration, impatience and more." Unlike those who can make choices over their circumstances, Sandy warned, caregivers cannot move out of harm's way. For most caregivers, once in the combat zone, there is no deliverance until the "war" is over.

Sandy went on to say that the caregiver's dilemma is this: She cannot leave her beloved charge, while at the same time, the physical and emotional demands are too often excessive. This sets the stage for unremitting stress. Non-stop stress is *not* a benign condition, and must be reckoned with.

From a scientific perspective, the chronic stress response is dangerous. The overproduction of cortisol directly impacts the adrenal glands—the system that regulates our stress hormones—and the result is constant fatigue, emotional exhaustion and lowered immune response. In fact, chronic stress plays some part in all illnesses. An Ohio State University study found that older caregivers of family members with dementia did not respond well to vaccines, had less defense against viruses as well as more inflammation and accelerated aging of their cells compared with adults who were not caregivers.

Part of the reason caregivers get locked into the stress state is the culture lacks models for aging gracefully and honorably. The *care receiver* resists aging and chronic disease. The *caregiver* is likewise affected by these negative emotions, and feels powerless to change or even talk about the situation. Thus, chronic diseases among the elderly have two victims: the patient and the caregiver. Working with caregivers who provide care for loved ones with Alzheimer's disease, Sandy notes typical patterns among caregivers that contribute to the locked-in state. "Caregivers focus more on the person they care for than caring for themselves. Caregivers do not take care of themselves. And it is very difficult for caregivers to ask for help, especially from family members."

Environmental Stressors

Environmental stressors or demands are said to be at the very core of the caregiver burden, as are complications from social, financial, medical and other sources. Some stressors have to do with excessive hours of work, others with the medical condition of their loved one. Still others result from lack of family assistance, costs of care and sheer physical demands of care. What stands out is the high proportion of women giving care for 85 hours or more weekly (51 percent), as well as those who have given care for four years or more (63 percent). Many were wholly responsible for the entirety of the home-based medical and personal care their loved one received, with little or no respite for most of the women. While no single activity is likely to send a person over the brink, consider what a full-time schedule of services to a frail, dying or demented person could do to anyone courageous enough to take on such tasks.

Among caregivers, care-related stressors primarily centered on three issues—a weak or inadequate network, a perception of being overwhelmed by demands and a sense of not measuring up to the role. How can one begin to measure stress levels among these caregivers? Physiological tests exist that can accurately measure an individual's accelerated heart rate or blood pressure. One also observes stress firsthand: people talk faster, they may hyperventilate, or they may appear distracted or overwhelmed. Or, simply ask a person to describe their beliefs and experiences, which I did, inviting them to indicate their stress levels on a scale of one to 10. Here are several verbal observations from our caregivers.

Renae

I got tired of it, 24 hours a day, seven days a week—sickness, treatments all the time, also death. I've given up friends and family. I just wanted to get out, but I couldn't, so I gave up things that would have helped me. Yes, I'm up to a 10.

Faith

My stress level was 8 out of 10. I never looked for any other way of doing this and as a result I exacerbated my back problems. I still wake up thinking about Mother falling out of her wheelchair. I felt overwhelmed and lost my temper.

Mary Beth

I had very high blood pressure and exhaustion, mini-stroke and I couldn't write, couldn't speak. I got to the end of my wits and just screamed, 'I'll leave you.' Toward the end, my stress level was at 10.

Cindy

I didn't stay in touch with neighbors; no reason to be in touch. I was confused and frustrated in the responsible role struggling with multiple decisions every single day, and failing at any level of control and comfort in the decisions I did make. I had high blood pressure and essential hypertension. There was just no relief. I was a 10.

Mary Ellen

I was always exhausted. I was angry but I knew it had to be done. I cried a lot; depression, frustration and anger. So I fought with him and yelled a lot and today I am lonely [after her husband's death her stress level remained at 9].

Let's review the elements of anticipatory grief: a recognition of deep losses, the lack of boundaries in caring for a very ill or demented person, grueling hours, facing the death of a loved one, gender strain, inadequate medical services, money problems and even routine housework, cooking and home management. Add to this, high stress levels are *normal* and *frequent* experiences for caregivers, not extraordinary or occasional responses. Once the caregiver correctly assesses her responsibility as a social and personal fact, she still needs to make a choice. What will it be—embracing the good, while managing the bad or collapsing in the face of adversity?

Undoubtedly, some caregivers perceive caring as an unrelieved burden. Others focus on the benign or positive aspects (a point we explore in the final chapter). On one side, negative emotions flood the overburdened caregiver. On the other side, positive perceptions reduce the burden to manageable proportions. According to the classic stress model, those with unabated negative emotional responses are most likely to experience high stress, to become seriously ill, to ignore self-care (e.g., no exercise, poor diet) and develop poor coping responses. For example, the caregiver's behavior is at odds with sensible self-care (e.g., refusing help, watching television all night, engaging in heavy drinking or drug use). Or, she may withdraw from former friends and organizations, rather than seek outside support. Here, the model predicts an increased risk of physical and psychiatric disease.

Caregivers often experience "compassion fatigue," a state of irritability and exhaustion. If left unattended, this state can easily lead to burn-out, where the caregiver abandons all hope of providing effective care. I ran into such a case recently at a caregivers' conference when an overwrought caregiver described how she learned to cope by giving up. Jennifer's "solution" to the burden of caregiving was to take a three-week vacation, and leave her dying husband to cope "on his own."

Warning Signs of Caregiver Stress

In earlier chapters, I documented some of the hazards and risks of caregiving in a highly medicalized and technologically sophisticated milieu. At the same time, we live in a modern world that is fractured. We are invariably pressured to do and be more, allow ourselves to become overloaded with responsibilities and confront rapidly changing technologies that divide our attention. According to research from the Alzheimer's Society, the extent to which caregivers manage stress indicates successful versus unsuccessful coping. In my study, the warning signs of burn-out were only too clear, and include denial, anger, social withdrawal, anxiety, depression, emotional exhaustion, sleeplessness, irritability, lack of concentration and serious health problems.

Caregivers frequently **denied** both the disease and its effects on the person being diagnosed. Carla, a 50-year-old wife and mother who recently returned to college, willingly took on the responsibilities of caregiver for her friend.

> It seemed normal, natural, like taking care of kids at home, not really so different. Taking care of my friend with breast cancer gives me satisfaction, knowing I'm helping someone else. I thought it was interesting—gave me a chance to meet people at different stages of their lives. It was a good experience, if it does nothing else but show how you can appreciate people who care for others.

But after one-and-a-half years, her friend's cancer came back and she died rather abruptly. Carla reflects differently on this phase of the caregiving experience.

> But thinking back on it, I'm frazzled, tired, trying to finish up school [university degree]. I'm still married, kids have grown up. I don't

think it's something I want to do now. One day I'll probably need someone to look after me. I don't know if it was a healing experience for me. It helped me to know, 'This too shall pass.'

Many caregivers expressed **anger** at the person with the illness or other loved ones when no effective treatment or cures could be found. They also confessed to feeling *obligated* to take on the role of caregiver, rather than making a considered choice. Cindy, whose voice we first heard in Chapter 6, cared for her father, an alcoholic, who suffered from dementia for 25 years. Because Cindy was the eldest child, she felt duty-bound.

> *I was haunted by a childhood of morning wake-up calls—my dad vomiting. During the time I was caregiving, I ranted and railed with emotional outbursts. I had no feelings of compassion for him. He got what he deserved, but today I feel guilty.*
>
> *When he was in the care facility, I only saw him once a week... I am guilty.*

Other caregivers withdrew from friends and activities that once brought pleasure. Joanne was told by the doctors that her mother was going to die. Instead, her mother lived with a bad heart and osteoporosis for seven more years. Joanne gave up all outside activities to care for her mother—with devastating results.

> *I just took care of business* [mother's care]—*zero clubs. I quit League of Women Voters, totally lost touch with my friends. I was over there at the nursing home every single day, but Mother was unable to have a conversation. I suffered from mental health problems.*

Countless caregivers described the **anxiety** they felt about facing another day and what the future might hold. Jean had trouble relaxing during her interview. Years of caring for her mother, who had Parkinson's disease, osteoporosis and dementia, had led to her constant sense that something *could* and *would* go wrong.

> *I worry about money. I just get home* [from visiting mother], *and I start worrying about having to go back and visit her. I worry about the dementia getting worse, which means her needs will increase. I*

want to do a good job, but my dreams are vanishing the older I get and the longer she lives. I'm running out of time. Will I run out of money? And I'm not taking care of myself.

Depression about the ability to cope was all too common. Rose, age 75, is a strong-willed woman who feels undone by years of caring for her difficult, aged mother, who has made non-stop demands on her.

> *My basic value in life is independence. I've lost that through caregiving… I think it's really hard to reclaim your sense of self when you're caregiving.*
>
> *I even get despondent about her loss of self. Mother was always a controller. She always pulled my strings and I'm aware of it, so I can't express sympathy. I've just learned not to blow my own temper. I think if I walked more, I'd be better off. I wonder if the action of [mother's] temper isn't the action of dementia.*

Caregivers often complained of feeling **emotionally exhausted** over the impossibility of completing necessary daily tasks or coping with unforeseen situations. Sandra, age 42, whom we met earlier, was considerably younger than her dying, elderly husband. She admitted to a sense of overwhelming stress and utter exhaustion. She was especially devastated when she realized her husband had withheld important financial matters from her.

> *His expectations were always higher than what I could achieve. I didn't know about his financial stuff until after it happened. I cried a lot in private and felt helpless and frustrated—overwhelmed, just overwhelmed. I'd barge through every situation, and only thought about things when it was over.*
>
> *Then I'd break down and feel guilty about feeling bad, and not being able to make him better. The emotions, the high stress, just did us both in, long before he died.*

Now, in her mid-eighties, Catherine confesses to feeling tired and exhausted most of the time. Simply maintaining the house and looking after her ill husband and an extended group of relatives was more than she could manage.

I was so tired. I just wanted the day to end, the routine to be over so I could take my Vicodin. I did what needed to be done, and put us both to bed early. I broke both my wrists [lifting her husband], *so I need to manage my pain and make constant compromises. I'm so tense and so tired. I try to rest, so I can do things for other people. The hardest part of the day is getting up in the morning with no energy and being in pain.*

With a seemingly endless list of concerns, **sleeplessness** is a fact of life for numerous caregivers. Faith experienced the 24/7 caregiver consciousness—the sense that everything that happens to your loved one is your responsibility. Sleep seemed out of the question.

I still wake up in the middle of the night reliving the trauma. Caregiving leaves a life imprint. When I was caring for Mother, I would lie awake listening for her to fall down. She was very tall, five foot, ten inches, couldn't walk and hard to pick up after a fall. I managed by drinking coffee and tea—looking for energy. I felt responsible for every bite she took.

For two-and-a-half years, Marsha took care of her father with Alzheimer's and cancer. But it was those last weeks of his life that were the hardest for her.

My whole life was disrupted for three months. Instead of work, I was caring full-time for another person. Toughest time was the middle of the night from two to six a.m.; he was up constantly. As a result, I didn't sleep much. I didn't do very well taking care of myself.

Sleeplessness soon gives way to **irritability**, moodiness and an increase in negative reactions. True of most caregivers, Mary Beth recognized that her highest intentions could easily be undermined when confronting the daily grind, and invariably contributed to her feelings of irritation. Suffering from dementia, her husband's demands often seemed unbearable.

The hard parts were bathing him, and his not knowing what was going on. I never had even one minute to myself. He would talk and talk and talk, and every night he would start about 7:00 p.m.: 'Is it time to go to bed yet?' for two hours until finally at nine I would go to bed. I was just unhappy and tied in an unhealthy way to my husband. He wouldn't accept respite care, so I put him in a home, which I regretted.

Caregivers often suffered from a **lack of concentration**, making it difficult to complete even the most familiar tasks. Performing the same routines over and over, along with having no personal time, typified most caregiving in the home setting. Rosanne, who exemplifies the devoted daughter, is a consultant who works out of her home. She exhibited a typical response to the problem of home care in her struggle to stay focused.

My husband and I began with enthusiasm taking care of mother, but with dementia came entitlement feelings, and soon I was on a short leash with little freedom, loss of work, loss of money and an inability to concentrate. I guess I gradually believed there was no time for myself.

Finally, a host of **health problems** take their toll on the caregiver, both mentally and physically.

During the time Clarice cared for her father, who had heart problems, she suffered from multiple ailments. Negative emotions clearly played a role in Clarice's medical condition.

Caretaking has taken over my life. I had high blood pressure from no exercise, and a bad TV dinner-diet—planned for the times I completely crashed. My back problems were chronic from transferring [lifting] my dad. I felt trapped and depressed and exhausted. I watched Shrek to relax and Valium helped, as well.

Another caregiver, Charlotte, experienced various illnesses throughout the ten-year period in which she cared for her husband of 40 years. Finally, she succumbed to the realization that she could no longer give home care, and moved both of them into an assisted living facility.

I think my poor health is due to... getting older, more stress, more worries, little relaxation. For example, today was a very stressful day. We just got over the stress of moving and now we have the stress of

placing him in an Alzheimer's unit—one major adjustment after an-
other. I've had multiple sclerosis for 31 years. During caretaking I've
had bladder infections, surgeries, cataract surgery for both eyes, high
cholesterol, diabetes, hearing problems, high blood pressure and neu-
rological problems. I finally joined my husband in care.

Nora cared for her 89-year-old mother with Alzheimer's and heart failure, as well as her father, also 89, with heart problems and depression. Perhaps adding to the complexity and apparent endlessness of caregiving, Nora was designated caregiver for her manic-depressive sister. Nora's way of life was threatened by the sheer volume of caregiver tasks, but she felt unable to change her situation for more capable coping.

No doubt about it, dealing with my emotions is the most physically
and emotionally demanding part. I'm depressed when I'm there with
Mother, bottling up my feelings and needing to get away from it.
We've already gone through the grieving process and they're still alive.
They have been dying for four years. The emotional toll is terrible. It's
getting harder and harder and I can't find any solutions.

Stress of Illness for Partners

Considering the array of illnesses and negative events some caregivers experienced, one questions whether the sick should be nursing the sick or the old taking care of their even older loved one. In fact, this situation is so grave that a groundbreaking, nine-year study of 518,240 older couples, published in *The New England Journal of Medicine*, painstakingly documents the "stress of illness" for the partner. The research extends the notion of the "widower effect"—a condition in which a spouse dies soon after being widowed. The article indicated that, while this been common knowledge as early as 1848, new research also suggests that spouses of people who are simply *hospitalized* have a greater risk of dying than the spouses of healthy people. Additionally, care receiver problems that affect physical or mental ability, like dementia or hip fracture, are worse for the partner's health—findings applicable to almost anyone in a close relationship.

Dr. Nicholas Christakis has worked with Hospice patients and their families, and observes how illness, health risks and death in one person can have similar consequences for others in a person's social network. Dr. Christakis has paid special attention to married couples, observing the high death rate that occurs for the well partner when one partner becomes seriously ill and requires hospitalization. I refer to this as the "affinity effect," which implies extreme mutuality. After all, close relationships entail distinct connections forged with sympathy, mutual attraction and empathy.

Married couples are not the only ones affected by this affinity effect. In fact, it can impact any close relationship. An afflicted person affects entire families. In a word, *living with*, *caring about* or *caring for* a sick person can contribute to illness or even premature death, unless— and this is a very large UNLESS—caregivers unravel themselves from their care burden and seek another way. These findings are clarified over and over by our caregivers' experiences.

A recent call from Rhoda, a caregiver who "simply didn't have the time to devote for an entire interview with me" is a case in point. A self-professed "professional" caregiver, she has presided over the deaths of her parents, three brothers and a host of fellow church members. Now, she cares for her 55-year-old husband, who suffers from a rare auto-immune disease, and is required to use a wheelchair. Rhoda and her husband, Andrew, have strong religious beliefs, as well as an abundant social network to sustain them. But recently, their son has taken on "peculiar" behaviors that threaten his well-being, as well as his relationship with his wife.

Rhoda wanted advice about what to do, because her son believes he has a number of dreaded diseases, has been inappropriately self-medicating, acts out deep anxiety in a number of ways and can no longer function as an autonomous adult. The logical question is: How can family members stay well despite being deeply connected and/or giving care to their sick or dying relative? We'll look at strategies for easing caregiver grief, as well as avoiding the affinity effect later.

Empathy and Emotions

Daniel Goleman writes in *Social Intelligence* that in today's psychology, the word *empathy* carries three distinct meanings: *knowing* another person's feelings, *feeling* what that person feels and *responding compassionately* to another's distress. The caregiver may act out of compassion or a strong sense of duty, and effectively carrying out this task ultimately depends upon empathy, a "feeling into." Goleman argues that in an important sense, "We experience the other person's emotions in our own body."

This process can occur at an unconscious level, and helps to account for the frequent statements by caregivers that they were "at one" with their care receiver, failed to differentiate themselves from their ill or dying loved one or tended to use the "we" pronoun to describe their caregiving activities.

By any definition, these family caregivers have *empathy*. They have given time, money, strength, attention, love and devotion to the elderly loved ones in their care. While their efforts usually remain invisible, except to family members or immediate friends, they play an incredibly significant role in managing periodic crises and relieving the burden of elder care for other family members. But such sacrificial giving involves more than heroic measures. Giving selflessly comes at considerable cost. Sometimes, it can actually result in a loss of sympathy and compassion. What originally served to motivate and energize the caregiving act has been turned upside down.

When Pain and Grief Are Acknowledged, But Unresolved

Here is a poignant story from Candace, a former student of mine (and not part of the original interview group). As a therapist, she knows very well that caregiving is highly stressful. Still, she felt wholly unprepared for letting go of the loved one at the end of life. Social expectations do not help, she concluded.

Social expectations dictate that family, especially women, know how to be caretakers, [a conviction that] *is both unreasonable and unjust.*

For society or governments to expect a caregiver to put her life aside and be joyful about doing it is ridiculous and unrealistic.

She calls for a change in policies and services to relieve the "unnecessary suffering of the caregiver." Her larger story confirms how the affinity effect extends beyond marriage or the nuclear family.

As the only 'available' female for my aging aunt, I offered to move her to Bellingham [Washington] *where she could be near to me after she began experiencing disorienting TIA's* [transient ischemic attacks]. *Her son, an only child, lives in Missouri and moving her there was not an option due to her preference—and his. Although they had a wonderful relationship, it was made clear that he and his wife did not have the capacity or desire to provide care.*

Of course, I volunteered. As a retired therapist, I recognize that I am a 'caregiver' by nature and training. But regardless of my many years of training and professional ability to detach, I was not emotionally prepared for the changes that caregiving would make in my life. I wish that I had had the aforementioned [aging class] *material before I said: 'Sure…move her here. I'd love to have her closer.' Our situation became fairly textbook.*

Auntie was 90 at the time and I was 53. I worked full-time in a clinical setting. The retirement facility (not a nursing home or assisted living) was across the street from my office, which we assumed would be handy for both. However, as my aunt's condition deteriorated, she became more dependent upon me and demanding, which was out of character for this previously vibrant, independent woman. Because I worked across the street, she could see my vehicle and would know if I was at work and available to come over, and confront me if I didn't.

I soon found myself feeling the loss of independence and self-control—and guilty when I tried to take time for myself. Her son would occasionally fly into town long enough to 'fix' something and be gone in a day or two, which did not give me a break from the responsibility. His response was: 'Well, you're good at dealing with her emotions, and I'm not.' I found myself becoming resentful of his ability to come and go as he pleased. I was stuck with her 3:00 a.m. tearful, disoriented phone calls and notices from the residential facility that she was out wandering the halls and pounding on doors when other residents were trying to sleep. My stress levels increased exponentially. Over the next year, I began to have sleep disturbances and headaches.

I noticed a steep decrease in auntie's cognitive ability about the time of an unfortunate accident on the [facility's] activity bus that resulted in fractured ribs. The x-rays from the accident proved fortuitous because they identified a malignancy within the lung. At the end of two weeks, the malignancy had spread to her other lung and a breast, and she began to complain of increasing headaches and back pain. It was determined that she had a fast-growing malignancy, which was rapidly metastasizing. The medical professionals 'guessed' that some of her worsening disorientation was likely due to a malignancy in the brain, but a CT scan was not ordered, since it would only serve to identify a source. It could not offer any treatment or resolution of her symptoms, and the procedure would potentially terrify her. Every now and then, I would get a glimpse of my wonderful aunt when she would be cognizant—and I would grieve each time she lapsed back into her disorientation. We, my family and I, rode an emotional roller coaster every day for six months.

Candace experienced more agony when her aunt died in her absence. Her reactions were anger and guilt, typical responses when caregivers can't meet impossible demands.

She passed away when I wasn't at her bedside, because I had taken a much needed break. I felt guilty and sometimes I still do. I didn't want her to die without family at her side. Initially, I was angry with my cousin for leaving, but I know that he did what he had to do for himself. I don't recall being angry with my aunt at any point—frustrated at 3:00 a.m., but not angry. I was angry with the disease that was destroying her beautiful mind. It was a difficult and trying time for me and my family—even with my advanced skills. I'm grateful that I don't have another aging relative to consider caring for.

Lessons Learned

Although it seems impossible at times, combating stress through enlightened *self-interest* and *self-loving* could well be the caregiver's first priority. The caregiver is the one who must take control of the situation. Regardless of circumstances, the caregiver cannot sink into emotional despair. These "shadow emotions," as Deepak Chopra calls them, must be allowed to surface, confronted and only then will they dissipate. After all, they're only energy configurations. We CAN change them.

Sandy Stork recommends caregivers view themselves as CEOs, chief executive officers, in their management of self and their care receiver. The process starts with a strong identity, a positive self-image, and a set of practices that enhance well-being. I recommend three basic—not always easy—stress reduction practices:

1. Change your approach to the care receiver—show a happy face.

2. Alter your routines to include taking care of yourself. Certainly, you are as important as the loved one. Keep a schedule book to include regular activities that can renew and refresh you. Where have you been on your calendar?

3. Reach out to others, including friends, family and support groups. Talk to someone you love or admire every day to re-energize yourself.

Because grief has a life of its own, you need to embrace it—never repress it. Consider Sandy Stork's inspired idea that feelings are "the garden of the soul: beautiful ones, thorny ones, bitter ones, sweet ones—all are a part of the natural order." I cannot say enough about working with your negative emotions. Your task is to recognize these feelings and work with them. Sandy offers a prescription for letting go of these negative feelings by *acknowledging* them, *listening* to them and *responding appropriately*. She includes additional stress reduction practices to unbury those emotions. The final chapter explores caregivers' emotions in greater detail.

1. Name your feelings—any and all feelings are important to recognize and label.

2. *Recognize* these feelings as normal and natural. Everyone has them at some time or other.

3. *Don't ignore* the feelings, because they are the source of stress. Ignoring or denying the feelings feels like self-protection, but this approach only contributes to increased stress.

4. *Take the charge out* of the feeling by allowing it to surface. Feelings need to come out. How? By *weeping, words* and *sharing.* Go to a person or group where it feels safe to share your grief. Have the *courage* to share. Grief needs to be witnessed for it to be fully expressed, and then released.

5. *Practice daily meditation*, which should include deep breathing. This practice reverses the stress response and offers a relaxing influence. Try to breathe in *calm* and breathe out *kindness.*

The good news is that despite struggling with chronic losses and grief, most caregivers found ways over time to transform their situation from an overall negative experience into a positive or even uplifting experience. They discovered it is, indeed, possible to move beyond grief into a more optimistic state of mind. Such a shift made them more likely to find workable coping strategies. Instead of withdrawing from friends, they sought them out. Rather than neglecting family celebrations, they welcomed them. They insisted on keeping their jobs (if important to them), which helped them maintain a sense of balance.

Keep in mind that negative feelings are not harbored by caregivers all the time. Mitigating influences—a strong network with supportive relationships, engaging in outside activities and accomplishments and having good self-care practices—can reduce the stress reactions. These can also contribute to positive beliefs about yourself and the caregiving experience, as well as decrease the overall risk for physical and psychiatric disease. Another very practical approach is to advocate for your loved one. Let's find out more about this in the next chapter.

Chapter 10

Advocating for Elders in Nursing Homes

Nursing homes are environments of isolation and disempowerment. They dictate when to get up, when to go to bed, when and what to eat, when to take showers, and who will help, and when and if to leave.

— Barry Corbet, "Nursing Home
Undercover: Embedded." *AARP Magazine*

To ask the hard question is simple.

— W.H. Auden

The Hard Question—The Simple Answer

The hard question—when to place Jim in 24-hour institutional care—nagged at me for months. With its multiple stairs, thick carpet and narrow doorways, our home proved unsuitable for his wheelchair. Reviewing the situation in therapy, I made the decision to bring Jim home—but not in the house we had lived in for 25 years. After more than a year of house hunting in my very hilly town, I found a home in April 2001 without outside steps. A wide doorway from the garage into the home allowed for wheelchair access. An open floor plan and bedroom on the lower floor accommodated all our living needs. The upstairs loft could be reserved for the grandchildren, and the two upstairs bedrooms worked for a study and guest room. The neighborhood was lovely and quiet, and trees surrounded the development. Even the wrap-around deck was perfect for enjoying summer days and outdoor eating. I looked forward to a summer of gardening and indoor painting, and preparing myself for full-time caregiving in the fall.

In the meantime, Jim was located in an assisted living facility—a place he earlier ruefully referred to as his "prison," and he the "chief inmate." As his health deteriorated, we hoped that through the family's encouragement and frequent prodding, he could build himself up to the point of once again sharing a home with me. Month succeeded month, and although I was ready to have Jim move in, my son thought he wasn't "quite ready." Finally, the Thanksgiving holiday rolled around. It was time to bring Jim "home." "Welcome to the new house, Dad and Grandpa," the family shouted out. Jim's response was to look confused and desolate.

As the meal proceeded, Jim began to look desperate. He seemed unable to cut his meat, and after Tim cut it, reluctant to eat it. He turned down the potatoes—they stuck in his throat. The salad tasted "raw" and his untreated teeth prevented him from chewing the crispy carrots and seeds. His eyes lit up momentarily when Susan's pumpkin pie showed up at the overladen table. But in a short while, he began fidgeting in his wheelchair. "What now," I asked? Jim turned to our oldest son, Tim, and said in a monotone:

"I need to go home now." The family's response was shocked silence. I realized what was once his prison had now become his nest.

The hard question—when to seek institutional care—had a simple answer. The patient knew when it was time. A few months later, we began the tortuous process of looking for a skilled nursing facility.

The Need for Institutional Settings for Elder Care

Today's medical arrangements present us with a muddle. Regardless of how serious the illness, hospitals today allow only for short stays. Taking care of the newly released patient at home is often not possible. So, we are *dependent* upon skilled nursing facilities for the post-hospital recovery period. And we are *dependent* upon skilled nursing care to ensure that recovery is possible. But therein lay the paradox. No one is assured that nursing care in these settings provides the fundamentals for either rest or rehabilitation.

For many patients, an episode or two of recuperating in a rehab center may be enough. They return home healthier—or begin the journey into dying. Eventually, family caregivers confront a time when they can no longer manage the physical or mental care of their elderly loved ones. It could occur after multiple hospitalizations, as in my case. When the level of care becomes unbearable, putting the loved one into a nursing facility seems like the only alternative. Another muddle: it means having to choose between the lesser of two evils—excessive *care* burden versus excessive *cost* burden.

Gerontologists argue that there *should be* "adequate institutional alternatives." But what constitutes "adequate" is often left unsaid. Few families have the knowledge, practical experience, or sense of empowerment to know how to choose an "adequate" placement of their loved one, or what to do if *adequate* is *poor* or even *dangerous.* Placing a frail loved one in an institutional setting represents another phase of caregiving; another distinct extension of ourselves. I needed to give service to Jim, but in a different context—a context where I was definitely not in charge. I tightened my belt and swore in the spirit of service and the gift of both time and money to do my best—corral our children for assistance—and work within this new setting. I was ill prepared for what was to come. This phase of care was *advocacy,* an entirely new experience for most caregivers.

Experiencing Advocacy

As Jim became increasingly more ill my responsibilities expanded. I needed more information, more time and more training for managing ordinary caregiving tasks—giving medicine, assisting in showering, preparing meals, doing laundry and shopping. As for the extraordinary ones—handling legal papers, managing investments and learning new treatments—I felt overwhelmed. With Jim's deteriorating condition, I recognized that I could not maintain both my husband and myself for very much longer. I found myself increasingly exhausted and dispirited. I felt traumatized by the shift in his behavior from a fiercely independent person to a nearly totally dependent one—unable to walk, toilet, dress himself or manage medications. I suffered defeat by the sheer complexity of the medical demands. Thus, my journey into institutional caregiving and advocacy began.

No warning bells went off when we first placed Jim in care. The members of our family were novices, rank amateurs, who watched our loved one stumble from one facility of poor care to another. No one offered us a manual or a guide for "good nursing homes." Once on Hospice we still were not presented with guidelines for choosing a facility. So, we learned on the job—the hard way—by confronting threatening or damaging situations immediately. Essentially, we operated as crisis managers throughout Jim's three-year stay in a number of different care facilities.

Certainly, bad things happen to patients without good care. But how did we know what good care was? Where should we begin? I started with the legalities and economics of institutional care, and sought out our personal lawyer, who provided helpful information to plan for incapacity or disability, which happened in our case. This required three legal directives: (1) a General Durable Power of Attorney for financial purposes, (2) a Durable Power of Attorney for Health Care (I became the legal party that signed off on my husband's medical care), and (3) a Living Will. This last document directed the physician *not* to use extraordinary measures to resuscitate my husband in the event of brain death.

I am not alone in discovering that institutional medicine invariably employs feeding tubes, respirators and other lifesaving equipment on patients who would prefer to die. Heroic measures, as these are called, have become routine in hospitals and nursing homes. Without a personal advocate present to remind medical staff that a signed Living Will indeed exists, medical staff are likely to assume that dying people wish to continue living *indefinitely*.

At one point, I consulted with another, highly knowledgeable lawyer (a Seattle-based professor with a background in welfare law) about Medicaid's state and federal programs, which pay for long term-care in a family group home or skilled nursing facility. The attorney clarified that this program had a "spend-down" feature, requiring the married couple to reduce their estate to $80,000 (an amount subject to change), or for a surviving spouse, $2,000 before the government picks up the costs. Medicaid provides low-income elders with months or years of expensive nursing home care. Medicare, the federal program linked to

Social Security, has no clause for long-term care, since Medicare payments are linked solely to brief periods of follow-up care after hospital stays.

For our prudent middle-class family, who carefully saved for the rainy day, Medicaid simply did not work. Spending down means the surviving spouse (in this case, me) may experience deprivation, having used up the bulk of savings and pension. Moreover, the significant loss assures no inheritance will remain for the children. The state, as well, can put a lien on one's home, so after the surviving spouse's death, the state claims all monies they had paid out for medical and nursing care. Lawyers reminded me that assets can be shifted to children or other relations over a few years to achieve the reduced level of income to qualify for state aid. But this abandonment of financial autonomy, I felt, is inherently unethical and probably illegal.

Advocating in Care Facilities

I awoke to the realization that for a variety of reasons, the law was overly restrictive in its capacity to speak for, defend or support my sick husband and our family. I stumbled upon some harsh realities. Supportive transactions are unlikely to occur in a court of law. Nursing homes are not likely to face the threat of a lawsuit if poorly trained nursing assistants fail to give the requisite shower or provide a liquid diet after the doctor ordered it. Care involves far more than a formal written care plan or an able body to carry it out.

Nursing care is fraught with human error. I am ever mindful that medication errors—among the most common medical errors—harm at least 1.5 million people every year. Even worse, sometimes overworked CNAs (Certified Nursing Assistants) can be cruel, intentionally negligent or indifferent.

Obtaining excellent care requires vigilant oversight by staff and family. My experiences with human error over the years Jim was in a care facility gave me an entirely new appreciation of the need for cultivating awareness, and for staying tuned into the distinct organization of nursing facilities. I realized over and over that nursing homes are grossly understaffed, and nursing assistants are both seriously under-trained and underpaid. Elderly persons with failing physical and mental faculties are routinely ignored or shunted aside. Fortunately, I also met some marvelous, compassionate people.

Some examples can clarify the "horror stories" our family experienced during Jim's stay in six different care facilities. In one instance, we were moving Jim from the assisted living facility, which required the elder to be reasonably mobile—and preferably continent—to a nursing home. Assisted living facilities resemble an apartment style arrangement, often with a nurse on duty, whereas a nursing home is reminiscent of a hospital, although with a more informal ambience. As we entered the beautifully appointed nursing home, I thought my troubles were over. The facility had a spacious, private room for Jim overlooking a meadow, complete with trees, birds and natural landscape. Contemporary furnishings and easy chairs gave me a sense of comfort and ease. Well-dressed administrators launched into a description of the facility's assets and activities, which appeared ideal. Now, he'll receive the level of care he needs so much, I thought.

Over the course of the next seven months, I learned I had to pay very close attention to his care in this would-be "model" facility. Indifference, incompetence and impersonality pervaded the setting. I learned a patient had been forgotten for 24 hours, left dead in her bed shortly before we arrived. I observed a woman who continuously requested assistance who was ignored because she was "so obnoxious," according to one staff member. The patient later died in that nursing home; a formal investigation followed. As a result, the facility was closed down for a time, and then reopened under new management with a new name. But justice was too late for her.

Night after night I observed a tall, very obese nursing assistant push Janie, a small female patient, from her doorway into her room because the patient would not "listen to orders." This same assistant shouted at me numerous times when I sought help for my husband or when I thought he had been neglected too long. I learned to smile and ignore her outburst—but not without my stomach turning inside out. The CNA was just as likely to turn on *us* at any time.

Dorie was a dear lady who had been confined to our shared nursing facility for more than five years. How I looked forward to her warm greeting as I walked down the hall to Jim's room. Unfortunately,

Dorie's refreshing salutations were perceived by staff as disruptive. Within minutes, Dorie would be summarily ushered from the open hallway to her little prison. In this setting, staff seemed reluctant to accept a resident who behaved normally.

Prior to this nursing home experience, Jim had moved to one of the few available short-term nursing facilities for recovery after hospitalization. This placement offered an entirely different ambience than the genteel but poorly staffed one we later encountered. Instead of soft music piped into rooms and staff speaking in lowered tones, this facility had a *frantic* quality. Resembling the infamous "Bellevue," the public New York City hospital for the indigent, the facility had unremitting noise. The lack of carpeting created a continuous din as non-stop loudspeakers transmitted messages from ward to ward, professional staff to assisting staff, from an insistent administration to an indifferent kitchen staff. Wheelchairs, pails and trays rattled by on cumbersome wheels and footsteps thumped outside the sickroom door. Who could rest in this hubbub?

The recurrent moaning of patients reminded me of Dante's fourteenth century version of Hell—*abandon hope all ye who enter here.* This particular facility had a sizeable number of late-stage dementia patients, who required total care, including feeding. As the first seating of patients completed their meal in the dining room, the second seating of severely cognitively disabled patients was wheeled in and lined up for feeding. Staff fed as many as four patients at one time, many patients with their eyes closed, utterly unaware of who they were, let alone what they were expected to do.

The perfunctory level of care extended to the patients' room arrangements. Few nursing facilities offer private rooms, and when they do, the price can be prohibitive for many families. Elders accustomed to their own space, surrounded by precious mementos and memories, must downsize drastically into a setting smaller than a typical hospital room. Confronted with a roommate they do not know, an illness they cannot control, an impersonal environment they usually did not choose and the loss of any vestige of autonomy, is it any wonder elders have been known to plead with their families: "Never put me in a nursing home!"

Institutional food for the elderly deserves widespread public attention. Food is often unappealing, unattractive, unappetizing, even revolting and contributes to patients' chronic dissatisfaction. Sometimes, the meals are counterproductive for older digestive systems and dental problems: overly starchy, meat too tough to chew, copious gravy on cold potatoes and mushy white bread. I observed the enormous amounts of discarded food left on the plates where Jim resided. The elders either could not chew the food or digest what they had swallowed. In some cases, the meal was not recognizable due to overcooking or because it had been draped in heavy sauces. I'll never forget Katherine, a 92-year-old woman in a wheelchair, whose look of dismay said it all. With a withering gaze, she stared at the pale canned peas, stiff and jellied pork chops and hard tack rolls, and righteously commented: "You'd think they'd feed us some decent food, since we're not long for this earth." Katherine often looked forward to her family taking her to restaurants, where she could finally make choices that suited her food preferences.

Sometimes, issues surrounding the food reached a crisis state. Our experience showed us that kitchens were not informed of a patient's change in health status in time to alter the menu. Standard meals were served to a patient who could not swallow or had developed an allergic reaction. Less lethal were rigid feeding schedules, whether in the dining room or in the patient's room, which rarely take into account the patient's changing appetite or taste preferences. What should be one of the livelier and joyous parts of the day—eating and exchanging greetings with table mates—turns into a depressing litany of complaints.

In his displeasure, Jim (or more likely, one of our family members) often led the charge against the food—at least in one facility—and may have encouraged others to loudly lament poorly cooked and monotonous fare. The cook began to hold a grudge against Jim, and started verbally abusing him. Our daughter Liddy popped into the dining room just in time to witness the event. The angry young cook was shouting and haranguing Jim, a shadow of his former self, because he was too slow in eating his dinner. The young man was summarily dismissed. But we had no idea how long this abuse had been going on. Our family was justified in pressing charges, but after consultation with the director, we agreed to let the matter rest.

In these facilities, I saw how dependent the elderly residents were on institutional benevolence. Most are fearful of complaining about anything because they fear retaliation. Remember: These nursing home residents are primarily drawn from the generation that endured the Great Depression and fought in World War II. They are accustomed to hard times. Some elders have such severe cognitive disorders they cannot find the language to address an institutional grievance. Others who have complained are often ignored, set aside as troublemakers or punished through neglect. I experienced many days in which personal services were so inept, I vowed to bring my husband home again, even at the cost of my health and sanity.

Without doubt, nursing facilities are not hotels catering to customer preference. Alas, they are also not hospitals aiming for highly sterile surroundings and low ratio of patients to nursing staff. Away from the visiting area, our family felt they exuded an oppressive sadness that weighed heavily on staff, visitors and patients alike. The sights, sounds and smells hit the uninitiated like a wall. One can easily be overcome by the tragic faces of demented patients or by the constant moaning and shouting of deranged elders. For the more cognitively aware, but stoic patient like Jim, the presence of so many mentally disturbed people acted as an added emotional burden to his physical pain. Bad odors are one of the more unnerving experiences for visitors and new residents. Many institutional wards emit the unceasing stench of human waste—blood, urine and feces—trapped in rugs, mattresses and floors.

Yet, a heroic quality often flowered in these squalid environments. When the care facility was truly caring, and when visiting family, friends and volunteers radiated love, concern and positive intention, everyone connected to make a difference. The difference was an emotional shift from feeling consigned to the lowest underworld of Hell to a reasonable—if physically and psychologically difficult—place some elders must accept as their final home.

Consider what institutionalized elders routinely need from staff. I found the list to be extensive: water, feeding (at least at later stages of life), medicine, diaper changing, bed changes and urinals emptied. Over the course of the day, staff must make frequent transfers for each bedridden patient from bed to wheelchair, from wheelchair to toilet, from toilet to bed, as well as check in every two hours to determine the patient's condition (This two-hour minimum meets Washington state requirement for patients confined to their beds). Add to this, nursing aides monitor machines (e.g., oxygen), and for those more highly motivated staff, drop-in to chat with lonely, and often frightened, patients. So much can go wrong with this picture.

Staff shift changes interrupted ongoing services. Over a period of only a few months, I observed a number of instances of exceedingly poor care. A patient was left on the toilet for more than an hour. Nursing notes omitted essential information, including failing to include new orders from the attending physician, which specified supervised toileting for the patient. Nursing aides had only inadequate training for the complexity of the job. For example, washing wounds and monitoring machines were outside their expertise. Some were simply too incompetent or indifferent to handle the work. They had problems at home, came to work intoxicated, experienced chronic fatigue or worked too many hours the day or week before. In some facilities I observed staff and administrators who were routinely hostile or intimidated certain patients.

Forgetfulness seemed endemic to institutionalized care, as floor staff attempted to answer multiple patient calls, confront emergencies, deal with difficult patients, while simultaneously carrying out their routine duties. Unless the staff person wrote down a patient's request (and very few aides did this), they may have forgotten it by the time they reached the end of the hall because of multiple interruptions. This became serious when the elder needed water or had been left in dirty diapers for a couple of hours—a situation we confronted too many times to count throughout Jim's years as a patient.

Without guidance or a conceptual framework—indeed, in the absence of language—I began my personal campaign of advocating for my husband, Jim. Only after I had fled from the poorly monitored facility did my family and I move to an assertive position. We then became vigilant at:

- Diligently watching staff behavior.

- Immediately intervening on behalf of Jim when inappropriate or poor treatment occurred.

- Speaking out to individual staff and supervisors.

- Complaining about treatment to responsible staff persons.

- Agitating to social workers and supervisory staff for conscious, compassionate care, rather than careless and indifferent treatment.

- Collecting information to better advise hands-on staff on the minutiae of care.

- Defending my loved one's patient's rights, but also other similarly affected elders (with less success).

- Admonishing individual staff for lapses in service.

- Inquiring about other patients' experiences through family members to find out whether I was dealing with an isolated situation or a widespread institutional problem.

- Connecting with Jim's physician and later, Hospice, to spell out the problem areas.

Intervening on behalf of another, seemingly so simple and humane, evolved into an all-consuming enterprise. Each care facility offered a distinct institutional format, one that had to be meticulously learned. How else would you have known whether you missed the weekly shower unless you knew that the window of opportunity for such care was a brief one hour per week? Some facilities welcomed family. They correctly perceived the positive value that family members brought to the elder's sickbed. Other facilities limited visiting because it interfered with institutional routines. They claimed visitors agitated the patient, put too many demands on the patient or wanted patients to engage in social interaction that complicated their care.

Few nurses, however, were as bold as the one who told me to keep visitors down to two persons maximum, as it not only interfered with care, but too many people around could be "dangerous" for the patient's health. As I discussed in an earlier chapter, medical staff can be very arbitrary. In this case, my advocating took the form of a non-confrontational nod at her inappropriate request. I then clarified the policy with administrators, who were far less restrictive. Our family of myself and six adult children, their spouses and children, finally resolved this unpleasantness by rallying round the overburdened nurse, and praising her for her nursing skills, kindness and concern about Jim and other patients. Her response: unalloyed joy and an entirely new repertory of interaction that was personal and pleasant.

Not all family members were equally sanguine in dealing with staff transgressions. Our son, Timothy, often flew into momentary rages when his father's care appeared inadequate. On daily visits, Timothy monitored the state of his father's well-being, and if it had fallen short, he strode purposefully down the hall to locate the offending staff person who had failed to clean, feed, hydrate or otherwise look after Jim. With Timothy's tap on the shoulder and direct eye contact, the aide usually jumped into action. But this was not always the case. We all became quite philosophical about recognizing Jim's immediate needs and whether we could do anything about them during our visit. We also came to understand the constant pressure on staff that contributed to slow or unresponsive service.

Empowering Caregivers: Knowledge About Elder Care Institutions

Personal experiences with elder care institutions helped us to clarify what constitutes "adequacy" of care. Being intimately involved with advocating in these long-term facilities gave us a greater sense of ease about how to develop strategies that helped Jim. Additionally, *advocacy* can entail large scale reform groups who speak out and lobby on behalf of families. Caregivers need to be alerted to typical failures.

The National Citizen's Coalition for Nursing Home Reform has written a manual, which needs to be on every family's bookshelf: *Nursing Homes: Getting Good Care There*. The manual identifies the seven most common problems in care. The Coalition pinpointed the following cause and effect risks for patients:

1. Not being taken to the bathroom according to individualized needs leads to incontinence (wet and soiled).

2. Not getting enough fluids to drink leads to dehydration (often thirsty and dry skin) compounded by drugs that contribute to excessively dry mouth.

3. Not getting enough to eat leads to malnutrition (weight loss, low energy and cracks in the corner of the mouth).

4. Not being groomed properly leads to poor hygiene (body odors, dirty mouth, dirty clothes).

5. Not receiving preventive skin care or failure to frequently turn bedridden patients leads to pressure sores (holes in the skin, which can penetrate to the muscles underneath the skin).

6. Not being helped with range of motion exercises or physical therapy leads to shorted muscles and chronic joint discomfort.

7. Not encouraged to retain independence leads to loss of ability to eat, dress, walk, bathe and get in and out of bed (increased dependency).

In fact, Jim experienced all of these conditions during his stays in both assisted living and nursing home facilities. Only after we settled Jim into his last nursing home, a long-standing and respected institution in our community, did we learn about the differences in such measures as patients' rights, quality of care and the role of the family as advocate. Of course, nursing homes typically broadcast patients' rights as fundamental, and cite a litany of features seemingly placing patients first—such as the freedom of association, right to dignity and right to self-discharge, among others.

Nursing facilities claim they pay attention to quality of care by involving the resident and family in care planning, engaging in problem-solving and taking individual needs into account. They also claim they welcome the outspoken advocate who steps up and speaks out on behalf of their loved one. In fact, states are now mandated to provide intervention by an ombudsman, should a consumer bring a complaint. Reality is a different matter.

What keeps concerned relatives from bringing formal complaints is related to the same set of issues that contribute to poor care. Care facilities for elderly and disabled people are typically for-profit corporate structures, invariably removed from the day-to-day supervision of care. Despite strict federal and state standards, resident abuse is widespread in U.S. nursing homes, and largely goes unreported and unpunished.

Since corporations are in the business of making money, shortages or low inventories provide one way of cutting costs. We found a lack of nutritious food, particularly fruits and vegetables, frequent outages of clean bed linens and towels and worker shortages among housekeeping and nursing staff.

It's no secret that nursing homes have a litany of shortcomings. Low pay, poor benefits, difficult working conditions and poor management lead to low morale and high staff turnover. Constant turnovers in the nursing staff—as much as 100 percent a year in some facilities—create another series of problems. This includes an overall lack of staff awareness of individual patient's needs, rigid scheduling, impersonal treatment, denial of responsibility, as workers "pass the buck," and slow-downs by overworked staff. These conditions confront patients and their caregivers everywhere.

In one facility, I observed staff routinely take their collective dinner break during the same time elders needed help with their after-dinner toileting. In such instances, a general sense of abandonment pervaded the environment, as elders in wheelchairs and family members went in search of elusive nursing assistants.

I blame the corporate model—with profit as the bottom line—as the culprit. Absentee ownership also creates a serious gap between a *care facility* and a *caring facility*. Sometimes, this contributes to absurd situations. One nursing home in our consistently temperate Bellingham, Washington community received directives from its central office, located in torrid Phoenix, Arizona. The care facility ran its air conditioning at the same level as in Arizona. However, in Bellingham, 72 degrees is likely to be a normal summer high. The results were predictable—hallways and dining areas were filled with shivering elders wrapped in multiple layers of sweaters or blankets. Over time, I felt the physical coldness was an apt metaphor for the psychological chill that pervaded the entire environment.

Another point is that nursing homes are run on a hierarchical model, typical of corporations and hospitals. Administrative supervisors give orders to lower ranking nurses, who in turn give orders to their underlings. This practice undermines team work and joint problem-solving.

It also leads to resentment on the part of the nursing assistants, who do the bulk of patient care.

On more than one occasion, I witnessed the frustration and rage of floor staff, who indignantly protested the impossibility of accomplishing the scope of duties they had been ordered to do. But if they failed to follow directions, they were docked wages or even fired. Certainly, having appropriate staff-to-patient ratios could have enhanced staff morale and patient care. And, unless facilities implement different management strategies, staffing shortages will remain endemic to the industry.

Another overlooked issue in nursing home care is the strong bias against the aged held by citizens and the medical profession alike. These negative attitudes may increase, as the number of elderly rise. Today, persons 65 and older account for more than half of all hospital stays and one-third of the nation's health care expenditures. Yet, few medical schools train students in geriatric medicine. As of 1998, as few as 14 of the nation's 126 medical schools require a course in geriatrics and only 85 offer elective courses in the area of study. Care for older persons is not reinforced professionally, and professional role models are largely absent. Irreversible physical declines and death may create an intrinsic reluctance among many health professionals to serve this needy population.

A final consideration for understanding the lack of good care in nursing homes involves the residents themselves. Because healthier elders remain in their homes or choose residential or assisted living facilities, nursing homes increasingly house the most seriously ill patients, namely, those who are most dependent and most likely to have serious dementia and physical disabilities. Patients' problems, especially among those suffering from dementia, often stem from having to leave behind a cherished home, friends and familiar activities. Patients are bedeviled by circumstances not of their making. They are clueless about their medical situation, and how it affects their ability to communicate or even take care of themselves. They feel perpetual anxiety over these "strange" living arrangements, and plaintively ask over and over, "when can I go home?" Feeling disconnected from all that is familiar and secure, it is not surprising that many succumb to hopelessness that contributes to withdrawal and maladaptive behavior.

The National Citizen's Coalition for Nursing Home Reform stresses, however, that many of these maladies can be remedied when the environment changes. I found their "Tips to Remember" particularly helpful for elder advocates.

- Nursing homes residents have the same needs as anyone else—namely, a need for recognition as an individual—in this case, one who has special needs because of physical and mental infirmities.

- Without individual recognition, residents can feel displaced and, without a sense of familiarity, can feel virtually homeless. Depression and withdrawal soon follow.

- Engaging the staff with individual residents remains the best remedy for elder dislocation in an institutional setting. Rather than asking the resident to change life-long individual habits, adjustments in routines need to be made by the *facility*. *Individualized care* is the basic tenet of the standards set forth by the federally sponsored Nursing Home Reform Law, and it applies to all nursing homes receiving federal money. Although individualized care has been lauded as the new standard, it only rarely translates into a new set of institutional practices.

- Nursing home staff can accommodate individualized care by carefully assessing each resident, and then developing a plan of care to meet that person's needs. The plan must then be publicized throughout the institution (i.e., kitchen staff, physical therapists, nursing staff) to ensure its implementation.

- Families play a significant role in nursing home advocacy, as well. They need to share information with the nursing staff, participate in care meetings and expect the facility to make reasonable accommodations for their relative's individual needs and preferences.

- Nursing homes need to be well-staffed to provide good care—a point that cannot be overemphasized. In addition, federal regulatory agencies should demand sufficient resources to enforce the standards of care.

Before the disabled elder moves into a nursing home, he or she must have an assessment. This assessment is a complex undertaking. It serves as the basis for grasping the person's ability to walk, talk, remember, bathe, see, hear, eat, dress and comprehend. The evaluation also determines the level of assistance required for toileting, wheelchair transfers, physical therapy and the like. A good assessment evaluates personal habits and preferences, such as the best time for waking up in the morning or favorite television shows. Familiar routines, activities, habits and relationships are precious reminders of our individuality. Nursing homes employing the one-size-fits-all model frequently ignore the "specialness" of each person in their care, which results in inadvertently undermining the resident's sense of self.

When Jim was strongly urged to be "more social" with various activities, such as Bible reading, musical performances by volunteers, exercise, movies, popcorn parties or ice cream socials, he strenuously resisted. Jim responded to suggestions that he should be forced to be cordial, even ebullient, when he preferred being alone, by overtly withdrawing. Jim chose the hermit role as his method of coping with illness and depression. The family agonized over his decision, gently encouraging him to participate in at least one or two activities a week. He finally compromised, attending periodic musical events (which often were not very good) or a special dinner (which sometimes were), as long as a family member accompanied him. But this was not always feasible.

The sure-fire way, we found, to integrate a recalcitrant elder in a nursing home was to send an enthusiastic member of the activities team to personally take the resident to the event, which happened a few times with Jim. Focusing on the solitary person's isolation and withdrawal does not work. The staff at a well-managed nursing home can work wonders to integrate even the most confused and difficult resident with gentle persuasion.

Institutional Care: A Universal Experience for Elders?

Nursing home living is not an isolated experience for the few. One-half of all women and one-third of all men will spend some part of their lives in a nursing home before they die—25 percent for at least one year and nine percent for five years or more. But not all nursing homes are alike—some are downright dangerous. The National Citizens' Coalition for Nursing Home Reform reports 30 percent of nursing homes have regulatory violations that have caused life-threatening harm or death to residents. Another 50 percent of nursing homes do not have enough staff to prevent residents from getting harmed. Nursing home abuses are endemic to the system, as reported by the Rand Corporation and the Alliance for Aging Research.

- Robert W. DuBois, principle investigator, uncovered medical death records of elderly patients dying in nursing homes, which reveals 27 percent had died because of improper medical care.

- Older persons are either over- or under-prescribed with medications, and drug reactions comprise more than one-half of all deaths.

- Persons 75 years or older are much less likely to receive prescriptions for reducing heart attacks compared with younger patients.

- Many elderly diabetics do not get recommended tests for their condition, suffering needlessly.

- For other patients, 20 to 40 percent of all hospital procedures performed on older patients were unnecessary.

- Two of every five of the nation's 1.6 million nursing home residents are malnourished.

Nursing homes and the challenge of long-term care—care which may extend for years—have exploded into national awareness. In 1999, Time magazine called conditions in some nursing homes "fatal neglect." Much earlier, Richard Garvin and Robert Burger authored *Where They Go to Die: The Tragedy of America's Aged* (1968). Nursing homes are "halfway houses between society and the cemetery," they said, a situation that has continued for decades. The Florida-based Coalition to Protect the Nation's Elders called for Congressional hearings on nursing home fraud and abuse. The Coalition argued that residents have been starved, beaten or left to die, while "giant nursing home chains are ripping off taxpayers with phony billing scams." The deep indignation expressed in the Coalition's statement reflects the anguish many advocates feel when addressing elders' unmet needs for safe, nurturing and cost-effective care. A recent legal response to the abuse/neglect problem in nursing homes has been offered by nation-wide law firms, which focus on litigation, affixing blame, not simply arranging money settlements.

Nursing home reformers blame the abusive treatment on a severe nursing shortage, low staff salaries and high turnover rates. Nursing aides, who perform most of the hands-on care, are often given only a few weeks training, and paid little more than fast food workers.

During my tenure as an advocate for my husband, I can recount a number of episodes confirming these findings. My husband fell out of his wheelchair *twice* in one day from weakness because of staff failure to secure him to the wheelchair or place him in a bed. This occurred after transitioning him from one facility to another. On another occasion, an elderly dementia patient in the same institution fell out of bed and suffered a concussion, because staff had failed to put up safety rails that prevented falls. In still another preventable situation, one patient, quite demented, assaulted another elderly person before staff could intervene. Overworked or forgetful staff may fail to complete rounds, and frail elders, too weak to summon aid, may not be bedded for the night until the late shift comes on. This may be a small matter to a healthy adult, but for an exhausted elder, it can create a major setback.

Fortunately, most negative episodes we encountered were not life-threatening, although some came close. As a family, we mainly appreciated the care, and tried to remain positive and raise morale in the ward. The issue of elder abuse, though, is deeply troubling, because older people, similar to small children, are exceedingly dependent on caregivers and the safety of their immediate environment. My overriding experience over the three years Jim lived in nursing facilities was a pervasive sense of frustration and disappointment, whether as an individual or as a family, to fundamentally change the institutional environment. What the sick elder needs is comfort in a home-like setting—what that elder receives is an uncaring institution. For the 50 percent or more seriously ill elders in our community living in nursing homes without regular visitors and contact with the outside world, life truly looks hopeless.

A Better Way?

What is needed is not more nursing homes, but more public commitment and finances to enable care to occur in the patient's home. To secure a well-trained nursing assistant from a good agency in my hometown of Bellingham, Washington requires a strong cash outlay. For the totally disabled elder, who requires care around-the-clock, the cost is $478 per *day*, or nearly $175,000 per *year*. Such expenditures eliminate almost all American families from this care option.

As a society, we need to rethink basic practices for long-term care. We need to mount a revolution in elder care treatment—not only for more effective and publicly supported home care, but also for nursing home care. Nursing homes will continue to be a necessity, but we should be prepared to make some fundamental changes in their organization. A shift from the current corporate model to an enlightened cooperative or client-based model would be a step in the right direction. Liz Taylor, a former *Seattle Times* columnist and speaker on aging issues, optimistically refers to the "big progress" in elder care as "resident-driven" care—the standard in Sweden for more than 20 years. For the United States, this non-corporate model can be a reality, but only with fairly drastic cultural change, including public resources to make it work.

Let's look at some practices in the Swedish approach to long-term care. The Swedes emphasize that what is normal for a person at home should continue to be normal in the congregate setting—an approach emphasizing client autonomy and choice. Consequently, their service houses individual apartments, not semi-private rooms where neither party has privacy. Each has a full bath, not a bath down the hall. Nursing stations or utility rooms with soiled linens and garbage have been eliminated. Breakfast and dinner are taken into residents' apartments, so they are not forced to have regimented mealtimes according to a predetermined schedule set by staff. They are also allowed to get up and go to bed when they choose.

Research shows a significant increase in both autonomy and satisfaction on the part of residents, and many indicated they actually preferred living there. Perhaps more surprising, the Swedish model is no more expensive to operate than the standard American nursing home. Ultimately, if the United States were to adapt the Swedish perspective of privacy, dignity and autonomy for giving care in a congregate setting, we would most likely witness a sharp decrease in elder abuse, as well as greatly enhanced care for end-of-life patients.

Lessons Learned

Instead of feeling powerless, caregivers and their families *can* do something: Take on an advocacy role. This entails witnessing, speaking out and demanding competent care for their loved ones and similarly situated elders. With one of three nursing homes in America reported to fall below federal standards or to actually abuse or neglect patients, I believe the time is right for seeking changes in congregate living arrangements for end-of-life care. Until that happens, it remains critical for caregivers to be advocates. As a colleague said recently about institutional regimes for his mother-in-law: "If you have a team of advocates, you will be all right."

Chapter 11

Gifts of Caregiving

To have courage for whatever comes in life—
everything lies in that.

— St. Theresa of Avila, 1515-1582

It's not the load that breaks you down,
it's the way you carry it.

— Lena Horne, Jazz Singer

A Love Story

Jill, one of our caregivers, endured emotional abuse and rejection during her childhood, knowing her mother didn't love her. Yet, she rejected her oppressive childhood beliefs and overcame the nearly insurmountable limitations caused by lack of maternal caring and love. Jill succeeded in her life, and beautifully so, as an educator, friend, socially conscious and compassionate woman, as well as a powerful leader in the healing community. Her joy was infectious: she danced in the hallways and brought comfort to the afflicted.

How did she manage to do this? During the final stages of her mother's life, Jill was guided by her capacity to love and by her spiritual connections. She left her home and job for two months to sit patiently beside her mother's bed, to care for all her needs and, finally, to usher her mother through her end-of-life transition. Even on her deathbed, Jill's mother could not relinquish her early attitudes of hostility toward her daughter.

> *I believe in the basic goodness of people. I knew my mother didn't like*
> *me. She told me so. I tried to calm her, but she only insulted me. I*
> *couldn't make her happy and I abandoned my dream that my mother*

would have a change of heart—being nice to me. I prayed a lot and wondered why I chose her. She went to her deathbed never saying she loved me.

The best part of caring for my mother was that she was allowed to die in peace in her own home, to be surrounded by the people who loved her. She died in a good way and I finally got to see who she really was. I was determined to help her passage. I owed her the best care and I took the experience as a spiritual challenge; it was profound. Healing did happen for me because I came to a much deeper acceptance of who my mother is.

Love, as the quintessential spiritual value, can be expressed unconditionally in caring for another, as Jill has done. This level of benevolence reflects the highest form of faith: the willingness to forgive and go beyond limiting views by living from the heart—a life practice that turns out to be easier to talk about than to sometimes achieve.

Embracing the Shadow

Jill's love story is powerful. She shows you that when you give yourself out of love, you lose nothing. In fact, you discover the gifts that abound in what appears to be a hopeless state of affairs. Instead of hoarding negativity about her past, Jill surrendered to the situation. She abandoned the rejected self her mother had imposed on her and found her true self. She emptied herself of denial, resistance, hidden fears and impossible hopes. Her caregiving was forged through years of inner struggle, deep empathy, a bout with cancer and a life dedicated to teaching and healing. In this way, she overcame her abusive childhood. Faith, based on love and self-respect, allowed her to give time, energy and care without reservation to a bitter and unforgiving parent.

Jill's story demonstrates the spiritual capacity all of us have to transcend the inherent difficulties of caregiving. With its unceasing demands and inner conflicts, caregiving can easily plunge you into an abyss of guilt, fear and anger. You can wallow in your misery, and ignore the gifts of giving care. Alternatively, when you move beyond your dark side as Jill did—the unforgiving, unloving, fearful part of yourself—you can achieve spiritual wholeness. Only by embracing your shadow, can you let go of your losses, pains and bitterness. Now, you see clearly the gifts of caregiving.

The successful caregivers in our study developed their inner lives. Their self-acknowledged wholeness helped them to have balanced emotional lives, and to maintain their social connections and spiritual integrity. They could take an enlightened view of their caregiving task. As Catherine, a highly energetic caregiver, commented:

> *I think caregiving is a gift if you look at it in a positive way. It enables you to do something for another human being—especially one you love.*

Actively seeking the gifts of caregiving takes you on that miraculous yellow brick road, immortalized by Dorothy in *The Wizard of Oz*. Here fresh adventures await, new relationships beckon and novel ways of looking at yourself—and your loved one—emerge.

You may need some additional habits of the heart for getting to and staying on the miracle path. I recommend the following: *planning ahead, cultivating a positive attitude, having a sense of accomplishment, staying compassionate, being socially connected, expanding your health practices* and *developing a spiritual life.*

Planning? Who needs it? As a caregiver, you will need to become an overnight expert. The U.S. Army has a graceless, but truthful, adage that certainly applies to caregiving: "lack of prior planning leads to piss-poor performance." Why don't we plan for elder caregiving? Why are we surprised when the crisis comes? Why do we go into shock when our loved one is stricken with stroke or heart attack or dementia? Why do we have trouble accepting that our parents or older spouse are aging and may require us to step up on their behalf? Clearly, the culture and each of us are often in the shadow of denial.

Clearly, caregivers who planned ahead—who said they fully intended to serve their elder *before* the elder's current medical crisis—were the most ready and able to take on the job without emotional collapse. *Intention* plays a critical role here. It's a key feature for almost all successful or even moderately successful caregivers.

Another feature of the yellow brick road is the *attitude* you bring into the caregiving. Throughout the book, you can see how many caregivers are deeply conflicted about their responsibilities. I was dismayed to find that only one out of three caregivers said they had a significantly positive or optimistic attitude about their caregiving. What else sustained these caregivers?

More than 75 percent of caregivers reported they felt *respected* and *valued* for their work. This self-acceptance and self-respect kept them together, even when their optimism lagged. Caregivers are especially uplifted if the care receiver and immediate family appreciated their efforts.

Another way of staying on the visionary road is the feeling of a *sense of accomplishment*. Not an easy achievement at all. "Doing my best"— although most wanted to do significantly better—translated for most caregivers into: "I'm powerless to change what is happening to my loved one, but I'm doing the job to the best of my ability." At one level, the statement, "doing my best," can be interpreted as a positive, self-affirming assertion. For some women, though, "doing my best," really meant, "I'm no good at this job, and my best is pretty bad," and for a very few caregivers, "I feel sorry for my loved one that I can't do any better than this." Feeling dismal keeps you in the shadow. Instead, take your caregiving journal and before you go to bed, write down all the accomplishments you have performed throughout the day. No matter how trivial, each gesture of loving help counts as a triumph—a solid victory over negativity.

Who would argue that *compassion* must be an essential feature of staying on the miracle path? As expected with this empathetic caregiving group, compassion ranked high as a motivation for service. Nearly 90 percent responded very positively to the phrase: "I believe loving kindness is the best medicine." For some, compassion extended to advocacy, first, for their own loved one, and among some caregivers, for unrelated elders. Advocacy involved a range of activities, including speaking out to medical staff on behalf of their own or other patients, writing letters supporting particular policies and participating in caregiving support groups or patient-centered activities.

Virginia, an only child, delighted in the fact that her mother, with whom she always had a close, "sisterly" relationship, could join her household of two—her son and herself. Despite friends warning her that bringing her mother to live with her *would never work*, Virginia found her mother's presence comforting during all 15 years of caregiving. Her mother contributed love and goodwill, as well as funds to keep the household running. When her mother's health broke down at age 85, Virginia confronted the medical system, protesting the poor treatment given her mother by both her doctor and the hospital ombudsman. Virginia admitted that, although she couldn't help her mother medically, she could participate in her care by advocating for her in the system.

> *As an advocate on behalf of my loved one, I was more aware and determined to get good medical treatment, and insistent on having the right thing that needed to be done.*

I inquired about the level of *personal and community activities* among caregivers to determine if any of these supported their journey on the right road. Since isolation and long hours are most likely to contribute to negative attitudes and poor health outcomes, having outside activities could serve as an incentive to stay socially connected and mentally active. On both measures—personal and community activities—these caregivers demonstrated significant involvement. They enjoyed friendship groups, book readings and professional organizations. A word of caution: during the dying process of their loved ones (which could involve months), most caregivers were forced to abandon, first, their community activities, and next, their hobbies, reading and even their most cherished friendships.

Disappointed with standard medical practices, some caregivers turned to *alternative health practices*, such as acupuncture, massage and chiropractic, to reduce stress and stay centered on their caregiving. Yet, only one in three caregivers had ever tried non-traditional medicine, and among this number, use was limited to an average of five visits over the course of their caregiving. Most caregivers pointed out that they either failed to understand the medical value of these approaches, found them too expensive or derived little benefit. For many caregivers, religious or spiritual solutions to personal adversity served as their primary orientation for maintaining balance in their lives.

Overcoming Obstacles

Caregivers can transcend their suffering, and many do move into a sense of peace and wholeness. Rather than stay mired in passivity, feeling defeated and lost, they seek the high road. They know how significant they were to the well-being of their care receiver. You could say that successful caregivers were deeply aware that the power of one really matters. This knowledge sustained them through the toughest times.

Faith's story offers a classic example of an imposed caregiving role. Yet, she came to embrace her demanding situation, because she learned so many invaluable life lessons in the process. In her most recent incarnation as a caregiver, Faith has devoted herself to her mother, who has Parkinson's disease. Prior to this commitment, you might recall that Faith had an extended family history of being the "designated caregiver" for a sizeable number of her relatives, beginning in childhood.

Faith's commitment to self-reflection made all the difference for her. Confronting illness and death as part of life, she could let go of suffering and gratefully follow her inner calling.

> *What supported me was introspection. I'd been sent away to be cared for as a child, and learned to take care of my older relatives. So caregiving was a given role. I really feel a sense of connectedness with all others, a complete sense of democracy. No one is more privileged than the other. It's the rhythm of human life and I have a sense of personal responsibility as an intelligent and responsible woman. This was a healing experience for me. Caregiving has a cycle and a clear completion. I can go back to the times of great trauma and remember [them] with peace.*

Martha has a different story of achieving wholeness. She grew up as a Quaker and now pursues a Buddhist path in striving for an open heart. Her spiritual practice has permitted her to have a satisfying—even joyful—life while caring for her husband on a full-time basis.

> *I swim and paint, attend the Alzheimer's support group and practice yoga and meditate every day. I'd go to church regularly, but I'd have to get respite care for my husband. I'm very careful about my health and I love to walk. I eased into his diagnosis of Alzheimer's, taking*

one day at a time and learning to appreciate his new language—all his own. We've been married fifty years for better or worse. I look at rough times like the weather—it will pass.

Martha's deals with the vagaries of human existence by simply taking everything in stride.

Ogden Nash said: 'Which is worse, to have everything going well and know it will get worse or everything going terribly but know it's getting better?' It's the way you feel about it that's the key—there are no magic solutions.

Gloria monitored her husband's dosage of 15 to 17 prescriptions for heart disease. She needed five different medications for her chronic back pain, much of it related to the strain of caregiving. After ten years of providing care for her parents and then a nephew, she wholeheartedly left work and accepted full-time care of her husband, now going on for five years. Gloria has a gentle peacefulness and new awareness about her situation.

It's my whole life and I wouldn't have it any other way. I'm on a new path as a caregiver, with a new awareness of a new experience. There is some ambivalence. I wish it weren't happening, but I know I am becoming a much more patient person. I don't go to church. Rather, I express my spirituality in my beliefs and lifestyle—being kind, supportive of charities, enjoying the world and nature. I try to make the world as good a place as I can.

Nora looked into the face of suffering every day and night as she cared for her 87-year-old sister, who suffered from peripheral neuropathy. This is a rare nerve disorder that is characterized by chronic and unrelenting pain. Nora tried everything possible to ease her sister's pain, often without success. In desperation to provide comfort, Nora finally knelt on the floor beside her sister's bed. She soaked her sister's feet first in hot water, then in cold, gently massaging them with ointments afterwards. At last, ready for bed, her sister could now, hopefully, relax deeply into sleep. Nora admitted the circumstances were often beyond her ministrations, but acknowledged the significance of her daily efforts to comfort her dying sister.

It was all-consuming and sometimes I couldn't help her at all. Pain pills didn't work, nothing worked. I'd never been so close to someone suffering from pain. I loved my sister, she was my favorite. I just put my intention on the positive; that's how you get positive results. I tried to be more responsible with my actions and follow through on projects. This experience was necessary for my own growth and understanding. Without it, I would have less compassion for others ill or dying. I believe you create your own thoughts and it's important not to let yourself be pulled down into negative thinking.

Caregivers also reported that they could not surmount the daily tribulations of caregiving—with its vigilance, tight organization of time and activities and the sense that their life was held in suspension—until their loved one died. This was my experience.

As I dealt with Jim's slow, agonizing dying process that lasted for nearly three years, I had one major concern—Jim's denial of his own death.

My personal issue with Jim was that I could not bring death into any dialogue with him. It seemed as though there was an invisible, but powerful shield with the words emblazoned, 'see no evil, hear no evil, speak no evil,' which blocked communication every time I broached the subject of his finality with him.

I sought my own remedies for coping with his refusal to have what I considered the *indispensable* conversation.

He seemed to want no part in preparing himself and the family for his demise. I felt so alone in all this. But I believed that everyone should be prepared. Then, I decided to take my own crash course in death and dying, and found a remarkable collection of books and articles that really helped me prepare myself, and hopefully, the family, for his passing.

When the nursing home staff called one morning with the news that Jim had slipped into a coma, I contacted four of my six children who lived nearby, to meet me at the facility. I also contacted our parish priest.

I felt so reassured when Father Frank walked in. My daughters appeared traumatized by their dad's condition. Clearly, Jim was dying. Once my son, Tim, walked into the room with his three children, the priest began administering the sacrament, and then it seemed everything changed. The tension went out of the room. The room seemed full of light. Jim's labored breathing eased, and we all had the same experience—it was so palpable. Jim had finally let go and was at peace. That was a defining moment for me, because I could finally surrender and be in harmony with what was happening.

As I lay on my nursing home-rigged pallet on the floor next to his bed, Jim died later that night, breathing a final shuddering sigh at midnight.

The sequel to caregiving can be a positive and uplifting experience.

Taking my caregiving as a whole, I felt I had so much to master. It was like a whole new world. Increasingly, I felt more mastery in my faith, as well. Once I shifted my academic interests to aging, I began writing articles, giving lectures. I felt happy I could transfer my worries and concerns into something positive. I felt a new sense of pride that I could transcend my fears of inadequacy. I overcame the smells of the sickroom, my husband's depression, his dying (but it haunted me for days, weeks, even months).

Today, after Jim's death? I'm a more enlightened person, a writer and researcher of the caregiving experience. I'm far more creative. I'm a friend and partnered-centered person who makes strong distinctions among family members, recognizing their individual capacities and limitations. I feel now I have an opportunity to live a full life. I would say I have had a complete renewal.

For caregivers who have turned over their lives to the well-being of their care receiver, every opportunity to participate in their loved one's experience becomes a cherished moment. Anne confirmed her commitment to stay the course in being with her husband in his gradual decline.

We get to do this—discovering and witnessing of our loved one's struggle. We can never really predict the moment of death, but there are certain guidelines. I understand these as a Hospice volunteer. I am happy to be here with Mike as he ends his life. It is a privilege and an honor.

Following Anne's lead, caregiving becomes a loving presence, and not a "mop-'till-you-drop" project.

The Gifts of Emotions

We've all been raised to avoid one thing: expressing what we really feel. As a child, no matter how deeply we felt the injustice, the fear, the loss, the longing, we were supposed to "suck it up like a big girl or boy." That idea's been ingrained in me since I was a baby. "Hush, hush," to stop the display of feelings—especially anger and fear or when I was overcome by tears, told to "stop it right now" or "you're just a big cry-baby." Even as an adult, I tended to squelch my feelings, pushing my worries, angers, fears and anxieties well below my conscious ability to make sense of them or to figure out what they were trying to tell me.

Well, what if I told you these repressed emotions actually serve as the best indicator of our personal truth? Moreover, the awareness of our feelings gives us the ability to bring our inner resources to bear. Reading Karla McLaren's wise book on emotions years after my caregiving reminded me that for most of my life, I have not paid much attention to my feelings. I am not alone. Karen McLaren says that most of us learn to separate our mind from our emotions, and subsequently make poor decisions and even fail to deal with our environment intelligently. We also get wholly out of touch with our spiritual and visionary lives. Worse yet, we don't even know how to integrate meditation, daydreaming, prayer and contemplation into our everyday life of work, driving, loving and relating. No wonder most of us have such difficulty empathizing fully with another, or even to understand our own motivations, feelings, needs and inner strengths.

This was my story until I took up full-time caregiving for my husband. I had long put my intellect in charge, spinning and whirling full-time into endless planning, strategizing, scheduling, plotting, and obsessing. My highly active life provided an exhausting regime, with no time for emotions that drain energy. For the most part, I managed to handle my issues with little attention to what my feelings were trying to tell me. If something popped up that concerned me, I applied my most intensive *thinking* to "working it out." Of course, I was frequently sad, mad or glad about my life and various events, but I tended not to spend much time or thought on why these feelings erupted at inopportune moments, or how I should look at or listen to what they were saying. My tendency was to be critical about my feelings. I was deeply distressed when I couldn't control my rage, horribly embarrassed when the "crybaby" emerged, frustrated, sad and woefully isolated when shame wounded me with its presence.

But caregiving stopped all that. Being responsible for the man I lived with for more than 45 years and was deeply connected to put all my normal responses into disarray. I felt thoroughly ungrounded and disoriented. I had no idea where my life was going in the grand scheme of things, and absolutely nothing made sense to me anymore.

What had surfaced for me, as for many caregivers, were the host of unlived emotions I had shoved out of sight, out of mind, until a better day, perhaps. I would do it after I had raised my children, after my career had come to a close, after I had completed my world travels—and after and ever after. And now I was faced with the grand hordes, all galloping at once through my now shattered psyche. It took time, but eventually I learned the language of emotions, and began to sort out their often subtle messages.

After confronting and embracing my feelings, my world changed. Rather than drained from caregiving, I was renewed with lively energy and a measure of wisdom. The pain of loss was still there, but now I had more resources for coping with it. Let me tell you how I came to recognize that these repressed emotions, once acknowledged and expressed, could actually work for me. After we take a good, hard look at the most formidable emotions caregivers typically confront—anger, fear, sadness, and grief—I will show you ways to get in touch with and release those emotions to benefit both you and your loved one.

Anger—The Boundary Setting Emotion

First, I learned that healthy anger is a protective device that restored my boundaries or created new ones. I was bolstered by the realization that anger was as irreplaceable as sadness or joy and must never stay in the shadow. It needed my undivided focus to stop, look and listen—bring it to consciousness and determine its meaning. Passive acceptance in view of the injustices I faced merely repressed the anger, and stripped me of the energy that the thrust of anger provided.

Caregiving opened the door to a wide spectrum of my angers and resentments—recycled childhood grievances, neglectful nursing home staff and unwarranted put downs by medical providers, among others. I was offered daily reminders of my wounded experiences of growing up in an alcoholic home. The unpredictability of Jim's illness, the sudden imminent sense that I had absolutely no power over the disease, reminded me of the level of chaos that prevailed from my broken parent. I seethed with impatience at the overworked and often indifferent nursing staff in the many facilities Jim visited. I was livid when a geriatric psychiatrist suggested I needed to better manage Jim when he refused to take his medications ("Why can't you keep him on his meds schedule?"). I felt as though anger had taken root in my soul, and was suffocating the flower of compassion I had so laboriously developed.

Although I was tempted to hurl that anger at others—nursing staff, psychiatrist and even unhelpful daughters, I channeled it into other energies—finding a spiritually evolved counselor, organizing the children to spend more time with their Dad, keeping an eye on staff behavior and even laughing at the naivety of the psychiatrist who somehow believed that an elderly person with dementia was tantamount to a badly behaved child. The best part: Jim and I created a funny story together about the psychiatrist's "strange" outburst, after Jim's abrupt dash out of the doctor's office. Our story offered us both a moment of solace during a particularly difficult summer. I learned a valuable lesson about anger. It could be melted with just the right ingredients of hope, love and humor.

Fear—The Focusing, Intuitive and Action Emotion

Two kinds of fear drive us. We've all encountered the first duo: the rigid, immobilizing fear of anxiety and the nonproductive activity of worry. The other is free-flowing fear, which is a different matter altogether. Instead, when you're experiencing an outpouring of fear, you take notice. You slow down, and test the waters. You're cautious. You move differently, more deliberately. You feel focused, centered, capable and willing to move into action. Fear is associated with our core values that are clustered around energy. This lifesaving energy is deeply invested in *security/survival, affection/esteem and power/control.*

Of course, fear has another side. When we perceive our most cherished values to be threatened, we can easily overreact out of our unconscious desires. What's wrong here? Once the current of fear is trapped into an habitual response, it becomes fossilized. This means our energies are damned up, and no longer flow with the situation. Instead, we recycle ourselves into worry and, at worst, an anxiety disorder.

We caregivers have much to be fearful about, so it's important to keep this channel open. Our fears are legion: problems around financial security, social position, ability to keep on with the grueling caregiving schedule, loss of power, energy and control over ourselves and others, just to mention a few. As losses mount up, our fears grow, and our courage to change shrinks. This is precisely why we need to pay attention to these feelings. We must ask: *What* is this feeling? I need to acknowledge it. *Where* is this feeling in my body? *Why* has it surfaced now? *How* can I get a handle on this new situation? *What* do I do about it? Since fear can bring a surge of adrenaline, it can be used to mobilize us into action. Intuition will come forward, as well. You *can* do the right thing without thinking deeply about it—if you allow yourself to let your feelings of fear guide you.

I must confess my most fearful moment of caregiving occurred after Jim's return home from rehabilitation following a series of hospitalizations. After settling him into my former study—which had been transformed into the sick room—I felt well-prepared for the wheelchair, the friendly porta-potty next to the bed and my bedside assistance whenever Jim needed it. I had even provided him with a loud-ringing bell to wake me up—the kind you call the cows with! What I was totally unprepared for, though, was the dementia that led to Jim's confusion, his failure to call me and his subsequent fall as he staggered in the dark to locate the commode. "The best laid plans...." I thought. "What shall I do now?" In the interlude between my adrenaline rush and the emergence of a realistic plan, I shifted into a full-blown anxiety attack, which raged unimpeded for at least an hour.

What to do with the unconscious patient on the floor? How can I reconcile my whipping him out of the rehab center against the better judgment of the medical staff? Where should he go now? Once the emotional smoke cleared, I realized that even with my son's help, we could not move him without possible damage to both Jim and ourselves.

The decision turned out to be obvious: call 911 and move him back to the rehab center. The cherished gift of free-flowing fear ignited my intuition and energy to make exactly the right phone calls and start to settle myself down to a good cry and an abundance of bodily shaking that helped quiet the inner roar. I followed it up with some cheese and crackers to prepare myself for the long ordeal awaiting me in the hospital emergency room.

Sadness—The Release and Rejuvenation Emotion

Sadness is no laughing matter—literally. It's a signal that something desperately needs releasing; surrendering the concern to a Higher Being or simply letting go. When we cling to our sadness, we can easily fall into despair and despondency—and lose whatever power and control we had over our situation.

When caregivers lead with their sadness, they compound their burden, rather than lifting it, and feel brokenhearted. I've certainly observed caregivers, who, stuck in their sadness, continue to recycle their feelings month after month without hope of resolution. Their labors appear futile as they struggle with physical and emotional instability, have round after round of lingering hurtful memories and anxieties, endure unworkable relationships and face excruciating loneliness. "I have no one to turn to," is a frequent lament, even when they're surrounded by people.

I found that deeply wounded people hang on to their sorrows, often presenting themselves as an incurable victim. When confronted with the sacrifices of long-term caregiving, they are likely to collapse into despair—"my life is meaningless," "why did this happen to me?" or "I'll never be happy again." Caregiving is *not* the time to break through despair and woundedness. Instead, they tend to inflict their misery on others: the sick or dying elder, family members and friends.

During my early caregiving weeks, I remained mired in sadness when I continued to insist on living in the same way, regardless of how poorly the lifestyle fit with everyday reality. I had a compulsive need to keep things as they were. I said to myself: "Jim *will* eat at the dining room table, and he *will* carry on a scintillating conversation—even if I have to hide my scribbled notes of happy conversational topics." I pushed this agenda for weeks. What a mistake! My dear one's energy was so depleted that simply sitting up in a chair took everything he had. The entire drama ended badly. Jim neither ate nor spoke, our dinner was a lonely and futile affair and my frustration knew no end.

But once I moved into meditation and took a deeper look at what was happening, I really felt the intensity of the losses I was experiencing. I plumbed the vein of sadness to release outworn expectations, and let go of completely unreasonable demands on myself and Jim. I realized how close I had come to the "nothing works" program, where I could have interpreted his withdrawal as a personal affront to me. I wish I could say I had found an instant solution to the eating problem. That was not the case. But now I had the energy and will to keep trying other approaches, sometimes successfully, and often with the help of family members or home assistants.

Grief—The Immersion Emotion

We've already considered grief—the mother of all emotions—in Chapter 9. You'll recall I said that grief can trigger bouts of bottomless stress. But there's more to the story. Grief has a number of facets. We know that the most obvious form of grief is the powerful emotion of loss that arises when death occurs, whether it is an actual death or the death of profound attachments, ideas or relationships. Grief can also stem from something we are supposed to take for granted, but no longer have—our health, strength, security, even a happy childhood. We've all felt the overwhelming sensation of grief when we failed to achieve a cherished goal or faced the shocking betrayal of trust by a close friend.

Let me tell you that when you are living with or caring for a beloved person, whose well- being has been deeply compromised by illness and debilitation, you can also experience *their* grief, sometimes so intensely it takes your breath away. The beautiful, lyrical writing of Karla McLaren depicts grief as dropping a person into the "river of all souls," the deepest place we will ever be. And for caregivers, that river contains *both* of you—caregiver and care receiver.

What is the message of grief? McLaren says that grief "asks us to become quiet and stop all forward movement, so we can dive into the depths." Be prepared for a conflict between head and heart. Our intellect pushes us to move forward—find a distraction, practice our addiction, anything but sit still. Our body and emotions guide us differently, insisting that we stay put and submerge ourselves in the healing currents.

Pain, illness, trauma and grief are natural and meaningful processes. Why have we pushed them to the edges of social life? We rarely honor a death by wearing black garments, or even observing a mourning period. By contrast, every preliterate culture offers a rich array of grief rituals—shouting, crying, chanting, music, dancing, eating. I grew up when wakes were in fashion. Mourning was an important occasion. First, participants were expected to cry openly and unashamedly as they viewed the open casket. Then, remembrances of the loved one were trotted out, followed by liberal doses of good Irish whiskey—for the adults—and a bountiful table of food for all. Only in our current Western culture are we expected to take death and dying "like a man," or treat death as simply an occasion for "celebrating" one's life—social practices that exclude us from lowering ourselves into the river of grief.

Now, here's the hard part, which I mentioned earlier. Long-term caregivers are very likely to experience what psychiatrists recognized as "complicated grief." This occurs when the caregiver suffers for many months or years as they witness and emotionally share in the progression of the disease or aging process that slowly erases the personality and will of their loved one. To abandon this grief would mean to disconnect from their dear one. Their hearts would close down. Without the emotional attachment, though, caregiving is just another job—and a burdensome one at that. But without social recognition that honors the grieving, the caregiver is treated as mentally ill, possibly needing medication.

To keep silent, as I had to learn to do in all my social circles (who needs to hear Nanette's caregiving saga again?), simply built up my sense of tension and isolation. I woke up to my dilemma. I have always embraced Christianity's long-held image of the sorrowful Mother of God as an icon—and the sense of suffering that goes with it. An alternative healer I was seeing regularly insisted that I "stop grieving immediately, because it's too hard on the heart." Yet, grieving with Mother Mary felt like my sole hope in a heartless world. The practitioner's attack on my deepest feelings first baffled me, then alerted me to the reality that I needed to go elsewhere to express myself—to make myself feel more alive and resourceful. That's when I sought a healer trained in India who would genuinely listen to me, and could work with my bodily symptoms. I also rediscovered the healing energies of prayer and religious ritual.

Giving Up Grief

Let's be frank. Normal grief does not last indefinitely, nor should it. None of us are able to stay in that river forever. Because we are earthly beings who aspire to be heaven-bound, we shouldn't dwell in those deep waters endlessly. Besides, caregiving demands so much of us. We must conserve our precious energy to do the heavy lifting that's required of us. And after our loved one has died, we will need to summon our strength and motivation to begin life anew without the structure of caregiving or the presence of the departed loved one. Even during the most difficult periods of care—in and out of hospital or nursing home, keeping the dementia-driven patient within the confines of home or other restricted space, or facing the slow dying process of a loved one with cancer or heart disease—we keep a remnant of ourselves, a glimmer of consciousness that reminds us: "I am alive," and "I will live through this." And perhaps the most powerful invocation of selfhood— "Despite my utter fatigue and exhaustion, I *can* and *must* get over this unbearable sorrow."

Such thoughts may be uttered in secret, only to oneself. Sometimes, they may be shared in a support group, or much less likely, among intimate friends. Simply thinking this—much less giving voice to such an admission—can be a dreadful source of guilt, a sense of shame that washes over us at the very idea that we can't alter the course of the disease or impending death. Guilt is not so much a feeling as it is a *recognition* of a personal shortcoming, an injury to another, even a violation of the moral order. But this is exactly the nature of long-held grief. It can distort reality, and turn it upside down. In this state, you can even ask: "Why do I deserve to live?" "Why can't I do more to save my loved one?" "What did I do that made this person so ill?" We call this reaction *survivor's guilt.*

Survivor's guilt is a mental condition that occurs when a person perceives himself to have done wrong by living when others did not. This disorder occurs during combat, terrorist attacks and natural disasters when death is widespread, but can also be found among rescue and emergency service workers. Even therapists have reported experiencing this condition in the face of their patients' suffering. The survivor believes that he is to blame for not being able to do more to save a person from catastrophe. The pattern of symptoms can be immobilizing, including anxiety, depression, social withdrawal, sleep disturbances, nightmares, physical illness, emotional disorders, and for many survivors, post-traumatic stress disorder.

How common is this among caregivers? I believe that all long-term caregivers experience survivor's guilt to some degree. Caregivers who reported chronic illness coupled with a loss of interest in life, numbness and inability to take care of themselves suffer from this disorder. Survivor's guilt is *not* a normal response—even if occurring frequently among caregivers—and should be treated as a serious mental condition if it persists. When I realized I was holding on to a sense of unyielding guilt over Jim's circumstances, I stopped and asked myself some essential questions. What more could I have done, really? How could I have turned around this disease? What can I do *now* to make his life more bearable? Once I stayed focused in the present—and only with the help of a therapist—could I change this highly negative belief.

A final recognition: Jim's disease had clearly monopolized our family dynamics for many years, severely limiting our interaction and ease with one another. We had too easily slipped into the error of allowing the disease to become our central organizing force. This awareness further assuaged my discomfort, prompting me into a fuller acceptance of Jim's illness and death. It also significantly freed me from the weight of guilt I had carried for so long.

Lessons Learned

Feelings are the caregiver's special gifts that make it possible to offer yourself generously and lovingly to another. Self-sacrifice and kindness are special qualities caregivers bring to the bedside of the dying. They are not without costs, though. One way to reduce this burden is to pay close attention to your emotions. These energy streams rise and fall with all the daily situations faced by the caregiver. If allowed to flow unimpeded by cultural strictures, our feelings can aid and abet the deep commitment we make to caring for another. To participate in the final drama of our loved one's life is to open the door to great courage and joy. Illness and death do not negate life, but are an essential part of it. Caregiving works as a celebration of all of the darkness of disease and the lightness of human connection, and not only a fragment. In this way we honor the human spirit in each of us. The ultimate gift of caregiving is that you can wholly and completely love, accept and respect yourself and all your loved ones without reservation.

Epilogue

Meet the Caregivers

Lord, make me an instrument of your peace;
Where there is hatred, let me sow love;
Where there is injury, pardon;
Where there is doubt, faith;
Where there is despair, hope;
Where there is darkness, light;
And where there is sadness, joy...

– Prayer of St. Francis of Assisi

Let me introduce the women whose stories you encountered throughout these chapters. The brief profiles reveal information about the caregiver, her care receiver, some of the circumstances surrounding the giving of care, and in some instances, caregivers' words of wisdom that helped them through difficult times. A reminder: all names, except my own and my assistant, Anne Mikkelsen, have been fictionalized to preserve confidentiality for participants.

Anne (written by her husband, Mike): Anne was a 100 percent atypical, fully engaged mother of four; she is now a 100 percent fully engaged caretaker. The main difference in the roles is her ability to treat me as an adult, capable of making decisions for myself, even though I am incapacitated by Parkinson's disease. She encourages me to continue doing what I am still able to do and she does not fret over what I cannot do. All the while, she continues to care for herself physically, intellectually and spiritually.

Antonia: A life-long caregiver, Antonia's first memories are of looking after her single mother. Enduring a life-threatening accident at age 12, Antonia believes she lived because she had a higher purpose—"I have always felt I survived for a reason." Today, she serves as a professional administrator in a care facility, as well as takes care of her elderly stepfather. She remains upbeat while confronting her own health challenges. Her advice: "Give and get a lot of hugs so you can recharge—and look at the lighter side. Even in the darkest moments, hold a spot for laughter."

Betty: An elementary teacher, Betty shared the caregiving of her 88-year-old mother in assisted living with her sister. Betty's life continued as normal, with no dreams abandoned, no losses, no regrets, no guilt, and a stronger relationship with her mother. She continues to feel valued. "I know that I did my very best to assist my mother in her final challenging years of life."

Billie Mae: An independent, retired business woman, Billie Mae became frustrated with the management of her inept 24/7 "care force" for her husband with Parkinson's, blindness and heart disease. Billie Mae abandoned nothing and always moved forward with gratitude. She retained the inadequate care team, but took over more and more of the everyday care. She was her husband's eyes, his driver and companion. He "finally gave up at 95." She adds, "I have only been a widow for one week and though my feelings are deep my greatest loss is the death of my husband."

Carla: A professional caregiver, Carla took over the care of her positive, appreciative 60-year-old friend with terminal breast cancer. Although she tried to live in the moment, Carla was overwhelmed by the denial of the patient's daughters. She remained grounded by her religious beliefs as her friend's cancer kept coming back. Eventually, she helped her friend prepare to die and stayed through to the end. "I owed her the best job I could do. One day, I'll probably need someone to look after me."

Carmen: A professor, Carmen served as a facilitator for six years for her 75-year-old friend with Alzheimer's. Since home care was not an option, she chose a nursing facility that focused on "the gentle care approach." This emphasizes communication as an important tool to learn the activities and memories that add comfort to each resident's stay. She was frustrated by the disease, the deterioration of her once independent, capable colleague and the lack of professional input. In the latter years, she felt trapped and a sense of danger that finally merged into relief as she faced the loss of a friend and a fine mind. "Try not to think of yourself, think of the other person's needs and comforts. Don't lose your identity, but recognize this person's life isn't going to last much longer and you have time to do other things."

Carrie: As soon as she could walk, Carrie was a caregiver—first for her mother with multiple sclerosis, then her father, then a sister, then a neighbor, then children, all the while postponing so many dreams. She has never known anything else, but remains philosophical. "Everything is temporary. Everything changes, it all passes—physical reality, emotions, life… it's all temporary."

Catherine: A competent, creative manager and working professor, Catherine remains socially active, and for ten years, has managed to happily fold the care of her 85-year-old flexible, uncomplaining mother into her professional and personal life. She provides social and spiritual stimulation, denying nothing pleasant either to herself or her mother. "I just kept up a normal life, interweaving my life with my job, weaving many threads together to form a pattern of life; hers was one of beauty. I suggest learning all you can from the person you're caring for."

Charlotte: A nurse who has multiple sclerosis, Charlotte has been married for 40 years. With good skills and a supportive family, she serves as caregiver for her 71-year-old husband, who has Alzheimer's. Charlotte's role changed from physical to emotional. "When I had no legs, he held me up. I didn't owe him, I just wanted to take care of him. It was reciprocity. I was sad to lose him but grateful for the time we had. I recommend worrying efficiently."

Cindy: A nurse, mother and reluctant caregiver for her alcoholic father, Cindy felt annoyed and inconvenienced, with no support and no relief in sight. She dreaded the fights, as well. After three years, she placed her father in assisted living with much remorse and guilt and little contact. "He got exactly what he asked for."

Claire: An extrovert, walker and homemaker, Claire is also a resourceful and accepting caregiver who speaks of the "wheel of life." Claire suffered a stroke, kidney failure and high blood pressure during the care of her husband. She accepted their way of life, and truly felt loved and supported by her husband. She said she believes in a Higher Being. "Live so there are no regrets. We always assumed that we would go on forever. Now, I sort of live day-to-day."

Clarice: A never-married student with a 19-year-old son, Clarice reiterates that her siblings all believed "no one was good enough for Dad." Before Clarice "got custody" of her 79-year-old father in 2003, their relationship was distant. She moved him 2000 miles to her home. Caregiving ultimately took over her education, her finances, her home, her health and her emotional stability. "I just had to do it: get dressed, put on red lipstick and go do it. I believe there is a bigger plan, bigger than I and I can play that plan."

Claudia: As one member of a beautifully choreographed four-sibling team caring for their mother, Claudia and her siblings allowed their roles to be determined and adjusted by their mother from her room in a nursing home. She felt fortunate that her mother was able to demand help from her children, and raised her to know that, "…this is the best thing I can do with my time." She adds, "Let your life be your message."

Denise: In her middle years, Denise enjoyed sailing and sharing quiet times with her husband and two boys. But in later life she was struck a bitter blow when a son committed suicide, and her husband developed inoperable lung cancer. The tragedies she faced led to serious illness, and eventually the inability to speak for months. Despite the setbacks Denise has encountered, she has done much inner work and feels healed and renewed. "It was such a difficult time; I felt so alone, but I felt good about helping him through the dying process. I kept my promise—to help him through the end."

Eva: A product of the circle of abuse, Eva was angry, guilty and overwhelmed. She also suffered from multiple personality disorder. She admits to having "a lot of hang-ups." While caring for her mother, she wished she would die, yet still wanted to make her mother happy. Ultimately, she felt healed as a result of caregiving. "Let it go, let it go, let it all go, and it does."

Evelyn: Having retired early to care for her husband with

Alzheimer's, Evelyn accepted her role. I "never gave it a thought, it was no sacrifice. I never longed for anything else. He was grateful. Other people were very kind. We couldn't live in a condo—nothing for him to do. It was peaceful knowing I was doing the right thing: fulfilling God's will."

Faith: A community health educator who retired early, Faith became the designated caregiver for her very difficult, negative, 87-year-old mother—an alcoholic with Parkinson's, heart failure, dementia and blindness. When Faith was nine, on crutches from polio, she began her caregiving career with multiple family members. After a lifetime of commitment, Faith felt "a sense of finality of care, an internal feeling that it was as good as it could be." She acted on her strong sense of connectedness with others and her complete sense of democracy. She believed that no one was more privileged than the other, and accepted the rhythm of human life. An intelligent and caring woman, she was proud of having a sense of personal responsibility.

Fran: A 61-year-old with two knee replacements, Fran has been trying to prove herself to her husband and his family. She has been married for ten years to a demanding husband with Crohn's disease and short bowel syndrome, who is numb from the waist down. Fran inherited the care of her mother-in-law, as well. Her husband's two unresponsive grown sons said, "You married him—you get Grandma too." She has experienced both mental and physical devastation and almost complete isolation. "No care for this caregiver. Restoration? I go to Costco and get help loading the car."

Gloria: Remaining positive and upbeat despite her own health challenges, Gloria provided care for her husband, who suffered from heart disease, as well as her 85-year-old mother, a quadriplegic in a nursing home. She expected to care for her husband, adjusted to their new lifestyle of illness and traded their separate independent lifestyles in favor of companionship, interdependence and sharing of interests. "What gets me through? Be appreciative of what you have now—you really have to live in the moment—next year I may be looking back and saying, 'I never had it so good.' Stay grateful and positive. It doesn't help you to look back. Find something positive to be and do."

Hazel: A Catholic housewife who once worked as a welder during World War II, Hazel is a self-sufficient woman who lives an uncomplicated, small-village life in Mexico. She has an ideal, holistic support team. She is a willing, yet no-nonsense caregiver of her husband, who had a debilitating stroke. "If he fell out of bed, Carlos came over, put him back into bed. If we needed food, Louis arranged for it. When I needed a lifting device rigged up, the kid across the street built something. If I got fed up, I took my grief outside, walked it around, waited fifteen minutes, it was over. I didn't have to make any changes, kept playing cards and feeding the birds, just used common sense. That's the way to deal with things."

Helen: A homemaker and skeptical Christian with a good income, Helen consciously took on the role of caretaker for twelve years. Her husband of 60 years, an academic who was always pleasant—"a saint"—had neuropathy. "Love conquers all. Do and say the most loving thing at this moment for this particular person no matter what."

Ina: A retired teacher, Ina cared for her husband of 48 years, who had mesothethelioma, a lung cancer caused by exposure to asbestos. She had a good son for support, and was able to maintain a normal lifestyle, never feeling confined or having to live alone. Her husband made most of the decisions and the future was simply not a topic. "Life changes completely during caregiving—just stop in your tracks. Do the best you can."

Jane: A self-described angry, out-of-control, highly stressed, bi-polar and driven daughter, Jane was often in denial about the consequences of her caregiving commitment to her father. Jane left her own young family to care for her abusive father with Alzheimer's, making choices "he can't argue with." She adds, "I'm going to keep trying until *he* gets it right."

Janice: Janice never sacrificed her spiritual development, but learned how to give up household chores and hobbies for more time with her mother at the nursing home, a half-hour drive away. Janice says she slowed down, took deep breaths and brisk walks. She laments a loss of free time, but acknowledges that she gained a great opportunity to hear wonderful family stories. Summing up her caregiving, Janice said: "It was a positive, privileged, lucky experience."

Jean: A duty-bound daughter, Jean sees no end to the caregiving. While caring for her mother, she has struggled through the death of her best friend and confidant. She feels in a constant state of stress, anxiety and grief. She felt her own stages of life slip rapidly and regretfully away while her mother lived well past anyone's expectations. "The elderly are living so long."

Jill: Trying to remain spiritual throughout the trials of caregiving, Jill never felt loved by the negative, super-critical mother she cared for through the final passage of life. Jill triumphed because she knew well the skills of Eastern meditation. She practiced compassion moment-by-moment. She sought to see and appreciate the child-face of her mother before she was wounded by life. Jill believes, "You can't do any better than the best you can."

Joanne: An editor and Quaker, Joanne is enormously generous of spirit. She assumed the care of her 94-year-old mother, with whom she was estranged since the age of five. She embraced her final opportunity to know her mother, abandoning nothing, regretting nothing. "The world provides fascinating opportunities to ease the suffering. I did the best I could. I kept the covenant."

Joyce: Joyce tried to be a good person, even though she was deeply depressed. Her 94-year-old mother was a deaf, gullible, hard-hearted controller who was never loved as a child and showed little affection or appreciation to her daughter during the 14 years Joyce cared for her. "I'm so glad my mother's taken care of. I would feel terrible if no one had taken care of her."

Kali: Originally a residential care aide, Kali became a premature caregiver. She felt lonely, worried and bored, yet also validated by caregiving. She later moved in with her grandparents, providing care 24 hours a day. Soon, she realized she couldn't go home anymore. Kali's grandfather was contrary, obstructive and controlling, while her grandmother with Parkinson's was sweet, happy and appreciative. "I got to know her better, keep her warm. She was like a mother to me. I don't believe this is a just world. He even cheated at cards."

Kathy: A fitness trainer, Kathy moved into her parents' home to care for both parents, ages 102 and 92. She copes by meditating, praying and walking. Sometimes, she feels overwhelmed, tied down or wants to run. "How long can people live?" Kathy worked to change her thoughts, emphasizing intentionality, advocacy and self-care. "I can do this—take care of my parents, and I'll come out stronger, healthier and more in tune."

Kendra: Between the ages of 15 and 21, Kendra cared for her father when her mother left to care for her own father. Too young to make a conscious choice or to be a caretaker, she was left exhausted, sad, hopeless and helpless. Kendra remained a caregiver until her father's death. Her mother continues to be resentful, blaming and controlling, while Kendra feels "too mature" for her age and hopes to move on. "Don't sacrifice everything—save something for yourself."

Laura: Laura retired early from clerical work and didn't see herself as a caretaker. With multiple illnesses herself, she took on the complicated role of care in two separate locations for her 90-year-old mother with Alzheimer's and her 85-year-old father with stroke damage and depression. She spent countless hours driving over, driving back and delivering dinners daily. She learned much, though. "See the humor. You can laugh or cry—I chose to laugh."

Lenora: A professional caregiver who earns $250 a day, Lenora cared for her friend, who was adamant about staying in her own home. Lenora felt little disturbance in her life, did an adequate job of not wanting to "leave her in the lurch," and had a theory that things aren't as bad as they seem.

Marianne: A professional caregiver for two-and-a-half years with only weekends to herself, Marianne eventually got tired of the job. "(You) can't take on their energy. I realized it was time to get out." She could no longer make the adjustments necessary. "Take responsibility just for your own thing—not others."

Marsha: Marsha took medical leave for two-and-a-half years to care for her appreciative father, who had Alzheimer's and cancer. She says she has no regrets, doing it all because he had always cherished her. She loved having him around, appreciated the opportunity to hear his end-of-life storytelling and learned a new kind of patience and kindness. The downside? "I didn't do very well taking care of myself."

Martha: A 78-year-old retired researcher with high coping skills, Martha meditates and reviews her choices daily. She strives for an open heart, but lacks privacy and free time. She is usually patient and is sustained by strong friendships, good neighbors and an active support group. After years of coping with her husband's diminished capacity and the failure of the medical system to offer a remedy, she has learned "the bureaucratic dance." Her husband of 52 years with Alzheimer's has a Ph.D., but has never been a people person. Sometimes he can be positive, sometimes negative, but mostly he's living in a very confusing world. "We're on this earth for a short time; we've been given all sorts of gifts and it is up to us to use them. The natural world is incredibly wondrous. We need to be respectful of things in this world and not do violence to them."

Mary Beth: A retired high school teacher with high blood pressure and a history of mini-strokes, Mary Beth prepared herself for her husband's care. She retained a good lawyer, secured Power of Attorney, had access to a good pension and sought out a support group. She then chose her fights. She saw it coming—the Alzheimer's and Parkinson's—and experienced it all, from his memory problems to the controlling behavior. He became despondent, paranoid and argumentative, filled with self-doubt and worthlessness. He even threatened suicide. Happily, a transformation occurred during the final stage of his life. At age 85, he started to acknowledge her with "absolute appreciation," and repetitive apologies for any transgressions. "You are allowed to feel sorry for yourself for three minutes, then it's over—you cannot succumb to self-pity." *'You have to have friends, you have to have friends, you have to have friends'* (said with emphasis).

Mary Ellen: Mary Ellen went rapidly through the stages from happy wife, fun companion, blackjack dealer to that of an angry, resentful, burned-out, depressed caregiver of two, living on food stamps. Her husband has Alzheimer's, while her adopted nine-year-old son is totally disabled. "I believe in honesty. I pray and meditate. No one is perfect. I am surviving."

Maxine: A semi-retired secretary, Maxine "carried her 87-year-old sister on her back," to live and care for her at the YWCA. She says she did the best she could with no one else to help. Sometimes she was cross, sometimes frustrated and impatient. She survived by trusting in a "Higher Power" and by gaining understanding and compassion for someone suffering from indescribable, untreatable pain. "This experience was necessary for my own growth and understanding. Without it, I would have less compassion for others ill or dying. I believe you create your own thoughts and it's important not to let yourself be pulled down into negative thinking."

Melanie: Learning to view caregiving for two sets of grandparents and her father as an opportunity and an honor, Melanie experienced very few frustrations, inconveniences or losses. She successfully teamed with her mother and sister for round-the-clock care until the very end of life. "Everything in life has a reason and purpose. We may not know it, but it is there. Don't let the little things bog you down—enjoy them all!"

Nanette: A dedicated scholar and student of caregiving, Nanette felt inadequate and overwhelmed. She feared the ineffectiveness of medications, financial pressures and her children's reactions. She witnessed her brilliant husband's rapid deterioration, keeping him at home until he resisted living, and endured evasive and cynical professionals. She also saw her dreams of travel and a companionable old age dissolve with each setback. She will never forget her late husband's depression and the oppressive smells of the dying in the nursing homes. In the end, she learned the full range of care and life's expanding spiritual lessons. She urges all caregivers: "Get your story out!"

Natalie: A loving, responsible and compassionate daughter and niece, Natalie sacrificed her life for 10 years, even beyond her ability to care for herself. As a new bride, she took care of her father first, then her mother, then her uncle, seeing each commitment through with intentional grace and dignity. When alone, she shed private tears and expressed resentment for the little that was leftover for her patient, supportive husband. "Seek support, accept help. Don't isolate yourself from friends."

Nora: A nurse and eldest daughter, Nora became the caretaker of her 89-year-old mother with Alzheimer's and her 89-year-old father with depression and heart problems. The worst part? Not being able to fix everything, as well as her parents' constant crying and shutting down. "Am I a horrible person for not bringing them to my home?"

Patricia: A conscientious Mexican Catholic, Patricia is the wife of a very ill, deeply stubborn and profoundly controlling American husband twenty years her senior. She prays on her knees every day so she can talk on the phone with her distant family, to ask God to make her husband more cooperative and to take his medications. She also prays to get help from her husband's children, and seeks God's intervention to transform miserable people, such as her in-laws. "It is our commitment in our culture to care for all humans, no matter how difficult."

Rachel: A 63-year-old teacher, Rachel grew up caring for her suicidal, alcoholic mother. As an adult, she considered herself a burned-out caregiver. Rachel was detached, passively unable to cope, and decided to hand over the care of her husband with colon cancer to her willing and very capable adult children. "I recommend getting all the help you can, do no harm, and do everything you can to avoid grief."

Renae: A grieving rescuer and caretaker of three—son with Down syndrome, mother with Alzheimer's and sick live-in boyfriend—Renae has also recently dealt with the death of her former husband. Renae was conflicted, uncomfortable and severely stressed, especially about caring for her boyfriend, who declined rapidly with pancreatic cancer only one-and-a-half years after moving in with her. "I lost myself in all the illness, gained weight, lost interest in everything, gave up."

Rita: Performing an act of love for her stepfather, Rita left her husband and children to fulfill her promise to let him die with respect and dignity in his home, all the while, allowing him to call the shots. "Keep your cool and all falls into place."

Roberta: A Christian who retired early from teaching, Roberta continued to be a friend and musician as she cared for her husband with dementia for three years. It was "like taking care of a toddler." She tried to think ahead and prepare, as well as advocated on behalf of Alzheimer's and dementia patients. "Don't try to do this alone. Get your spiritual life in order."

Rosanne: With a good husband, no children and a spacious home, Rosanne gave up her job to care for her mother. She felt very fortunate to have plenty of room for her mother—"to enjoy life and to sit in the sun." She and her husband tried their best to make her mother "feel like a duchess and look like a million bucks." But then her mother suffered frightening and devastating attacks of dizziness, possibly from mini-strokes, and Rosanne reluctantly had to place her in a care center.

Rose: Sometimes despondent, sometimes just worn-out, Rose learned how not to "blow her temper" while caring for her smart, cantankerous and opinionated 96-year-old mother. "Like mother, like daughter." Toward the end of her mother's life, Rose suffered from exhaustion and multiple stress symptoms.

Sally: A single mom of seven, with three children in college, Sally is an only child who rode the caregiving roller coaster for fifteen years. Her mother suffered from Alzheimer's, while her father had heart failure. Sally was sucked dry by three homes to finance, countless arguments, the unspeakable decline of her parents and wrenching life support decisions. At one point, her mother almost died, and then bounced back. The confusion and depression was overwhelming as Sally faced homes to sell and papers to shred. "It's a painful experience, like having a baby, but labor's easier when you know what to expect. You can make it through naturally, and always remember, you can't prevent it. Women I knew who weren't prepared for labor, screamed. I wasn't prepared for caregiving. I screamed, but that's the cycle of life."

Sandra: Sandra's unappreciative and negative husband was only 59 when he died of heart disease and cancer. Their relationship remained rocky throughout his illness for two years. "My intentions were there, but I didn't know what it would be like… financial stuff, guilt, his anger, no power, dreadful medical system, turbulence. Our emotions just did us in. Breakdown or breakthrough? I don't know. I only pray: God grant me the serenity to accept the things I cannot change, courage to change the things I can, and the wisdom to know the difference."

Sarah: A feisty, self-educated octogenarian and former actress/singer, Sarah began ten years of care for her blind, estranged husband, Jack, who lived in a separate but connected apartment. Sarah was anxious and tired, proud that she didn't put him in the veteran's hospital. At the same time, she did not feel any gratitude from him despite her sacrifices. "Gratitude? In a pig's eye." Meditation, movies, girlfriends, dinners out and making Jack laugh together made Sarah's years of caregiving easier.

Sharon: Married for fifty years, Sharon "never really worked" because her husband didn't want her to have a job. She became a willing but exhausted caregiver for her husband, who had lymphoma. "He would have done it for me, if I'd been the sick one." Sharon and her husband belonged to Compassion & Choices, but physician's assisted suicide was not available. Eventually, her husband died of pneumonia. Sharon makes crafts for sale and belongs to a co-op. "I get lonely sometimes, but I know I've been fortunate all my life—blessed. I feel he shouldn't have died, but we all have to do it."

Sylvia: An exhausted 86-year-old retired secretary with strong family support, Sylvia is happy for a "good day"—that is, one without unmanageable pain from her broken wrists. She cares for her 93-year-old husband with congestive heart failure, memory problems and despondency at home. "Sometimes when he gets out of line, I used a little shock treatment: just do what has to be done, but pleasantly, and put us both to bed." Sylvia suggests something she deems "healthy neglect." "Let people do as much as they can without trying to help them."

Teri: A premature caregiver of her grandparents, Teri felt impotent and angry at those family members who normally should assume the role of caregiver, but declined. Teri lost an important stage of early adulthood, but through faith and belief in God, did the best she could with the limited tools, power and respect she was granted. "I believe it's good karma—that somewhere, somehow, it's good to do good deeds."

Theresa: A retired librarian, recovering alcoholic and intentional caregiver, Theresa felt no burden and learned from her mother's example of how to give. Caring for her 94-year-old mother was a privilege. Theresa relaxed by dancing with seniors in the nursing home where her mother played in the rhythm band. Together they shared support, convictions, values, expenses and a love of each other. "Give till it hurts. Love with all of your might and it will come back to you. Amen!"

Toni: After six years of caring for her 81-year-old mother, Toni feels resigned, frustrated, trapped and angry. Now facing menopause, she resents her loss of freedom and privacy, and feels there is no good part of care except fulfilling responsibility. She is simply not prepared to be the "mom." She said, "I expected to help but not do every single thing. Run around, run around, solve one problem, another pops up."

Virginia: A retired, divorced professor with an active social life, Virginia lovingly accepted the challenge of caregiving. She was always close to her mother, who had Parkinson's. What began as home care ultimately led to a nursing home. "Coming to the end, I could see it more clearly. I think I did my part—a job well done. I recommend: Don't look too far ahead, one day at a time. Your attitude affects the patient. Try to rise to the occasion."

Wendy: At 65 years old, this writer/illustrator and recent Christian convert took on the caregiver role to a complaining, unappreciative 93-year-old mother, who had been "whittled away by age." Wendy tirelessly continued to provide care until her mother died at 102. Somehow, she managed to resist the negative impact of her mother's resentment and disapproval. She stayed grateful for the opportunity to do something for her, to expand her love—a "strong element of my conversion." She has gently lived out St. Francis of Assisi's prayer for peace, love and light.

Works Cited

Alliance for Aging Research. 2021 K Street NW, Suite 305, Washington, D.C., 20006 and Rand Corporation. See http://www.hsph.harvard.edu/pgda/resources.htm.

Alzheimer's Association. See http://www.alz.org.

American Academy of Medical Colleges. "Statement on Patients in Peril: Critical Shortages in Geriatric Care." Paper submitted to the Special Committee on Aging, May 12, 2002.

American College of Emergency Physicians. "Elderly Lack Medication Knowledge." *Annals of Emergency Medicine.* May 14, 2005. See http://www.acep.org.

American Medical Student Association. "The Senior Boom is Coming: Are Primary Care Physicians Ready?" May 14, 2005. See http://www.amsa.org/programs/gpit/seniors.cfm.

American Psychiatric Association. *Diagnostic and Statistical Manual of Mental Disorders IV, 4th Edition.* Arlington, Virginia: American Psychiatric Publishing, 2000.

Brunonia Barry. *A Map of True Places: A Novel.* New York: William Morrow, 2011.

Joshua Bartok (ed.). *Daily Wisdom: 365 Buddhist Meditations.* Summerville, Massachusetts: Wisdom Publications, 2001.

Melody Beattie. *Co-Dependent No More, 2nd Edition.* Minneapolis: Hazelden Foundation, 1992.

Karen Casey and Martha Vanceburg. *The Promise of a New Day: A Book of Daily Meditations.* New York: HarperOne, 1996.

Pauline W. Chen. *Final Exam: A Surgeon's Reflections on Mortality.* New York: Knopf, 2006.

Deepak Chopra and David Simon. *Grow Younger, Live Longer: Ten Steps to Reverse Aging.* New York: Harmony Books, 2001.

Barry Corbet. "Nursing Home Undercover: Embedded." *AARP Magazine,* January/February, 2007.

Nicholas Christakis. *Death Foretold: Prophecy and Prognosis in Medical Care.* Chicago: University of Chicago Press, 1999.

Nicholas Christakis. "Mortality After Hospitalization of a Spouse." *The New England Journal of Medicine* 254, 2006, pp. 719–730.

Nanette J. Davis. "Cycles of Discrimination: Older Women, Cumulative Disadvantages and Retirement Consequences." *Journal of Education Finance* 31(1), Summer 2005, pp. 65–81.

Nanette J. Davis. "When a Spouse Becomes a Caregiver." Chapter in Anne Cutter Mikkelsen, *Take Charge of Parkinson's Disease.* New York: DiaMedica, 2011.

Family Caregiver Alliance. "Women and Caregiving: Facts and Figures." June 7, 2006. See http://www.caregiver.org/jsp/print_friendly.jsp?nodeid=892.

Dorothy Foltz-Gray. "Stress: Embracing the Good, Managing the Bad and Keeping it from Getting Ugly." *Natural Health*, December/January 2011.

Marilyn Gardner. "Caregiving May Mean Overcoming Frayed Ties." *Christian Science Monitor,* July 11, 2004.

Richard Garvin and Robert Burger. *Where They Go to Die: The Tragedy of America's Aged.* New York: Delacorte, 1968.

Atul Gawande. "Letting Go: What Should Medicine Do When it Can't Save Your Life?" *The New Yorker*, August 2, 2010.

Daniel Goleman. *Social Intelligence: The New Science of Human Relationships.* New York: Bantam Dell, 2005.

Jane Gross. *A Bittersweet Season: Caring for Our Aging Parents—and Ourselves.* New York: Knopf, 2011.

Harvard Health Letter. "Diagnosing Alzheimer's Disease." Volume 36, Number 9, July 2011.

Harvard Women's Health Watch. "Prolonged Illness and Grieving." Volume 18, Number 7, March 2011.

Harvard Women's Health Watch. "When Patients Suddenly Become Confused." Volume 18, Number 9, May 2011.

Karen V. Hansen. *Not So Nuclear Families.* New Brunswick, New Jersey: Rutgers University Press, 2005.

Michael E. Hirsch (ed.). *Coping with Grief and Loss: A Guide to Healing.* Big Sandy, Texas: Harvard Health Publications, 2010.

Gregory James, O.D. "Addressing Barriers to Health Care for Our Elderly." American College of Osteopathic Family Physicians. See http://www.acofp.org.

Johns Hopkins Medicine. "Health After 50." Volume 23, Issue 5, July 2011, p.7.

Nicholas D. Kristof. "Medicine's Sticker Shock." *The New York Times,* October 2, 2005.

Elizabeth Kubler-Ross. *On Death and Dying.* New York: Scribner, 1997.

K. M. Langa, *et al.* "National Estimates of the Quantity and Cost of Informal Caregiving for the Elderly with Dementia." *Journal of General Internal Medicine* 16(11), 2001, pp. 770–778.

Nancy L. Mace and Peter V. Rabins. *The 36-Hour Day, 3rd Edition.* Baltimore: The Johns Hopkins University Press, 1999.

Reinisa MacLeod. "Tool for Grande Prairie's Parkinson's Support Group." *Parkinson's Post,* September/October 2011.

Karla McLaren. *The Language of Emotions: What Your Feelings are Trying to Tell You.* Boulder, Colorado: Sounds True, Inc., 2010.

Susan Moon. *This is Getting Old: Zen Thoughts on Aging with Dignity and Humor.* Boston: Shambhala, 2010.

National Citizens' Coalition for Nursing Home Reforms. "Nursing Homes: Getting Good Care There." See http://www.nccnhr.org.

National Mental Health Association (NMHA). "Co-Dependency." Mental Health Resource Center, 2001 Beauregard Street, 12th Floor, Alexandria, VA 22311.

Northwest Regional Council/Area Agency on Aging. "10 Warning Signs of Caregiver Stress." *Family Caregiver Support Project,* 2011.

Chokyi Nyima Rinpoche and David R. Shlim. *Medicine and Compassion.* Boston: Wisdom Publications, 2004.

Teepa Snow. "Problem-Solving the Challenges of Caregiving When Someone Has Dementia: Getting Out of the Box." Workshop presented at Alzheimer's Society of Washington, Bellingham, Washington, April 29, 2011.

Tallahassee Democrat. "Florida Nursing Homes Should Allow Nursing Home Cameras." March 18, 2002.

Liz Taylor. "A Small Hospital's Big Progress in Eldercare." *Seattle Times,* November 6, 2006; and "Culture Change is on the Horizon for Long-Term Health Care." *Seattle Times,* November 13, 2006.

Mark Thompson. "Shining a Light on Abuse." *Time,* August 3, 1998.

Terri Trespicio. "10 Thoughts on Whole Living." *Whole Living,* May 2011.

Robin West. "The Right to Care." Chapter in *The Subject of Care: Feminist Perspectives on Dependency.* Eva Feder Kittay and Ellen K. Feder (eds.). Lanham, Maryland: Rowman & Littlefield Publishers, 2002.

Andrew Weil. "Caring for the Caregiver." *Self-Healing.* August 2003.

Anne Wilson Schaef. *Meditations for Women Who Do Too Much.* New York: HarperOne, 2004.

Accolades for *Blessed is She*

"Even a quick review of **Blessed is She** might give today's caregivers and those who care for them hope, and lend support and information for their lives."
— Marsha Sinetar, Ph.D., author of
Don't Call Me Old, I'm Just Awakening

"Without sugarcoating the issue, **Blessed is She** offers strategies and affirmations to those who take on the tough responsibility of caring for a loved one who is in declining health."
— Barbara Lloyd McMichael,
Pacific Northwest Book Columnist

"**Blessed is She** is a treasure trove for those who currently are caregivers and for the rest of us who, as women, likely will one day become caregivers or receivers."
— Kathleen F. Slevin, co-author of
Age Matters: Realigning Feminist Thinking

"In her book, it is clear that Nanette Davis 'gets it.' When veteran family caregivers meet, they quickly bond because they share a special connection. **Blessed is She** brings these intimate insights to everyone. The stories reveal the secret known to seasoned caregivers… the challenging experience also provides joy, rewards and profound transformational learning. A must-read for all Baby Boomers."
— Louise M. Morman, Executive Coach
and Founder, eldercarelearnings.com

"Nanette's book, **Blessed is She**, inspires us by showing how varied yet courageous the caregivers she interviewed are, and how their bravery transforms them."
— Liz Taylor, former *Seattle Times*
Columnist and Founder, agingdeliberately.com

"Indispensable reading for anyone giving care to a loved one."
— Jennifer Lois, author of **Heroic Efforts:
The Emotional Culture of Search and Rescue Volunteers**

"Any caregiver will benefit from a reading of this very approachable book."
— Larry Richardson, Ph.D.

www.ingramcontent.com/pod-product-compliance
Lightning Source LLC
Chambersburg PA
CBHW060840280326
41934CB00007B/862